Dan Gookin
Sandra Hardin Gookin

SAMS

Teach Yourself Microsoft® Windows 2000 Professional in 24 Hours

SAMS
A Division of Macmillan USA
201 West 103rd St., Indianapolis, Indiana, 46290 USA

Sams Teach Yourself Microsoft® Windows 2000 Professional in 24 Hours

International Standard Book Number: 0-672-31701-X

Library of Congress Catalog Card Number: 99-62613

Printed in the United States of America

First Printing: January, 2000

01 00 99 4 3 2 1

Trademarks

Warning and Disclaimer

Associate Publisher
Angela Wethington

Acquisitions Editor
Chris Denny

Development Editor
Chris Denny

Managing Editor
Lisa Wilson

Project Editor
Dawn Pearson

Copy Editors
Kate Talbot
Mary Lagu

Indexer
Amy Lawrence

Proofreader
Katherin Bidwell

Technical Editor
Bill Bruns

Team Coordinator
Karen Opal

Interior Designer
Gary Adair

Cover Designer
Aren Howell

Copywriter
Eric Borgert

Editorial Assistant
Angela Boley

Production
Steve Geiselman
Louis Porter Jr.

Contents at a Glance

Contents

About the Authors

DAN GOOKIN considers himself a writer and computer "guru" whose job it is to remind everyone computers are not to be taken too seriously. His approach to computers is light and humorous, yet very informative. His favorite quote is, "Computers are a notoriously dull subject, but that doesn't mean I have to write about them that way."

Dan's most recent titles include the best-selling *Word 2000 for Windows for Dummies*, *PCs for Dummies, 7th Edition*, and *Dan Gookin Teaches Windows 98.* He is the author of the original Dummies book, *DOS for Dummies*. All told, he's written over 75 books on computers. Dan holds a degree in communications-visual arts (okay, let's be honest: Art!) from UCSD, and currently lives with his wife Sandra (see below) and four sons somewhere in the Pacific Northwest.

You can contact Dan at his e-mail address:

`dang@wambooli.com`

SANDRA HARDIN GOOKIN has a remarkable ability to make difficult tasks easy to understand. This comes from her speech communications degree from Oklahoma State University, but mainly from having to communicate with her five boys (four children + one husband, Dan).

Sandra has been working with Dan for six years. Her current task is to make Windows 2000 easy for you to understand.

Sandra's other books include *Parenting For Dummies, How to Use Excel 2000, Discover Windows 95,* and *The Illustrated Computer Dictionary For Dummies.*

You can contact Sandra at her e-mail address:

`sandyg@iea.com`

Together, Dan and Sandra's number one commitment is to their children. However, you can also find them directing and acting in their great community theatre, the Lake City Playhouse.

Acknowledgments

To Jordan, Simon, Jonah, and Jeremiah, our beautiful boys. Thanks to their love and support, they keep us young, happy, and completely knowledgeable on everything Star Wars and Power Rangers.

To Shirley and Virgil for their extreme flexibility, great dinners, and love. Too bad they fear playing dominos with us.

Special thanks goes to Jordan Gookin, our 12 year old. He is the one who researched and assembled all the bonus questions in this book.

Tell Us What You Think!

As the reader of this book, *you* are our most important critic and commentator. We value your opinion and want to know what we're doing right, what we could do better, what areas you'd like to see us publish in, and any other words of wisdom you're willing to pass our way.

As an Associate Publisher for Sams, I welcome your comments. You can fax, email, or write me directly to let me know what you did or didn't like about this book—as well as what we can do to make our books stronger.

Please note that I cannot help you with technical problems related to the topic of this book, and that due to the high volume of mail I receive, I might not be able to reply to every message.

When you write, please be sure to include this book's title and author as well as your name and phone or fax number. I will carefully review your comments and share them with the author and editors who worked on the book.

Fax: (317) 581-4770
Email: `opsys@mcp.com`
Mail: Angela Wethington
Associate Publisher
Sams
201 W. 103rd Street
Indianapolis, IN 46290 USA

Introduction

Welcome to Sams Teach Yourself Microsoft Windows 2000 Professional in 24 Hours. Finally, a book that doesn't assume you want to know every little nuance of Windows 2000. Who does? We promise to tell you exactly what's important in Windows so that you can immediately start getting work done and happily ignore the rest. Because honestly, Windows 2000 is a massive program. Do you really want to know all that stuff?

Of course not! You want to know what's important. You want to know it now. The other stuff? Forget it. Just getting the job done in the quickest way possible is the philosophy of this book. The other stuff, the details and boring technical matter, are all omitted—not even glanced at here. And don't be surprised if, on the way to getting the most from Windows 2000, you have a little fun as well. This book educates and entertains. Two perks for the price of one!

Does This Book Really Teach Windows 2000 Professional in 24 Hours?

Yes, it teaches the basics of Windows 2000—all the things you need to know to get work done.

Now please: Don't take us literally. You do not have to spend a continuous 24 hours reading this book. Instead, spend an hour every day perusing each lesson. The lessons are designed for easy consumption in the space of an hour, including all the to-dos and exercises.

What You Need

To work with this book you will need the following:

- A computer running the Windows 2000 operating system

Also suggested are

- A cup of coffee
- A package of Oreos
- Nice fuzzy wool socks
- A comfortable chair

Warning: The Authors do not advocate eating and drinking around your computer. Accidents do happen all the time.

Note: The Authors recommend Starbucks House Blend coffee and regular Oreo's (none of that Double Stuff—yuck!).

It's assumed that you already have Windows 2000 installed on your computer. The best way for that to happen is for you to buy a new computer with Windows 2000 preinstalled. You can also upgrade your existing computer to Windows 2000. Give yourself a full day to do that.

Conventions Used in This Book

This is what you'll find scattered throughout the book:

Icons. Three to be exact.

Tips. Bits of information to help make tasks easier or just to better your day.

Notes. Clumps of information that the Authors thought you should know, but the information really didn't fit in the outline anywhere.

Cautions. Just a few.

Screen Shots. These give you an idea of what you should be seeing on your screen. Keep in mind that there may be slight differences in what you see in the book and what you see on your computer.

Tear Out Cheat Sheet. This sheet is two-fold in its purpose. One, take it with you shopping for your Internet shopping needs. Two, keep this on your desk to help you remember the weird shortcuts that are a part of Windows 2000.

At the End of Each Hour...

Each hour will end with the following elements.

Summary. Read the summary carefully. If there's a concept in there that you didn't walk away understanding, go back and read the lesson again. You don't want to miss anything here.

Q&A. The questions and answers at the end of each hour come from a database of information that we as Authors keep. These questions are real questions other Windows users have had and have asked us. So you'll end up benefiting from their dilemmas.

Quiz. Test yourself at the end of each hour. Don't cheat! The answers are found in Appendix A.

Exercises. Actual tasks that you need to perform. No one is going to be peeking through your window to make sure you do these exercises so don't feel pressured to do them. However, reading about something is a great way to learn. Hands-on learning will enforce what you've read.

Vocabulary. Gotta speak the lingo. There are only a few words at the end of each hour so you're not overwhelmed with vocabulary words. Practice these words on friends and family and see how utterly impressed they are.

Where to Start?

You can start this book with any hour that you want. Here are a couple of suggestions though. If you need to cover some basic computer concepts, for example, how to use the mouse and how to work with text, then start with Appendix B. If you're buying this book because you really only need the hour on Networking, then by all means, go right ahead and start with the Networking hour. If you want to be thoroughly initiated into Windows 2000, start at the beginning and work your way through. There are several cross references throughout the book so if a concept is introduced that you don't know about, you can easily skip over to the other lesson.

PART I

So This Is Windows 2000?

Hour

HOUR 1

PC Basics

"The clock struck midnight, and I sat down in my dimly lit study. The twelfth chime still echoed in my head as the steady *tick tock* drove me onward. In the next twenty-four hours, I would learn and master Windows 2000. I licked my thumb and carefully turned the page."

No rule says that you must start with the first hour of this book at the first hour of the day. No, it's much better to pick a random hour to learn any of the many lessons this book offers. And you don't need to work the hours in order, either. Take a break!

This hour is about review and orientation. If you're new to computers and Windows 2000, you'll get valuable background information here that will help you understand the rest of the book. If you're an old hand, you'll appreciate the brush-up.

The highlights in this hour include the following:

- General information about your computer system
- Windows 2000's role in your computer system
- How Windows helps you use the computer

Your Computer System

The computer isn't a single thing. The full orchestration of the computer is actually many things all working together to help you.

Yes, help you. The idea behind the computer is to help you do things: get work done, accomplish some task, be entertained, or get educated. It slavishly obeys your every whim, taking on toil and repetitive tasks without as much as a frown. That's why computers are useful.

The two main parts of the computer system are referred to as *hardware* and *software*.

- Hardware is the physical part of the computer, the boxes and cables and electronics.
- Software is the mental part of the computer. It consists of instructions that tell the computer what to do.

Where you fit in the picture is sort of in the middle, between the software and hardware. You use the hardware to tell the software what to do. The software then tells the hardware how to do it. It's like a confusing Marx Brothers comedy, but with the end result of something other than chaos (you hope).

Of the two, it's software that's ultimately in charge of the computer. The main piece of software, the head honcho, is the operating system. It sits high and mighty, controlling both the computer's hardware and all the other programs that run on the computer.

On your computer, the operating system is known as *Windows 2000*.

Typical PC Hardware

What you have on your desk is a PC, or personal computer. True, a Macintosh or a Nintendo game console are also personal computers. But, in computer industry lingo, *PC* is accepted to mean a computer that runs the Windows operating system.

Most PCs consist of several basic pieces of equipment:

- *The console*—This is the main computer box, also called the *system unit* or sometimes (incorrectly) the *CPU*. The console contains the computer's main circuitry—the motherboard, RAM (memory), and microprocessor. It also houses the floppy drive, hard drive, CD-ROM drive, and other internal options.
- *The monitor*—This is the device that displays information, the computer's output.
- *The keyboard*—This device is what you use to communicate with the computer. Most of your interaction with the computer is done by typing on the keyboard.
- *The mouse*—Like the keyboard, this provides your input from you to the computer. Computer mice are necessary when using a graphical operating system, such as Windows 2000.
- *The printer*—Another output device for the computer is the printer. It produces *hard copy* of the stuff you create inside the computer. This is the end result of your PC labors.

Other, optional, equipment could be included with your computer: a scanner for reading in graphical images or photographs; a digital camera; external disk drives, tape drives, CD-ROM drives, and so on; modems for communicating with other computers and the Internet; and a host of other interesting devices.

The Network

A *network* is a collection of computers, each of which can access common resources (disk drives and printers) and share information. This is often called a *local area network* (LAN), but could be some other form of network (with the appropriate hardware and three-letter acronym).

There are essentially two types of networks. The first (illustrated in Figure 1.1) is the *peer-to-peer* network. This is a basic form of network where computers share information and resources. The computers can be PCs running Windows 2000, Windows 98, or even DOS. It can also include Macintosh computers.

FIGURE 1.1
The peer-to-peer network.

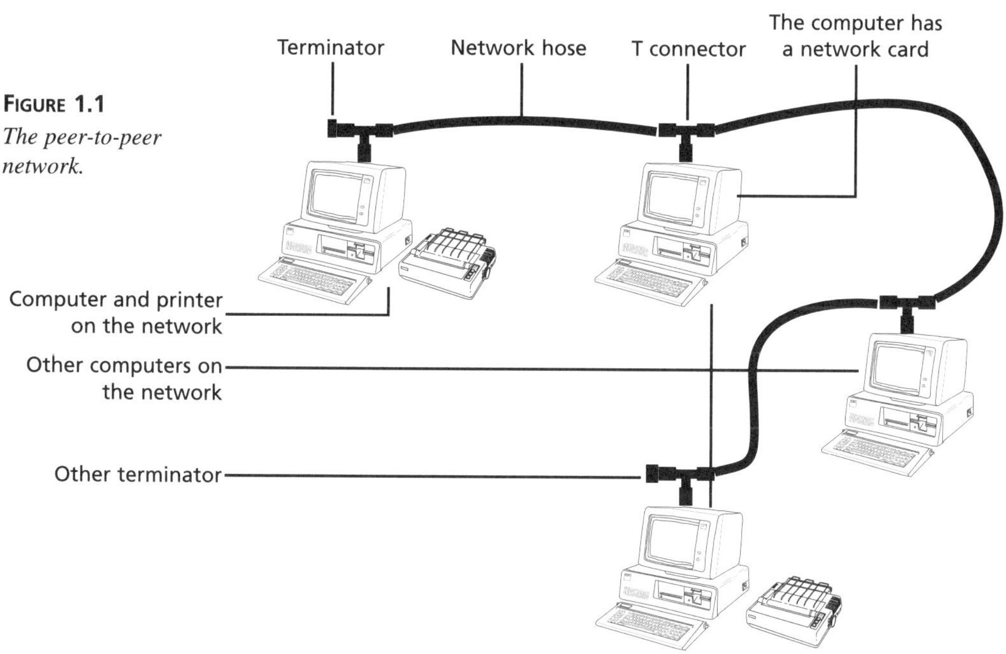

The second type of network is the central server type of network. In this network, one or more computers serve as a central storage place for files, programs, and other resources. This book does not cover this type of networking specifically; if you have any questions about such a system, your business or location most likely has a network manager to whom you can refer network-specific questions.

Your computer may or may not be connected to a network. If not, great. If so, even better. Windows 2000 is geared to work either way. So, if your computer has networking hardware and is connected to a network, you're ready to go and there's nothing more you need to do (other than learn how Windows does networks).

The Internet

The Internet is a grander network than a LAN or other basic computer networks. The Internet is essentially thousands upon thousands of computers all over the world. Actually, millions of computers – just a whole heck of a lot. The computers communicate with each other, sharing and storing information. Using software that comes with Windows 2000, you can access the Internet and get at all that information.

Some folks confuse *network* with *Internet*. Although they are similar, there is a major difference: The Internet means "the whole enchilada." Your company's network might have Internet access, but that network—your computer, the boss's computer, order entry stations, accounting, and all that—is local. The Internet is *every* computer on the Internet.

An Overview of Windows 2000

Windows 2000 is software that plays the role of an operating system inside your computer. Regardless of how powerful your hardware is, it's really Windows 2000 that calls the shots. Windows 2000 controls all the hardware and software in your system, and it is through Windows 2000 that you communicate with your computer.

Windows 2000 is a direct descendant of Windows NT, Microsoft's "advanced" version of its Windows operating system software. Windows has several versions of Windows 2000. But the two primary flavors are Professional and Server:

- *Windows 2000 Professional*—This is the version of Windows 2000 covered by this book, the more common of the two versions. It provides all the features you need for an operating system, allowing one or several people to use a computer and common Windows software.
- *Windows 2000 Server*—This is the operating system designed to run computer networks. There are several flavors of Windows 2000 Server, each of which performs specific tasks for networks, the Internet, databases, and other companywide functions. Windows 2000 Server is not an operating system designed for individuals to use (although you could, but then again you could also use a 747 to drive your kids to school).

Other versions of Windows exist as well. As this book goes to press, Windows 98 is the most popular version of Windows, the "consumer" version.

Basic Windows Concepts

Windows is a graphical operating system, using images, icons, menus, and other visual nuggets to help you control your computer. Most people find this easier to work with than typing in commands at a prompt or yelling at the computer (which is stress relieving but rarely effective).

To manipulate the objects on the screen, you use the mouse.

Working with the Mouse

The mouse is an essential part of working in Windows. Yes, you can get many things accomplished without the mouse, but eventually, you'll need to get acquainted with the squat little guy sitting on the mouse pad next to your keyboard.

To Do 1.1: Learning to Click with the Mouse

▼ To Do

1. Roll the mouse around on the mouse pad.

   Notice the arrow on the screen moving just like your mouse? That is because when you move the mouse, you move the arrow.

2. Point the arrow to the word *Start*.

   The Start button is located at the bottom left of your screen. From this point on, when you see the phrase "Click the (*and then a word*)," it means to use your mouse to move the arrow to something and then push the left button on the mouse. So, in this case, it would read, "Click the Start Button."

3. Click the left mouse button while the arrow is pointing to the word *Start*.

   The Start menu opens.

4. Click the Start button again.

   ▲ And now the Start menu closes.

This might seem like a silly little exercise, but if you're not familiar with a mouse, the eye/hand coordination thing can be really tough.

The Windows of Windows

Windows gets its name from the graphical boxes in which it displays information. The window frames information displayed within the window.

Each program Windows 2000 runs appears in its own window on the screen, as shown in Figure 1.2. The windows can be moved or their size changed, and the windows typically have interesting parts to them that let you control either the window itself or the information inside the window.

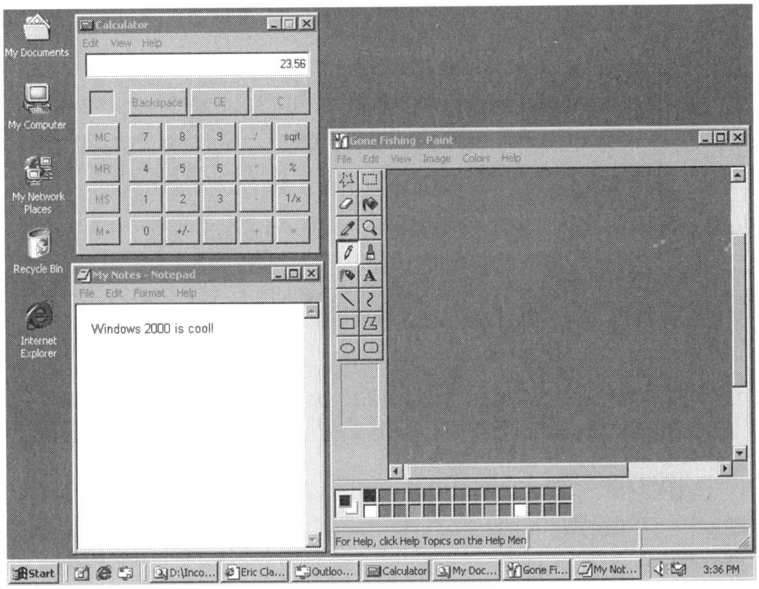

FIGURE 1.2
Multiple applications running in Windows.

Windows have specific parts, as shown in Figure 1.3.

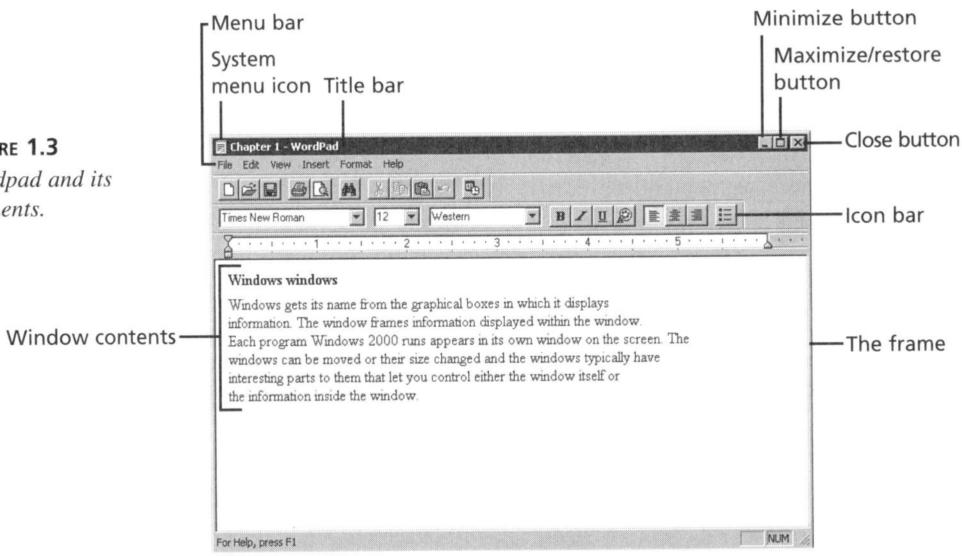

FIGURE 1.3
Wordpad and its elements.

Each of these gizmos controls how the window works and where it sits on the screen (called the *desktop*). Your programs and information appear in the window, and several windows may appear on the screen, allowing you to easily control several programs at once.

Icons

As an operating system, Windows 2000 controls information stored in your computer. The information appears in Windows as icons, each icon representing a file stored on the computer's hard drive. (A *file* is a single unit of information on a hard drive; an *icon* is a picture representing that information.)

Program icons represent programs or applications that do certain things in Windows. For example, the Internet Explorer is a program that accesses information on the World Wide Web. This program is represented as an icon in Windows, an icon you click to run the program (which appears in a window on the screen).

Icons also represent the documents or data files you create using various programs. So, for example, you write the Great American Novel or perhaps create a graphic illustration of "frustration" on the computer. That information is then saved to a data file, which Windows displays to you as an icon, or tiny picture.

The job of Windows is to help you organize and maintain these icons—your files and programs. That, and coordinating all the hardware in your computer, is what this book is about.

Menus

You tell Windows or its programs to do something by picking commands from a menu. There's nothing to type in and no commands to memorize. All you have to do is find the proper command on a menu—which becomes almost intuitive as you continue to use Windows 2000 and grow comfortable with its programs.

Figure 1.4 illustrates the Start menu, from which you can run programs or control Windows itself. The mouse is used to activate the menu, as well as to display submenus (the Programs menu in Figure 1.4) and choose items from the menu.

In Figure 1.5, you see a shortcut menu, which "pops up" at various times in Windows when you press special keys or the right mouse button. This menu contains commands that control specific items, such as the icon pointed at in the figure.

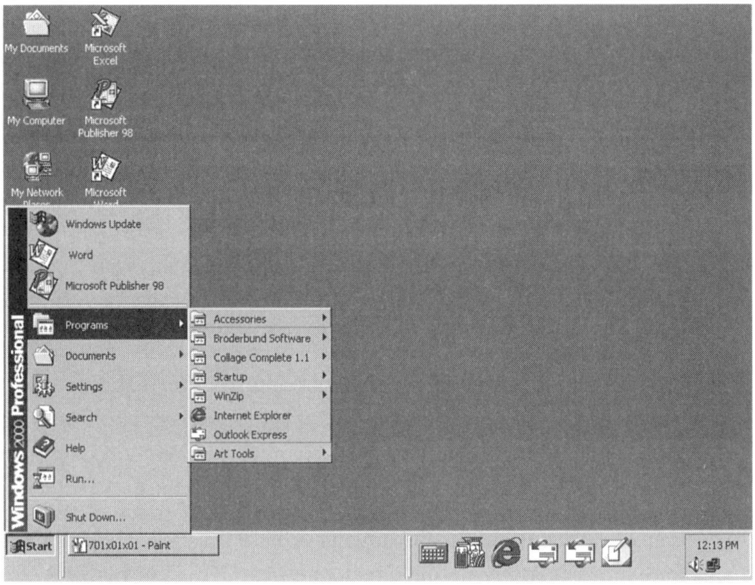

FIGURE 1.4
The Start menu.

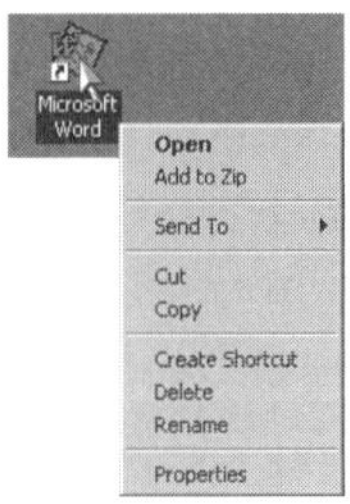

FIGURE 1.5
The shortcut menu for Microsoft Word.

Finally, most programs have a menu bar on which several menus appear. Each menu contains a list of commands that control the program or somehow manipulate the information you create in the program. Figure 1.6 shows the menu bar in My Computer. Not all menu bars show the same information, so read each one carefully.

FIGURE 1.6
The menu bar in My Computer.

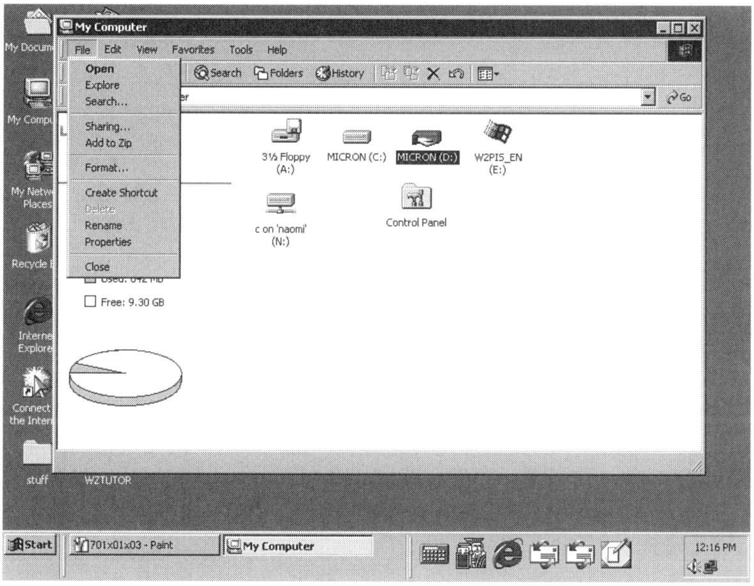

All these elements—windows, icons, menus, and other graphical gadgets that exist in Windows 2000—help you control your computer.

Summary

Your computer system consists of hardware and software. Controlling both those items is the operating system, Windows 2000. The operating system helps you control the computer's hardware and software and to maintain the multitude of data files (documents, graphics, and so on) that you will create and collect on your computer. Know how to effectively use Windows 2000, and you know how to control your computer.

Q&A

Q Is a CD-ROM disk hardware or software?

A The disk itself is hardware. All disks are hardware, even the hard disk. The information *on* the disk, however, is software. For example, Windows 2000 comes on a CD-ROM disk. The disk is hardware, which you stick into your computer to install or update your computer's operating system. The operating system that comes on that disk is software.

Q Is everything in Windows either a window or an icon?

A No, Windows uses lots of graphical goodies and whatnot to display information and let you control your computer. The windows and icons are merely the most common parts. This book shows you the other parts, how they work, and when they should be used to get the most from your computer.

Workshop

The workshop includes quiz questions to help gauge your grasp of the material and exercises to help reinforce your learning. You'll find the answers to the quiz and exercises in Appendix A, "Answers."

Quiz

1. True or false: All Windows 2000 computers come with a network.
2. Where is the Internet?
3. How does Windows 2000 display information about your computer?
4. *Bonus Question*: Who was the only president not born in the United States?

Exercises

1. Determine whether your computer is on a network. (You might have to ask the office computer manager this question, and if you have to ask the office network manager, the answer is probably yes.) Determine whether it's a peer-to-peer network or file server network. If it's a file server network, ask to see the file server. (This isn't important for running Windows 2000, but it should thrill the network supervisor that you're interested in such things!)
2. Determine how your computer will connect to the Internet. Will the connection be through the phone lines and an Internet service provider (ISP) or a national service like AOL?

3. Locate an icon in Windows, such as the My Computer, My Documents, or Recycle Bin icons found on the Windows desktop. Double-click the icon to see a window displayed.

Vocabulary

console—This is the main computer box, also called the *system unit*. The console contains the computer's main circuitry: the motherboard, RAM (memory), and microprocessor. It also houses the floppy drive, hard drive, CD-ROM drive, and other internal options.

internet—The Internet is essentially millions of computers all over the world. The computers communicate with one another, sharing and storing information.

keyboard—This device is what you use to communicate with the computer. Most of your interaction with the computer is done by typing on the keyboard.

monitor—This is the device that displays information, the computer's output.

mouse—The mouse, like the keyboard, provides your input to the computer. Computer mice are necessary when using a graphical operating system, such as Windows 2000.

network—A network is a collection of computers, each of which can access common resources (disk drives and printers) and share information.

printer—This is an output device for the computer. It gives you *hard copy* of the stuff you create inside the computer, which is the end result of your PC labors.

HOUR 2

Let's Get Ready to Rumble…!

When you turn on a TV, it's ready to rumble. Turn on a car and it actually rumbles! But a computer? No, it's not as accepting as other devices. The computer is suspicious. The chore of turning on a computer isn't really simple. You have to show ID, and there's paperwork and something about logs that have nothing to do with timber or fireplaces.

Turning off the computer can be just as difficult. It must be done properly. And then you have a choice: Do you shut down or do you hibernate? Log off or do a mere restart? Or maybe you just put the computer into a trance and convince it that the simple days of turning a switch on and off were actually a positive thing.

A whole hour devoted to turning your computer on and off? Is it that important? Yes. Windows 2000 can be customized, allowing several people to use the same computer. And the computer is more than just a toaster or a mere television set. Things must be done properly.

The highlights in this hour include the following:

- Starting your computer
- Logging on
- Quitting Windows
- Logging out
- Shutting down the computer

Starting Your Computer

The computer is off. It's safe! It's not misprinting phone bills or logging you into a porn Internet site. Ahhh.... Maybe you should keep it that way? Or maybe you should turn it on? Yeah, turn it on. That's a good place to start.

To Do 2.1: Starting Your Computer

To Do

1. Flip on the computer switches.

   At minimum, turning on a computer involves two switches, one for the computer box itself and one on the monitor.

   Turn on the monitor. Find its switch, which is usually on the front, bottom-right.

   Turn on the computer box, which is officially known as the *console*. (Review Hour 1, "PC Basics," for places where the on/off switch may be located.)

   If you have a printer, and any other external device—modem, scanner, external disk drive, whatever, turn on those switches as well. And turn on the light in your room if it's dark.

   The computer gently purrs to life....

2. Choose your operating system.

   This is an optional step if you've upgraded to Windows 2000 from an earlier version of Windows. You'll see choices displayed on the screen, listing the earlier operating system(s) or Windows 2000:

```
Please select the operating system to start:

Microsoft Windows 2000 Professional

    Windows NT Workstation Version 4.00

    Windows NT Workstation Version 4.00 [VGA mode]

Use the up arrow and the down arrow to move the highlight to your choice.

Press Enter to choose.
```

Press Enter. Because this is a Windows 2000 book, that picks the proper option.

(Note that this book does not transform itself into a Windows NT or Windows 98 book, should you choose those options.)

3. Watch your computer wake up.

   The screen might go blank for a moment. Be still! The computer is thinking. Eventually, dots march across the screen to confirm that the box isn't dead. Things come to life.

   The wait here depends on how much stuff is crammed into your computer's innards, or how much paraphernalia you have attached, or the phase of the moon. Sometimes interesting things are displayed; sometimes the computer chugs and churns in what sounds like the electronic equivalent of indigestion.

4. Windows 2000 rears its pretty head.

   Windows 2000 shows up with a "splash screen." It must be starting up. It even says that on the screen. This is followed by more splash screens and more waiting.

   (If the TV took this long to get going, all the shows would have to start at three minutes after the hour.)

5. Please wait.

   You should practice this on your own.

6. Welcome to Windows.

   Windows 2000 is designed so that several people can use the same computer. This is covered in detail later in the book, but when you first start Windows—even if you're the only one using the computer—you'll have to log in.

   To log in, press Ctrl+Alt+Delete, all three keys at once. (It says this on the Welcome to Windows screen.)

   Windows can be configured so that you skip this step. In fact, it might already be "skipped" for you. If so, you're done with startup. Skim ahead to the section titled "Doing Something."

7. Log in.

   All prisoners must identify themselves to the warden! The next dialog box prompts you to identify yourself and your password (to confirm that you are who you say you are).

   Logging in to the computer is a topic that needs more attention. Hour 15, "Juggling Multiple Users," covers logging in to the computer with more detail.

Getting Started with Windows 2000

If you're a new Windows 2000 user, a helpful screen with some nifty animation is displayed. This is the first time screen, shown when you first log in or start Windows 2000 for the first time. There are three options:

- Register Now
- Discover Windows
- Connect to the Internet

Choose one to see more information. There's even a nice lady to narrate these areas for you, too (through the computer speakers, of course; the nice lady just doesn't show up at your house or anything).

Register Now

Click on the words *Register Now* and Windows will whisk you to the place where you can register. Wow, that was fast. This requires an on-line registration, so I suggest that you wait until you read Hour 10, "Doing the Internet," which covers Internet stuff.

Discover Windows

Click on Discover Windows and you'll be asked for your Windows 2000 CD. The CD contains a Windows tour.

Connect to the Internet

Click these words and you're taken to the Internet Connection Wizard. Again, I'd wait on this until you have a chance to read Hour 10.

If you dare to take the Windows 2000 tour, click the Exit button when you're done.

> The Help screen is called the *Discover Windows 2000 Professional* tour, as shown in Figure 2.1. This screen automatically pops up when you start your computer for the first time. The tour can still be accessed at any time if, for some reason, you don't see this Help screen. Skip to Hour 5, "Getting Help," and go through the steps to open Help. Then click on the Contents tab, Introducing Windows 2000 Professional, and What's New? Look on the right side of the screen and click on the blue letters that say *Welcome Screen*. This will start this tour at any time, should you get an urge to see it again.

FIGURE 2.1
The Getting Started window.

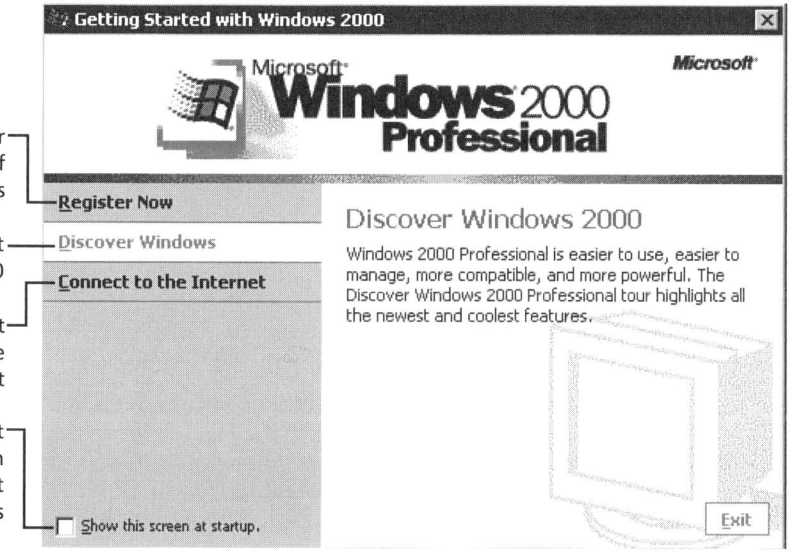

> You can save a lot of time and hassle by plugging all your computer gadgets into a single power strip. One button then turns everything on at once! Power strips can be purchased at any hardware or office supply store. Be sure to look for power strips that offer surge protection, as well as spike protection and other goodies designed to guard your electronics from the evils of electricity.

Doing Something

Windows 2000 exists to help you use your computer. After you go through the turning-on phase, you use Windows 2000 to get something done.

Ah, but that's the subject of the rest of this book. This is the on/off hour. So the next thing to do is to turn the computer off.

Quitting Windows

There is a difference between shutting down the computer and actually quitting Windows. Weird, huh? That's because the brains at Microsoft realized that sometimes you just want to stop for a while, but not actually end your computer time. So you have options. You might not have all the options listed in the following. It really depends on how the installation is configured. And you might have to activate the options at some time (such as Hibernate). But the following list does give you an example of what you can look forward to. Your options for quitting Windows are

- Shut Down
- Stand By
- Hibernate
- Log Off
- Restart

> You might not have the Hibernate option in the Shut Down Windows dialog box. You can add it yourself: Double-click My Computer. Double-click the Control Panel. Double-click the Power Options box. Click the Hibernate tab; then, click in the box to add a check mark. Click OK. This tab will not be available to you if your computer doesn't support this function.

Shutting Down

Shut Down both quits Windows and shuts down the computer. This option is covered in the section "Turning Off the Computer." You'll notice in Figure 2.2 that you actually have several options.

FIGURE 2.2
The shut down menu.

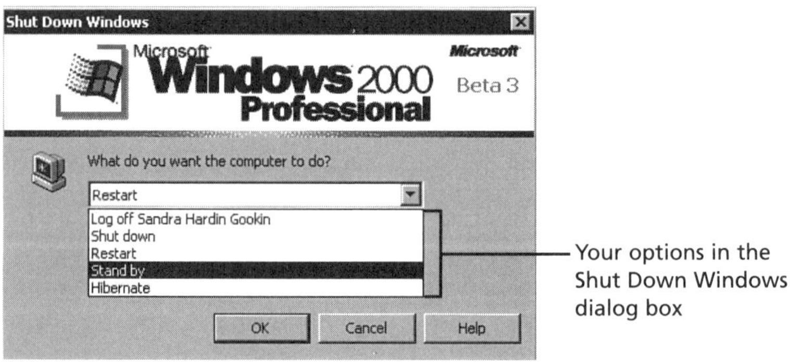

Stand By

Putting your computer on standby, the energy-saving option, turns your monitor and hard disks off, thus using less power.

To Do 2.2: Putting the Computer in Stand By Mode

1. Pop up the Start menu.

   Click the Start button or press the Ctrl+Esc key combination.
2. Select Stand By from the drop-down list.
3. Click OK.

   If you change your mind, click No, and Windows returns to normal.
4. Windows powers down.

   You can hear that Windows is slowing down, and it actually looks like the computer is off. But punch the power button, and your computer comes back to life just as you left it.

   If you plan to be away from your computer for a short while, standby is the place to be. And just as "Stand by for these commercial messages" is your signal to head for the fridge, the standby mode on your computer signals a good time to go make yourself one of those big ol' Dagwood-style sandwiches.

> Save your work before you go into standby. Unsaved information will be lost if you don't take this precaution.

Hibernation

Hibernation is the lazy person's dream. This option gives you the luxury of just stopping what you're doing and walking away (well, after you follow the steps below). No more saving everything you've done and closing all your programs. Nope. Hibernation saves all your work to memory, turns off your monitor and hard disk, and then turns off your computer. When you restart your computer, your desktop is put back just as you left it. And life is like a hammock just a-swinging in the breeze.

To Do 2.3: Putting the Computer in Hibernation

1. Click on the Start pop-up menu.
2. Choose Shut Down.
3. Click the down arrow to bring up other options.
4. Choose Hibernate.

   Notice the information below your selection. Microsoft wants to make sure that you know what you're doing.

5. Click OK.

   If you change your mind, click Cancel, and Windows will return to normal.

6. Windows powers down.

   Again, you can hear that Windows is slowing down. You get a little note reminding you that Windows is saving all that work you had going before you put your computer in hibernation.

   Just punch the power button when you're ready to go back to work, and your computer comes back to life. This time you get a message informing you that your computer is putting things back just as you left them.

   Windows has locked up your system so that no one else can get in. Just punch the Enter key to get past this annoyance.

   Wow! There it is. Just as you left it. Even if you left it a half-done mess.

> Several people have had trouble with the Hibernate function with Windows 98. People have written to me stating that Windows 98 goes into hibernation and then doesn't want to come out. It seems to go into some kind of coma. I'm a little difficult to wake after a really good nap, so I have to say I understand, but I can't honestly say whether Microsoft has fixed this problem, so be aware.

Turning Off the Computer

When you're really, really, definitely "fer sure" done for the day, you can quit Windows and turn off your computer.

To Do 2.4: Quitting Windows

1. Click on the Start pop-up menu.
2. Choose Shut Down.
3. Select Shut Down.

   This should already be your option, but if it isn't, click the down arrow for a complete list of options.

4. Click the OK button.

   If you change your mind, click Cancel, and Windows will return to normal.

5. Possible questions about saving work appear.

   If you haven't saved any documents to disk, you'll be informed of that now and given a chance to save. If you wait too long, a message appears saying, basically, that you are waiting too long and Windows isn't going to end this program until you decide whether you want to save the changes you've made to your work. All right, all right! Click End Now or Cancel, depending on whether you want to save.

6. Shutting-down messages appear.

   Windows displays a message that it is shutting down, just to make sure that you know what you did. Of course, there are no other options at this point, so if this isn't what you wanted, too bad. So sad. Now you have to flip back to the beginning of this hour and start all over.

7. Turn off the monitor.

   Turn off the power switch to the monitor, plus anything else attached to your PC, such as a printer.

> See Hour 8, "Working with Programs," for information on saving your valuable work.

Summary

This hour is dedicated to starting and stopping Windows 2000. The big question of the day is whether you standby, go into hibernation, or shut down completely. Decisions, decisions. There's always the option that you just leave your computer on and walk away from it. That's pretty simple, too.

Q&A

Q How do I know whether my computer will support hibernation?

A The only way to know whether your computer will support hibernation is to follow the preceding steps and see whether the Hibernate option is highlighted. If it looks faded, your computer isn't made to support it.

Q Do I have to turn off my computer?

A No. If you use your computer frequently, you don't have to use any of these suggestions. You can leave it on and walk away. Just make sure that you use one of the screen savers that Windows offers. Hour 21, "Adjusting the Screen," discusses a tad more on power management options so that completely turning off your computer is not your only choice.

Workshop

The workshop includes quiz questions to help gauge your grasp of the material and exercises to help reinforce your learning. You'll find the answers to the quiz in Appendix A, "Answers."

Quiz

1. What should you plug all your computer gadgets into?
2. How many characters can your password be?
3. What is the only option you have for shutting down that does not require you to save your work first?
4. *Bonus Question*: What country is Mount Fuji in?

Exercises

1. Turn on your computer and log on. Play with some programs.
2. Follow the steps for hibernation and discover whether your computer is equipped for such a thing.
3. Do ten jumping jacks and try to touch your toes.

Vocabulary

domain name—The name you will type in on the computer screen to log on to your network. Also, two vaguely rhyming words that I am going to try to work into my next poem.

fer sure—An idiom popularized in the mid-1980s as part of the so-called Valley Girl fad. Loosely translates as *definitely*, *with certainty*, *really really really*. Often vocalized with a sarcastic tone and poor pronunciation.

surge/spike protection—Protection from a power surge, or pretty much any change in the flow of electricity into your computer, or whatever you're protecting. It is an important characteristic to look for when shopping for a power strip. Can save your computer's life in the event of a lightning storm.

HOUR 3

Getting to Know Your Computer

Welcome to the tour of your computer. Everyone, stay together. No talking, no lagging behind, no taking pictures. We're walking, we're walking…

Time to get familiar with your computer. This hour is dedicated to making you more comfortable with the major aspects of your computer. The things that make this baby work and the areas where you'll probably be spending most of your time.

The highlights in this hour include the following:

- The desktop
- My Computer
- My Documents
- The Start menu
- The Control Panel

Basic Identification

There are some basic elements to Windows 2000, the "little stuff." These aren't the features boasted about on the box or in magazines. Instead, they're important places you should know about to get your bearings straight in Windows. There are five of them:

- The desktop
- My Computer (not *my* computer, but My Computer)
- My Documents
- The Start menu
- The Control Panel

Anything you can do with your computer is somehow connected to one of these five basic doodads.

The Desktop

If your PC were a large city, the desktop would be the airport. It's the place where you go to start things on your computer and where you return when things are finished. Most of the things mentioned in this hour—My Computer and the Start menu—are located on the desktop.

Figure 3.1 shows what's on your desktop.

FIGURE 3.1
The Windows desktop.

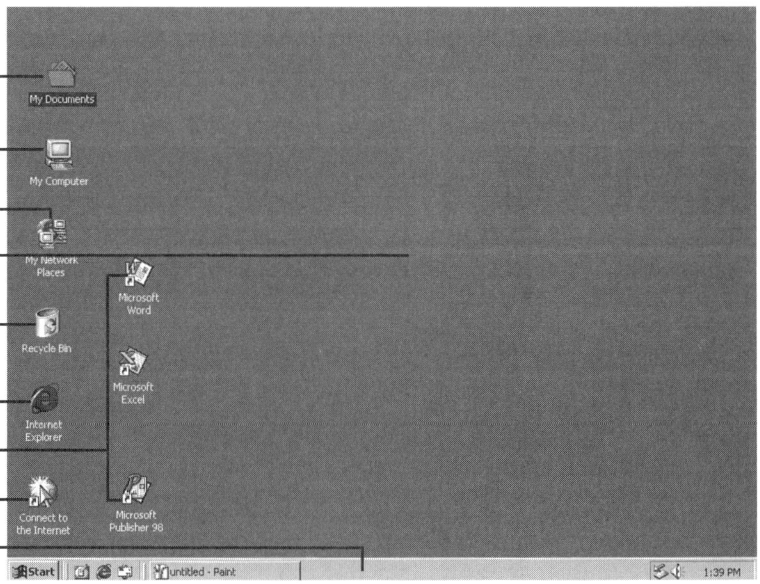

Screen Item	*Description*
Taskbar	The taskbar is located at the bottom of the screen. You use the taskbar to quickly switch between the windows, programs, or documents that you have open.
My Computer	My Computer is used to see everything on your computer.
Recycle Bin	The Recycle Bin is a holding bin for stuff you've deleted. You can go back and take things out of the Recycle Bin, should you have a change of heart about deleting something.
My Documents	This special folder will contain everything you create in Windows. All the documents, graphics, worksheets, and other files will be saved somewhere in this folder. It's *your* folder for *your* stuff.
My Network Places	The My Network Places icon lets you peek at the other computers on your network. The icon is there whether or not your PC is connected to a network.
Internet Explorer	Web browser software, which is your gateway to the Internet. This is really a program that Microsoft adds to the desktop for easy access. You can place other programs on the desktop as well, which is discussed in Hour 16, "Organizing the Desktop."

> The desktop shown in Figure 3.1 might look a tad different on your screen. If what you see is different and you want to change it, refer to Hour 16. You can change everything about the desktop because it is completely customizable.

My Computer

The My Computer icon represents all the *stuff* on your computer. Primarily, it contains icons representing the disk drives in your system: the floppy drive A, the hard drive C, and your CD-ROM or DVD drive, as well as other hard drives, removable drives, Sunday drives—you get the idea. Clicking those drive icons displays the contents of the drives, files, and folders, which are the sum of everything in your computer. (Hence the name, *My Computer*.) Figure 3.2 provides a quick tour of the desktop where you will find My Computer.

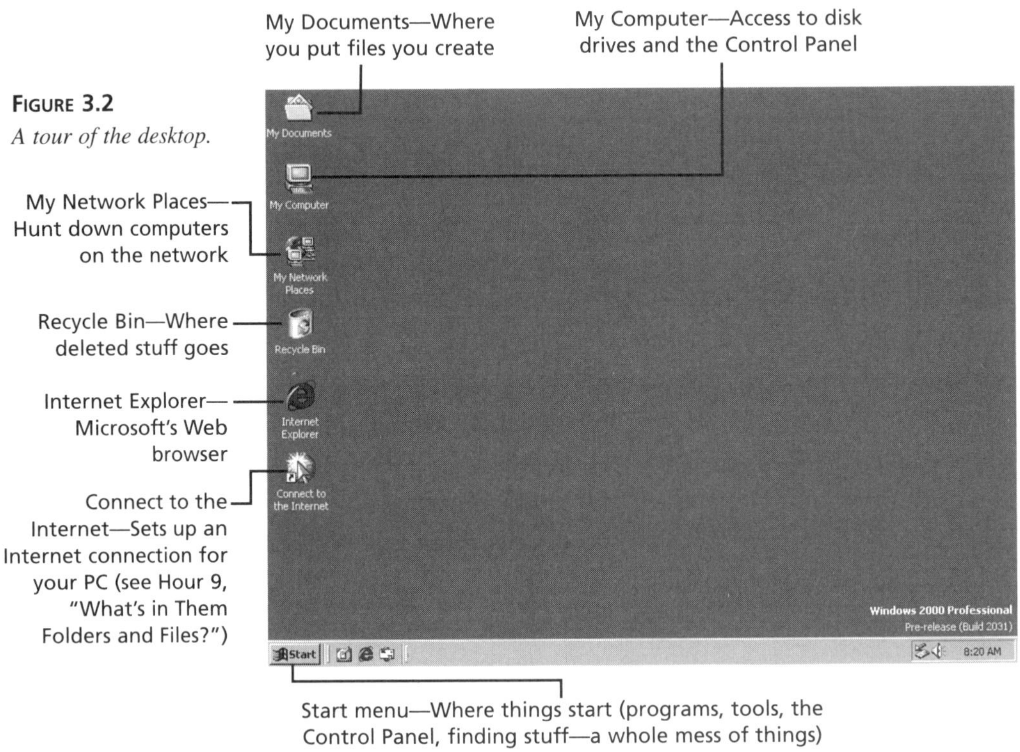

FIGURE 3.2
A tour of the desktop.

In addition to disk drives, the My Computer window also displays special folders, most notably the Control Panel (which is covered later in this hour).

> The My Computer icon is stuck on the desktop. You can move it around or rename it, but you cannot remove or delete it.

Peeking Inside My Computer

Double-click the My Computer icon to display the My Computer window, which contains a visual representation of your computer's hard drives. What you see should be similar to Figure 3.3.

FIGURE 3.3
The My Computer dialog box.

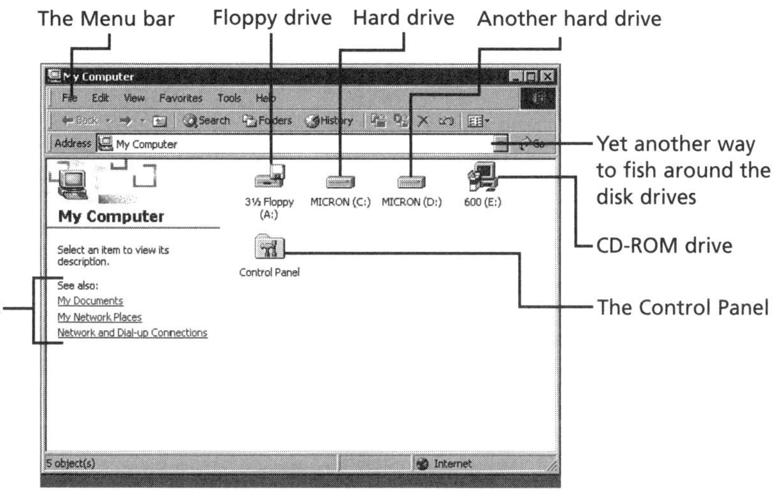

3

Look for the following things on your screen in the My Computer window:

- Your PC's floppy drive, A
- Your PC's hard drive, C
- More hard drives (if available)
- A CD-ROM or DVD drive
- Other types of drives, ZIP, JAZ, CD-R, and the gamut

The Control Panel Folder

The disk drive icons represent your computer's disk drives and the files and programs stored there. The Control Panel is used to control the appearance and behavior of Windows and the various hardware goodies your PC might have buried in its bosom or attached to the case.

Disk drives, no matter what type, are given letters and names. The letters have a colon after them and appear within parentheses. The names are optional and can be changed or deleted (see Hour 20, "Fixing Up Your Disk Drives").

The "serving hand" thing you might see under a disk drive means that the drive is up for grabs on the network, a shared drive. Likewise, a drive that looks like it's connected to the sewer system is a drive on someone else's computer on the network, one your computer is currently "borrowing."

> You can find more about this networking stuff in Hour 14, "Using the Local Network."

Be Bold! Open Up a Hard Drive

Windows displays the goodies inside your computer as icons. To see what's inside an icon—a disk drive or folder or whatever—double-click the icon with the mouse.

The window that appears after opening a hard drive displays files and folders on that hard drive. In Figure 3.4, you see the contents of drive C displayed, which consist mostly of folders with a few file icons tossed in.

FIGURE 3.4
The opened C drive.

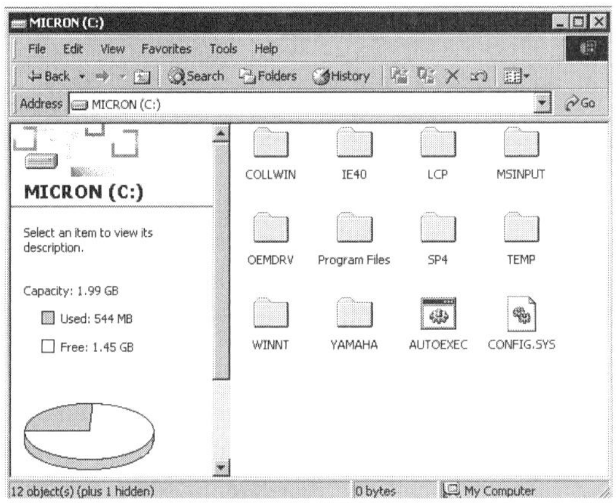

> I don't recommend opening files at random. Opening folders and snooping around is okay. Opening random files, on the other hand, might do something unintended. See Hour 4, "Working in Windows," for more information. Also, check out Hour 16 and Hour 18, "Maintaining and Cleaning Files." They are both about working with files.

Closing Various Windows

Close the drive C window; click its close button (the × button in the upper-right corner).

By the way, closing a window *does not* delete it or its contents. It just simply closes the window, just as closing a window in your house doesn't destroy the garden.

> You can close any window you like in any order; it doesn't matter which ones you opened first.

> All icons have names. The name is located beneath the icon. The icon picture clues you in to what the file does or which program created it.

Introducing My Documents

I want to introduce you to your new best friend: My Documents. My Documents is a folder that lives forever on your desktop. It's the folder where you'll store all the documents, all the graphics, or any other files you create.

Windows is configured to automatically take you to the My Documents folder whenever you use the Save command. It's also set up to display the My Documents folder when you use the Open command. This way, you can always find your stuff.

Inside the My Documents folder, you can create additional, specific folders for your stuff. Folders can be created for specific types of files and for projects, and you can create folders within folders within folders for several levels of organization.

More about working with My Documents can be found in Hour 9.

Accessing the Control Panel

The Control Panel was designed for *dinking*—you know, what men do with car engines when they have nothing else to do. They tweak and twiddle. You can do the same thing with your computer at the Control Panel.

▼ To Do

To Do 3.1: Opening the Control Panel

1. Click the Start menu button.
2. Choose Settings.
3. Click on Control Panel, as shown in Figure 3.5.

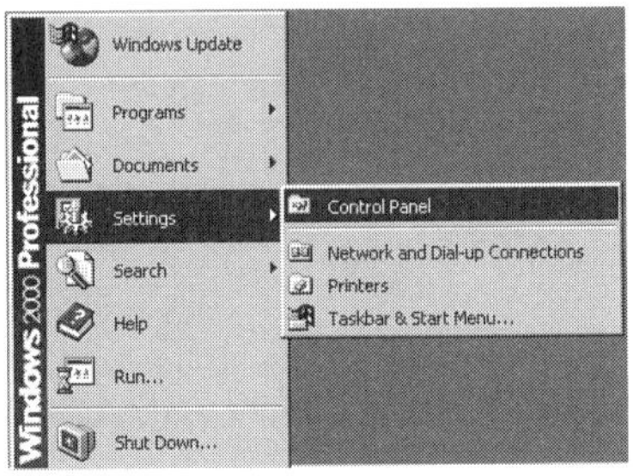

FIGURE 3.5
Finding the Control Panel via the Start button.

Or, you can…

1. Double-click on My Computer.
2. Double-click on the Control Panel icon, shown in Figure 3.6.

FIGURE 3.6
The Control Panel icon.

Both ways are equally acceptable and take you to the same place. (Actually, there are about half a dozen ways to display the Control Panel; you can find the other four on your own.)

The Control Panel contains icons that do a variety of things (all of which supposedly help you do your work better), including changing the way your desktop looks and setting the options for various devices in your computer.

What you see when you open the Control Panel might be slightly different from Figure 3.7. Certain programs may add their own icons to the Control Panel, and you might not see some specialty items, such as the Accessibility Options shown in Figure 3.7.

To work the Control Panel, you double-click an icon related to the part of Windows or your PC that you want to meddle with. Double-clicking an icon opens a window or dialog box where settings can be made or reviewed.

FIGURE 3.7
A typical Control Panel window. Double-click any of these icons to "open" them.

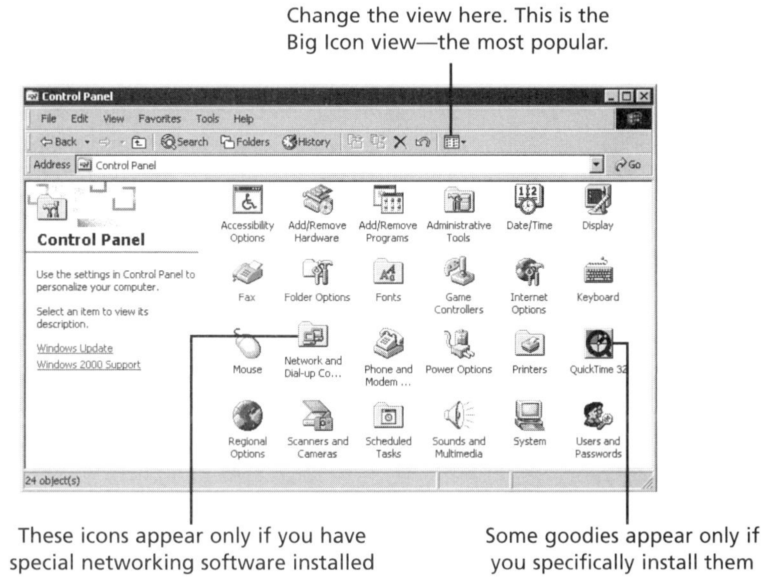

> If you want a detailed list of what each icon in the Control Panel is for, choose View and then Details from the menu. The icons are then listed with a brief description. If you want the icons the way they were, choose View and then Large Icons.

Table 3.1 outlines various Control Panel icons and their functions. Some are pretty nifty. Some are puzzles better left alone.

TABLE 3.1 Control Panel Icons

Icon	*Name*	*Description*
	Accessibility Options	Used to assist handicapped or physically impaired folk when they use Windows 2000.
	Add/Remove Hardware	Opens the Add Hardware wizard. Use this thing any time you add new hardware to your computer.
	Add/Remove Programs	Helps you install software. Really, all it does is hunt for the Setup or Install program on a floppy disk or CD-ROM drive.

continues

TABLE 3.1 continued

Icon	*Name*	*Description*
	Administrative Tools	Used to configure administrative settings for your computer. Not really necessary unless you need to get into the nitty-gritty workings of your computer.
	Date/Time	Opens the Date/Time Properties dialog box, used to set the date and time on your PC.
	Display	Summons the Display Properties dialog box, which controls the desktop.
	Fax	Used to set up your fax information.
	Folder Options	This icon is all about how folders look and behave.
	Fonts	The Fonts folder opens to reveal the fonts installed on your computer. There you can look at the fonts, print previews, delete fonts, or install new fonts.
	Game Controllers	This icon is just for fun. It adds, removes, and configures joysticks and gamepads.
	Internet Options	Configures your Internet settings.
	Keyboard	Customizes the keyboard settings for cursor blink rate, repeat rate, and important stuff like that.
	Mouse	Opens the Mouse Properties dialog box, where you can mess with the mouse and cursors.
	Network and Dial-up Connections	This icon connects your computer to other computers and networks and the Internet.
	Phone and Modem Options	Configures the way your telephone dials out and your modem properties.

Icon	*Name*	*Description*
	Power Options	Sets the energy-savings options for your computer.
	Printers	This folder is for adding, removing, and configuring both local and network printers. You can work with your fax here, too.
	Regional Options	Sets the standards for time, currency numbers, date, and so on, to fit your region of the world.
	Scanners and Cameras	Configures scanners and cameras that can be added to your computer.
	Scheduled Tasks	Schedules programs and certain operations to run automatically.
	Sounds and Multimedia	Assigns sounds to computer events and activities. Also configures sound devices for speech. (Your PC needs a sound card to make sound happen.)
	System	Detailed items providing information about your computer.
	Users and Passwords	Enables you to add users and set passwords.

There's a whole lotta dinkin' going on!

And Now, the Start Menu

Think of the Start menu as the starting place when you want to start something. Start working. Start a game. Start writing a letter. Start balancing your checkbook. All these things begin with the Start menu (provided that you have the appropriate software to do these tasks).

The Start menu is attached to the Start button, which you'll most likely find in the lower-left corner of your screen. It says (surprisingly) *Start*.

To see the Start menu, click the Start button with your mouse.

You can also use the Ctrl+Esc key combination to pop up the Start menu.

And if your keyboard has a Windows key (between the Alt and Ctrl keys), you can press it to pop up the Start menu as well.

There's a lot going on with the Start menu. Lots to do, lots to see. So I'm going to table this discussion and move any further conversation about the Start menu to Hour 6, "Everything About the Start Menu."

Summary

We hope you enjoyed your tour. Don't forget to sign the guest book! Buh-bye!

Now you know the basic what's-where of Windows 2000. Most everything you do from this point on refers back to the items mentioned in this hour. You should walk away from this hour knowing where My Computer, the Control Panel, and the desktop are located. If you don't, you weren't paying attention! Spend another hour after class and go back through the lesson. And spit out that gum while you're at it!

Q&A

Q What can I delete from the desktop?

A You cannot delete the My Computer, Recycle Bin, or My Network Places icons. You *shouldn't* delete My Documents, but beyond that, everything else can be deleted. My advice is to not delete anything until you're very familiar with Windows and know exactly what you do and do not need.

Q Is it possible to add programs to the Start menu?

A Absolutely. This is covered in Hour 6 and makes the Start menu very effective to use.

Q Can I delete icons from the Control Panel?

A No. There might be programs you don't think you'll use, but never, ever delete a program from Windows. Just ignore the darn thing if you don't think you'll use it.

Workshop

The workshop includes quiz questions to help gauge your grasp of the material and exercises to help reinforce your learning. You'll find the answers to the quiz in Appendix A, "Answers."

Quiz

1. Which item in the Start menu contains programs?
2. What type of icons will you find in My Computer?
3. How do you close a window in Windows?
4. *Bonus Question*: Who was the first Roman turned Christian emperor?

Exercises

1. Open My Computer. Open drive C. Continue opening folders and exploring their contents. (Don't open any icons, though.)
2. Double-click on My Computer, double-click on the Control Panel, and double-click on the Fax icon. Fill in the blanks in the User Information tab.

Vocabulary

Control Panel—Where you can go to dink around and customize your desktop.

jig—Any of a variety of lively dances performed in triple time.

My Computer—A virtual toy box where your computer keeps all its goodies. Also, a way of asserting your possessive spirit when referring to your computer.

HOUR 4

Working in Windows

The essence of Windows is to make it easy for you to get something accomplished, to do work. This is true, even though there are rumors floating around that Microsoft's real goal is to frustrate you and run the world. This is absolutely false: It's very possible to get work done without the frustration.

To make things happen in Windows, you have to start an application or run a program. This hour is dedicated to getting your work started with Windows.

The highlights in this hour include the following:

- Starting a program
- Quitting a program
- Using the Documents menu

Starting Something

Don't be fooled! Just because the button on the screen reads "Start" doesn't mean that it's the place where everything has to begin. The Start button is merely one of several places where things begin. It's obvious, but it's not like "Go" in Monopoly or the mob scene at the DMV.

> You can have Windows start some of your programs automatically when you first start Windows. Refer to Hour 6, "Everything About the Start Menu."

Starting with the Start Menu

The Start button starts lots of things, and one of those things can be a program in your computer. Just about every program, application, or utility has an item lurking somewhere on the Start menu. If the program isn't on the Start menu, you can always add it later.

To Do 4.1: Starting a New Program

To Do

1. Click the Start button.

   You can also pop up the Start menu by pressing Ctrl+Esc. If you have the kind of keyboard that has a Windows key, you can press the Windows key.

2. Choose Programs.

   The Programs submenu appears, as shown in Figure 4.1. The submenu lists programs and other submenus, organizing your entire computer's applications, programs, utilities, and games—everything.

   A program appears as an icon followed by the program name.

   A submenu appears as a special folder icon followed by the submenu's name. The name somehow refers to the submenu's contents, either a broad category of the name of a specific program (such as the Norton Utilities), a suite of programs (such as Microsoft Office), or a software developer (such as Adobe).

3. Find the program you want to run.

   Search for your program. For example, suppose that you want to run Paint so that you can doodle while you're talking on the phone.

   Paint does not appear on the main Programs submenu. If it did, you would choose it right now. Instead, you will have to hunt through the submenus.

   Because Paint is a Windows program, you should open the Accessories submenu to find it. That's where Windows keeps all its programs.

Clicking the Accessories item displays that submenu. You will see a list of even more submenus, beneath which are some of Windows own programs. You will spy Paint about halfway down the list of programs.

The submenu's name kind of gives you a hint as to what types of programs live there:Accessories contains miscellaneous Windows programs; Startup contains its own programs you want to add; Games contains games; and so on.

FIGURE 4.1
The Start menu and a submenu.

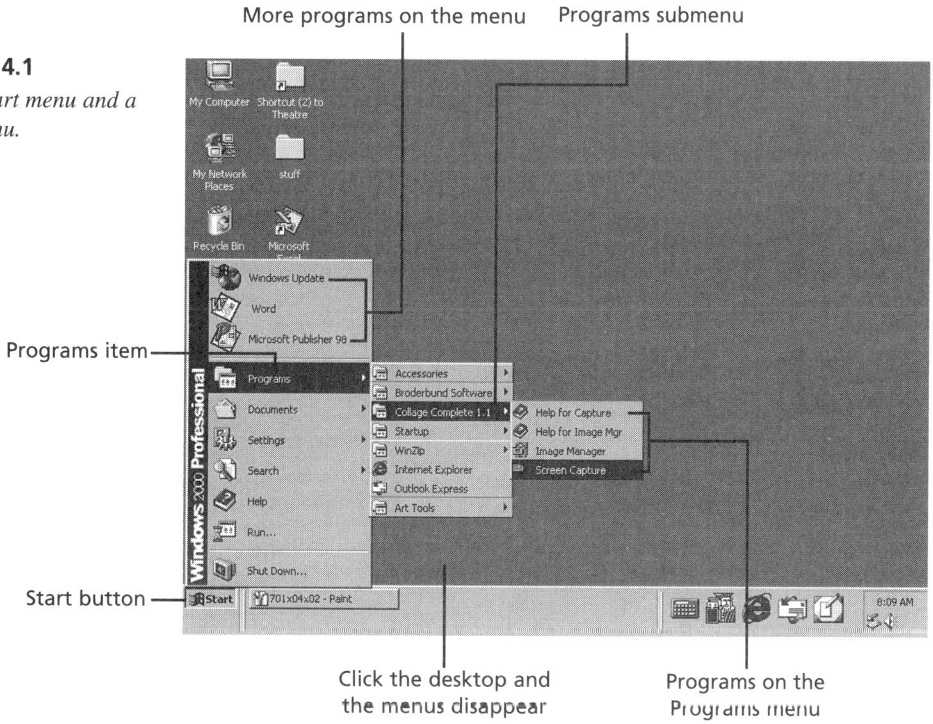

4. Click your program.

   This starts the program. If you choose Paint, you start Paint and can immediately begin doodling. (Choose File and then Exit to quit Paint. Because this is merely a tutorial, you shouldn't be doodling right now!) You can also jump to Hour 6 to learn more about all the goodies in the Start menu.

> These Start button menus and submenus are very mouse-sensitive. If you move the cursor off a menu just slightly, the menu might disappear. If the cursor hovers over another submenu item, that menu pops right up. It takes practice and a steady hand to work with these menus.

Another very handy way to start a program is to make your favorite or most frequently used program a part of the Start menu. Hour 8, "Working with Programs," covers adding programs to the Start menu. Then, when you want to start Word, for example, it will be sitting in the upper part of the Start menu. Easy, efficient, just wonderful!

Starting from an Icon on the Desktop

Some programs live on the desktop, pictured there as little icons. Windows comes with a few of these preinstalled, such as the icon for Internet Explorer.

To start a program (such as Internet Explorer), double-click its icon on the desktop. The program starts and quickly appears on the desktop.

In addition to Internet Explorer, you can add any program to the desktop as an icon. This is an incredible shortcut and makes running your most used programs a cinch.

Refer to Hour 16, "Organizing the Desktop," to find out how you can add programs and games to your desktop.

Starting a Program from a Window

You can use the My Computer icon or the Windows Explorer program to dive into the depths of a hard drive on your PC. Any time a program icon is displayed in one of those windows, you can open it to run the program.

To be honest, starting a program from a window is kind of dumb; there are much easier ways to do it. However, I'm required by the Computer Book Author's Guild to document everything. I have to mention it.

There are probably only two times you will start a program in a window. The first is when your program is on a floppy disk or a CD/DVD disk. The second is when you use the Find command to locate a file.

To get some practice, you can start the COMMAND program, which runs a DOS prompt window—the command prompt. Ah, the good old days....

The command prompt program is on the Start menu (in the Accessories submenu). Another way to start it is to browse the folders on drive C and then open that icon. Oh! Here's a task.

To Do 4.2: Starting a New Program in My Computer

1. Open My Computer (double-click the icon on the desktop to open it).
2. Open drive C.
3. Open the WINNT folder.

   If you don't see any files here, click the blue text that says Show Files. (This happens only if you're viewing your folders as a Web page.)
4. Open the System32 folder.

   Again, if no files are displayed, click the Show Files text.
5. Locate the CMD icon.

   Scroll down, down, down....
6. Open the CMD icon by double-clicking it with the mouse.
7. Fear not the command prompt. Type `Exit` and press the Enter key to banish it. Tremble not, gentle reader.

> Read Hour 8 for information on working with programs. It truly will expand your mind.

Using the Quick Launch Bar

This is easy. The programs you use the most should sit on the Quick Launch bar, where they're only a click away from being run.

The Quick Launch bar appears on the taskbar, typically right next to the Start button, as shown in Figure 4.2. Unlike the buttons on the taskbar, the Quick Launch bar displays program icons.

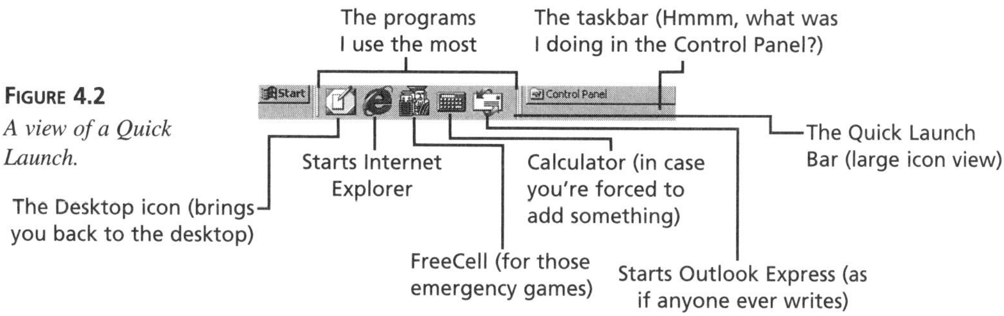

FIGURE 4.2
A view of a Quick Launch.

To start any icon on the Quick Launch, click it once. That instantly runs whatever program is associated with the icon.

> You can adjust the Quick Launch bar until it's organized and tweaked to your liking. More tweaking information is covered in Hour 16.

Windows comes configured with three items on the Quick Launch bar: Internet Explorer, Outlook Express, and a button that instantly hides all open windows and displays the desktop.

Using the Run Command to Start a Program

The Run command exists only for special situations, such as when you're asked to start a program with the Run command. For example, the documentation that came with your CD-ROM might request that you use the Run command. You can also use the Run command to find folders, documents, and even Internet resources. Bottom line: The Run command runs anything that's in your computer.

To Do 4.3: Starting a New Program from the Run Command

1. Activate the Start menu.

   You can also press Ctrl+Esc to pop that sucker up or click the Start button if a mouse is handy.

2. Click Run.

   The Run dialog box appears, similar to the one shown in Figure 4.3.

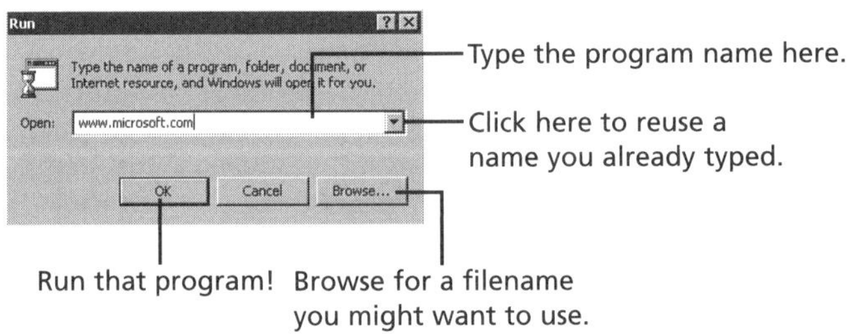

FIGURE 4.3
The Run command's dialog box.

3. Type the program's name.

   This is why this step is seldom done. You have to type the program's name in the Open box. Sometimes you even have to type the full pathname, which includes the disk drive, folders, a colon, and various backslashes—looks like the cat walked across the keyboard.

Your best help here is to carefully refer to whatever material is asking you to use the Run command to start a program. Games are a good example. The tiny manual in the front cover of the CD case will include a pathname you are asked to type into the Run command box. For now, you can run the Welcome to Windows program by typing the following into the Run dialog box:

```
WELCOME
```

Press Enter, and the Welcome to Windows dialog box opens, complete with annoying theme song.

Another case would be when you're browsing to a specific Web page. Then, you type the Web address into the dialog box, such as

```
www.microsoft.com
```

Press Enter, and in a few Internet moments, you're there!

> The drop-down list in the Run dialog box displays previous programs you've run. Choose one to run it again. (If Windows 2000 is new on your PC, you won't have anything listed in this drop-down list. Sorry!)

If the program can't be found, a rude message is displayed. Confirm what you typed and then try the command again. Remember that Windows is absolutely hypersensitive to every letter, number, and dot in the pathname, so you must be hypervigilant in your transcription.

> Sometimes you think that you're doing everything right, and the program still can't be found. You might want to refer to Hour 8 for help in tracking it down.

Starting a Document to Open a Program

Is the purpose of life to create? Or do we exist to serve? And what about those philosophers who state that the purpose of life is to discover life's purpose? Take a moment to ponder. Hmmm....

Now, think about a program's purpose. Programs, specifically applications, exist to create documents. And—hallelujah, Microsoft!—here's a secret Windows shortcut to creative fulfillment: You can start your work easily and quickly by opening a document instead of an application.

This is not a philosophical breakthrough; it's merely a shortcut. Why open a program and then open a document when you can merely open the document? You save one step! Of course, this works only after you've created the document.

Finding Your Document in the Documents Menu

Another Start menu submenu is the Documents menu. It contains the most recent documents you've opened or peeked at. You can choose one of those documents from the menu to instantly start working on it again.

To Do 4.4: Starting a Document from the Documents Menu

1. Click the Start menu button (or press Ctrl+Esc or that Windows button).
2. Choose Documents.

   Either press the D key or hover your cursor over the word *Documents*. This pops up the Documents submenu, shown in Figure 4.4, which contains a list of documents you've tinkered with recently.

FIGURE 4.4
The Documents menu.

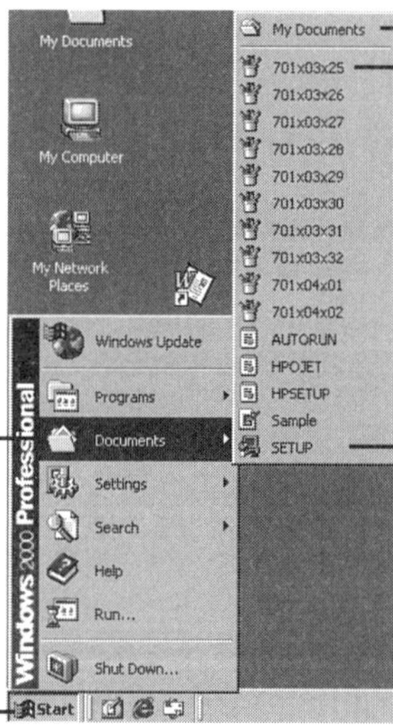

   If your Documents menu contains only the hollow word *Empty*, there are no documents to open. Oh, well. Get busy!

3. Click the document.

   Picking one of these documents automatically opens the application that created it.

4. Begin your work.

Cleaning the Documents Menu

As you continue to work, you will notice that the Documents menu continues to fill with the names of documents, up to the last 15 items you've opened or saved. Although not all Windows applications stick documents here, eventually this can get really junky.

To Do 4.5: Cleaning the Documents Menu

1. Click the Start button.
2. Choose Settings.
3. Click Taskbar & Start Menu.
4. Click the Start Menu Options tab.
5. Click Clear in the Customize Start menu.
6. Click OK to close the dialog box.

Finding Documents in My Documents

A special desktop folder is My Documents. It's really—shhh!—a folder on the hard drive, but it's the folder you and your applications use to store documents you create. Hence the name, *My Documents*.

You can open the My Documents icon on the desktop just as you open the My Computer icon. This displays the files and folders stored in the My Documents folder. When you find the document you want, open it by double-clicking with the mouse. This starts the application that created the document and loads the document for editing, printing, whatever.

Be a Quitter: Quitting Programs

Quitting a program is right up there with starting one: It's inevitable. In keeping with its reputation for having way too many ways for doing things, Windows has several ways to quit a program. Then again, humans have a variety of ways of saying goodbye: *buh-bye*, *adios*, *au revoir*, *ciao*, *sayonara*, *auf Wiedersehen*, and so on.

The Common Way to Quit

Most applications in Windows have the File menu. Sitting squat at the bottom of that menu is the Exit command. To quit any application, choose File and then Exit, and you're out.

The Exit command might be, in some rare instances, the word *Quit*.

If you haven't saved your stuff before quitting, Windows will alert you and give you a chance to save.

Refer to Hour 8 for more information on saving your stuff.

Quitting by Closing a Window

In Windows, closing a window is often the same thing as quitting. (This is why some Quit commands are called *Close*.)

You close a window by clicking the X in the window's upper-right corner. This is more abrupt, kind of like saying goodbye by walking out the door.

The keyboard shortcut for closing a window is Alt+F4. There is no justification for this keyboard combination other than it's consistent throughout Windows.

The Ctrl+Alt+Delete Way to Quit

Another option to killing off any program is to press Ctrl+Alt+Delete. This is the old DOS reset command, which used to restart the entire computer. Windows has changed that somewhat.

The Ctrl+Alt+Delete command in Windows 2000 takes you to a Windows Security dialog box to decide what you want to do: Shut down the computer, change your password, or stop a program that has locked up and is no longer responding to your commands.

When you first press Ctrl+Alt+Delete, you will see the Windows Security dialog box.

Summary

Windows is not the world. It's merely a path to your applications, which is why you use the computer. The applications can be started in a number of ways: from the Start menu, the desktop, the Quick Launch bar, or a window. You can also run an application by opening a document created by that application. When you're done, you close the program's window, which can also be done in a several ways.

Q&A

Q Is there really a best way to start a program?

A No, not really. The more you use Windows, you will come to realize that many times you start a program based on where you happen to be at the time or what you want to do.

Q Is there a best way to end a program?

A Yes, absolutely. Always end your program by clicking the File button and then Exit (or Close). This allows your program to officially close and properly shut down.

Workshop

The workshop includes quiz questions to help gauge your grasp of the material and exercises to help reinforce your learning. You'll find the answers to the quiz in Appendix A, "Answers."

Quiz

1. What three things are in My Computer?
2. What is the most common way to quit a program?
3. Other than clicking the Start button, what is a way to open the Start menu?
4. *Bonus Question*: How long was the Titanic?

Exercises

1. Start a program, create a document, and close the document and program.
2. Repeat.
3. Now, go to your Documents menu and clean away the documents you have just been playing with.

Vocabulary

desktop—What appears on your monitor after you have Windows up and running.

pathname—The full name of a file. The pathname includes the drive where the file lives, the folders, and then the file itself. The drive letter is followed by a colon, and backslashes (\) separate the folder names. For example, D:\Documents and Settings\All Users\Start Menu\Programs\Accessories\Games is the pathname for the game Solitaire.

submenu—A menu that appears after you choose an item from the primary menu.

Time Out 1

FreeCell: The Game for Real Athletes

One thing about Windows being graphical and all is that it opens the doors to some fun games. Just about everything you've ever played—in real life, in an arcade, or on any computer—has a Windows equivalent. Not only that, Windows itself comes with a handful of interesting games, wonderful toys to obsess over and take your time away from real work.

Right now, you deserve a little break. Every so often, this book will throw in a little Time Out session so that you can get familiar with the Windows games.

Where Are the Games Hiding?

If you look hard enough, you will find all kinds of games for all kinds of people. There are strategy games, blow 'em up games, adventure games, card games, board games, you name it.

Unfortunately (your boss might think otherwise), not all of those come with Windows. However, those games that do come with Windows can be fun and addicting, two of the highest qualifications of any good computer game. But, be aware: Many companies are suffering the effects of these addictions. Some companies have been known to delete all the games from computer systems. No way! Yes, way. So, keep a lid on this game addiction stuff.

> If, by chance, you go through these steps and you don't see FreeCell listed as one of your games, jump forward to Hour 6, "Everything About the Start Menu," and read about how to add a program to the Start menu. Then, come back here and finish reading this Time Out.

Follow these steps to find the games:

1. Open the Start menu.

   Click the Start button on the taskbar, or press Ctrl+Esc. These next few steps are a little long so feel free to take a peek at Figure TO1.1 (which illustrates these steps).

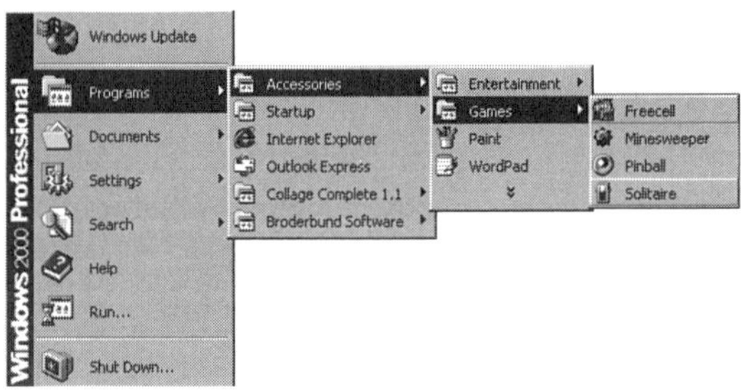

FIGURE TO1.1
The path to the games.

2. Choose Programs.

   The Programs submenu appears.

3. Choose Accessories.

   The Accessories submenu appears.

4. Choose Games.

   The Games submenu appears. You will see a list of the games installed with Windows, as well as any other games you might have added.

5. Click FreeCell.

   At this point, you can pick any game you want. This section is dedicated to learning FreeCell, so you might want to continue following along.

> There are three really cool things you can do with games: Add your favorite game to the Start menu, drag a shortcut to the desktop, or add a game of FreeCell (or any game) to the quick launch bar. You can have games all over the place! These nifty tricks can be found in Hour 8, "Working with Programs," and Hour 16, "Organizing the Desktop."

Learning to Play

FreeCell is a combination of a logic puzzle and solitaire card game. And if you become addicted, like most of the people in my family, FreeCell can keep you busy for hours at a time.

Perhaps the most annoying part about FreeCell is that every puzzle has a solution. Yes, every game has the potential to be won. Not that every solution is obvious or every game easy, but there is a solution, sometimes several. At times, though, you might have to give a good primal scream before you are able to see any. The irony is that the inevitable frustrations of FreeCell don't in the least diminish its addictive properties. If you're brave, check out Figure TO1.2 to get a glimpse of FreeCell. Warning: You'll be hooked once you see this figure.

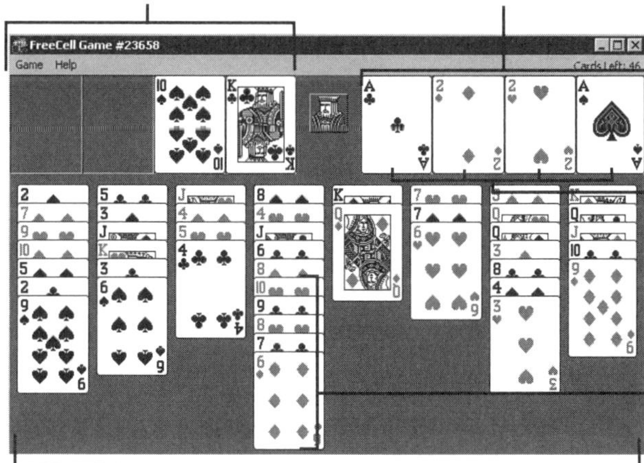

FIGURE TO1.2
A typical, highly frustrating FreeCell game.

The Object

The object of FreeCell is to move all the cards to the home cells (the area in the upper-right corner of the screen).

How to Win

You win by making four stacks of cards in the home cell area. The cards are divided by suit, and they are stacked in order, from lowest (the ace) to highest (the king).

Playing the Game

Move a card from the eight columns of cards by clicking the card you want to move and then clicking the stack where you want the card to go. The game will tell you whether it's a valid move, meaning that you've obeyed the rules of red on black (or black on red) and in numerical sequence.

Here are your options for moving cards:

- Onto one of the four free cells
- Onto a different stack
- Onto the appropriate home cell

> To move an entire stack of cards, FreeCell will automatically use all available space to move the cards one by one, re-sort them, and rebuild the cards back in order, in the new space. For example, if you have a stack of four cards that you are moving to a new stack, you must have three available spaces for FreeCell to move the stack.

Each free cell holds only one card, so you must have one free cell available to use it. You can also move a single card or a stack of sorted cards (for example, 5-6-7-8) to another stack. If you can move a stack of cards, the game will ask whether you want to move the whole stack or just the top card. However, because you can only place one card in each free cell area, moving a stack of cards depends on whether there is enough free space to allow the move.

Keep moving the cards around until you can start stacking the cards in the home cell area.

Tips and Tricks

Free Up Those Aces First!

Look for trouble spots, such as three of a kind in a row. That spells certain doom unless you can play all three cards.

Right-click a card to see what suit it's in. Sometimes it's difficult to see exactly what that red card is underneath that stack of other cards.

Try not to fill up the free cells, especially with high-suited cards, such as face cards.

If you can clear one whole column, you're halfway to winning the game.

You can move a card from the bottom deck of cards to a free cell by double-clicking the card.

Try to look several moves in advance.

If you get yourself into a pickle with only one legal move left, the title bar flashes, warning that you have only one move left.

Every puzzle has a solution! If you don't win the first time, try playing the same card layout again (it will ask whether you want to when it announces that you've lost). Don't be surprised if you have to play some games several times. Just remember to try a different approach each time so that you don't end up in the same losing position.

Here are a few options you have for starting a new game, which you'll want to do because you'll be addicted to this beyond belief:

- Push the F2 key to start a new game.
- Click Game and then Restart Game if you feel yourself heading down the wrong path.
- Click Game and then Select Game to pick a game number, or just work your way down the numbers. Start with game #1, then game #2, and so on.
- Click Game and then Statistics to find out how you're doing percentage-wise. If you don't like what you see, click the clear button and the score will be erased.

Hunting Down Other Games

If you have a modem and access to an online service or the Internet, you have an open door to thousands of games. Each of these Time Out sections will give you hints on where you can find more games.

Here is one place for finding games:

`http://play.yahoo.com/`

Hour 5

Getting Help

It's always been my belief that help systems are good only when you know what you are looking for. They never have entries titled, "That thingy that does that blocky thing for you," which, sad to say, is sometimes how I talk.

That being said, Windows 2000 does a good job of helping you find your topic when you have only a vague idea of what you want to ask.

The highlights in this hour include the following:

- Using the Help system
- Working with the index
- Troubleshooting
- Using the Find panel

Finding Help When You Need It

Help is everywhere. It's as quick as the "push" of a button or click of the mouse. This section is dedicated to showing you all the ways to find help. Here's a summary:

- Press the F1 key.
- Use the Help menu.
- Click a ? button.
- Access the Help system directly.

The F1 Key—The "Quicky" Way to Help

The F1 key is the Help key. Press it to get quick answers, whether you're stuck in a remote dialog box or off working in an application.

Sometimes the F1 key gives you a description or definition of your location and sometimes real information on getting something done. Figure 5.1 shows the F1 key giving help in the Paint program.

FIGURE 5.1
The F1 key type of help.

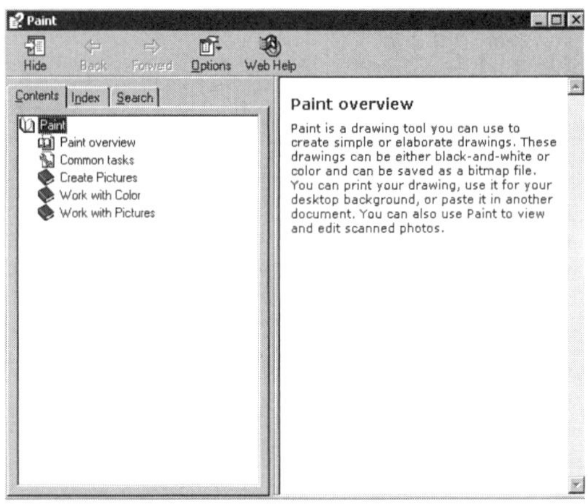

When you're done reviewing the information, press the Esc key to return to your document or click somewhere on your screen.

Help in a Program

You might be in the middle of something important, such as an intriguing game of FreeCell, when you need help. There is usually a Help menu, off to the right of the other menu items. Click that menu to see what types of help are available. (Unfortunately, psychological counseling is not yet available through Windows, not even Windows 2000.)

The ? Button

Some Windows programs and dialog boxes might display a little question mark button in the upper-right corner of the window (by the × [close] button). This appears most often in the various Office applications. Clicking the ? button activates a feature so that you can point and click anything in the window to get help on it.

Windows Help

You can also go directly to the Windows Help system.

To Do

To Do 5.1: Opening the Windows Help System

1. Click the Start button.
2. Click Help.

From this point, you can take any direction you want in order to find the answers to your questions. More about the Help system is next.

Using the Help System

The Windows Help system is designed so that you can look up information in the way that best suits you. There are several choices, most of which are represented by a tab inside the Help window:

- Contents—Look up help in a table of contents.
- Index—Use an index to find information.
- Search—Sift through the Help system for specific bits of text.
- Favorites—Bookmark topics that you keep referring to. The Favorites option is especially handy if you, like me, have about thirty trains of thought choo-chooing through your noggin at any given moment.
- Web Help—Click this button (no, it's not a tab in the dialog box) for Windows to hop out on the Web to search for information.

5

Figure 5.2 shows you the Contents panel in the Help system. This is where you see an organized overview of information in the Help system.

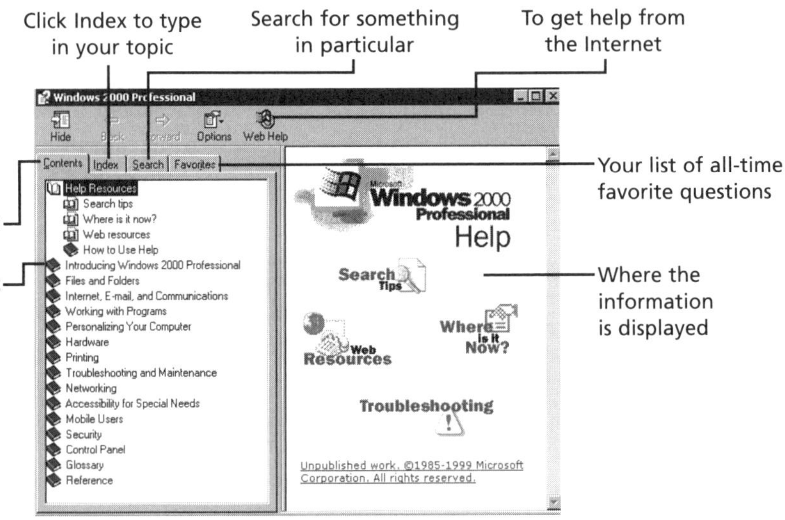

FIGURE 5.2
Working in the Contents tab.

> If you don't see the Contents panel, click the Contents tab in the upper part of the Help system window.

The Contents tab is organized as a table of contents. To open a category, click its name. This changes the icon by the category from a closed book to an open book and displays a list of topics in that category, as shown in Figure 5.3.

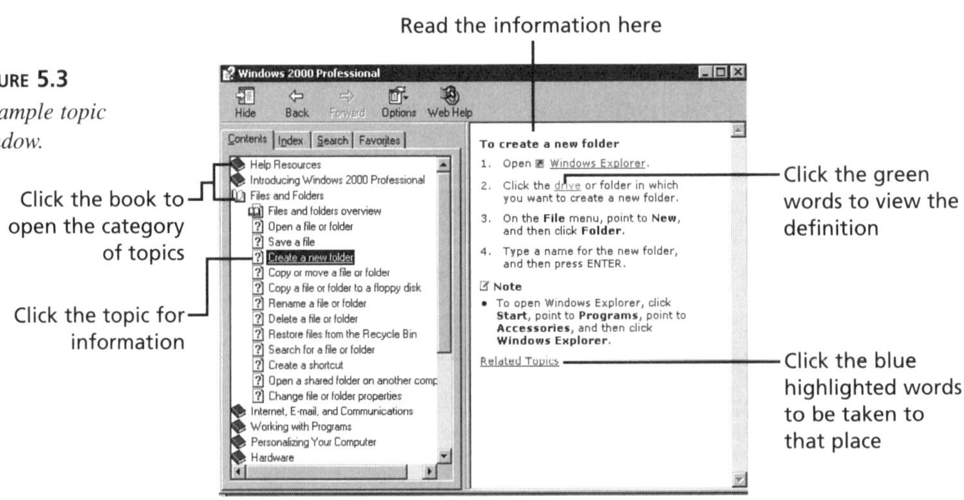

FIGURE 5.3
A sample topic window.

To close a category, and make the screen a little more readable, click the category name again.

To open a topic, click the topic name. This displays detailed information about the topic, often including step-by-step instructions in your native tongue.

Underlined text in the Help system means that you can click that text to see more information. *Blue underlines* are links, which display a topic or open another window. *Green underlines* highlight unusual terms or jargon that might baffle you.

To see a definition of the text, point the cursor at it. The cursor changes into a little hand with a pointy finger. Click once to see a pop-up definition, shown in Figure 5.4. Click again to make the definition go away. Do this enough times, and you will eventually be able to add to your resume "Conversant in Techno Babble."

FIGURE 5.4
A pop-up definition.

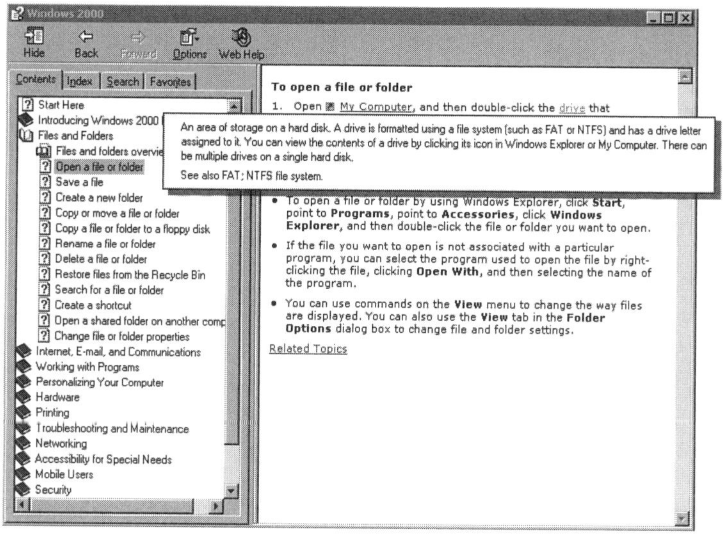

Using the Index

If the Contents tab shows "the manual," the Index tab would be the Index to that manual. All information about a specific program or Help topic is organized in that index.

You can use the index to quickly find a topic if you know exactly what it is. A note from personal experience: Microsoft has no entry beginning with the identifier "That thingy...."

To Do 5.2: The Index Tab

To Do

1. Click the Start button.
2. Click Help.
3. Click the Index tab.

   The Index tab part of the Help system displays an alphabetized list of items found in the Contents panel, as shown in Figure 5.5.

FIGURE 5.5
The Index panel.

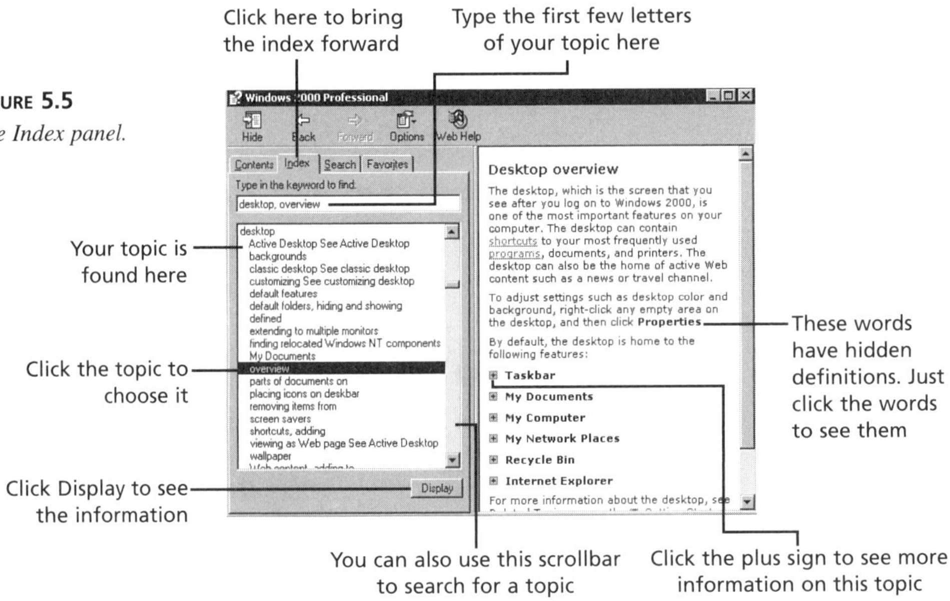

4. Search for your topic.

   Type the word you are searching for in the box at the top of the panel. As you type, notice how the Help system automatically scrolls to the first matching word, narrowing your search.

   If the topic or word you're searching for is not found, the Help system displays the next closest match (spelling-wise).

   If the topic or word cannot be found, trust me, it's not in the Help system. Try another related topic or word.
5. Click the topic or word in the scrolling list.

   In the scrolling list, locate the index topic or word. There may be several close matches, in which case you can click the closest match to highlight it.
6. Click Display.

If the topic has only one reference, such as a specific command, additional help information is displayed on the right side of the window for you to preview. If the topic has more than one reference, a second Topics Found dialog box appears, showing more topics. Click the specific topic you want and click the Display button.

Searching for the Right Word

Another way to hunt down information in the Help system is to use the Search panel. This locates every occurrence of any word or phrase anywhere in Help.

After opening the Help system, these steps are used to search for text.

To Do 5.3: The Search Tab

1. Click the Search tab.
2. Type in the word or phrase you want to search.
3. Click List Topics.

   A list of possible options is brought forward. Scroll down to find what you are looking for.
4. Click the word or phrase in the list.
5. Click Display.

   Your topic is displayed. Figure 5.6 illustrates this process of searching for a subject.

FIGURE 5.6
The Search panel.

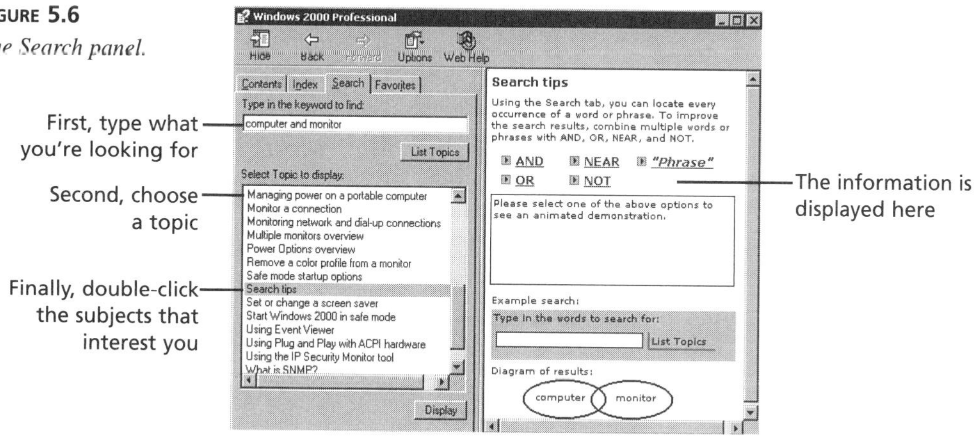

5

Search Tips

The following table gives directions on how to be more specific when using the Search panel in the Help system. When using the Search feature, you can search for *print*, for example, and Search will locate every occurrence of the word *print*. These tips help you better define what exactly it is you're looking for by combining words or phrases with *and*, *or*, *near*, and *not*.

Word	*Task*	*Example*	*Function*
And	Broadens search	*Computer and monitor*	Finds topics that use both words.
Or	Broadens search	*Computer or monitor*	Finds topics that contain either word or both words.
Near	Narrows search	*Computer near monitor*	Finds topics that contain both words in close proximity to each other.
Not	Narrows search	*Computer not monitor*	Finds topics that contain the word *computer* but not the word *monitor*.
"word"	Narrows search	*"computer monitor"*	Any words in quotation marks are searched for with that exact phrase.

Keeping Favorites

There are some things in Windows that you will never remember. Don't be embarrassed. It's a fact of life. I myself have a whole list. Having to grab something out of the Recycle Bin might be one of those things. Instead of constantly hunting down Recycle Bin information, you can find it once and then add it to your list of favorite Help topics.

To Do 5.4: Picking Your Favorites

To Do

1. Locate your topic.

   It's your choice how you find the information. You can use the Contents, Index, or Search tabs to find the topic you want to save in your Favorites panel.

2. Display the topic.

   This could mean clicking the topic and then clicking Display to show the information.

3. Click the Favorites tab.
4. Click Add.

   This saves the topic title and puts it in the topic list.

When you're ready to refer back to one of your favorites, simply double-click in the topics list to display that topic information, as shown in Figure 5.7.

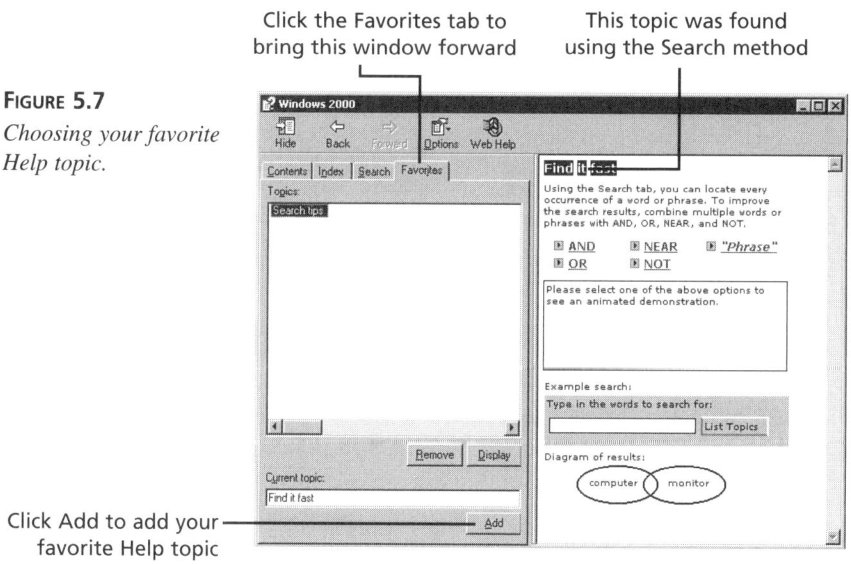

FIGURE 5.7
Choosing your favorite Help topic.

> When you're done with Help, simply click the × in the upper-right corner of the window. This is the universal Windows Close button.

5

Web Help

On the menu bar of the Help systems window is an icon called Web Help. This is a direct line to the Microsoft Product Support Services, located on the Internet. Yes, you need Internet access to use this.

This support service offers information about Windows 2000 that you might not find in the Help system and has a list of frequently asked questions (FAQs) that tend to be very helpful.

If you're hooked to the Internet, click the Web Help button, read the information, and click the Support Online link. You're in!

Summary

Don't be shy about spending time in Help. It's a great way to get to know Windows. The more time you spend there, the more comfortable you will become when looking up information. And, guys, don't worry, no one will know that you stopped to ask for directions.

Q&A

Q Is there a place to find out where the old Windows NT 4.0 and Windows 98 stuff has moved?

A Yes. Open Help, click Help Resources, and open the topic "Where is it now?" This section locates where these old components from these two systems are now.

Q Is there a way to print the information in Help?

A Why yes, there is. Right-click the topic you want to print (the information in the right side of the screen) and then click Print.

Workshop

The workshop includes quiz questions to help gauge your grasp of the material and exercises to help reinforce your learning. You'll find the answers to the quiz in Appendix A, "Answers."

Quiz

1. Which key offers the quickest access to Help (otherwise known as the *Help key*)?
2. What is the purpose of the underlined words in Help text?

3. How do you exit Help?
4. *Bonus Question*: What does Massachusetts mean?

Exercises

1. Using the Help system, find the Search Tips for using Help.
2. Choose three Favorites to add to your Topics List.
3. Browse through some of the "books" under the Contents tab.

Vocabulary

F1—The key used to summons help

Help system—The system used to display information about Windows 2000

topic—A category of information

PART II

Going to Work with Windows

Hour

HOUR 6

Everything About the Start Menu

Anchored to the wee li'l Start button is the mighty Start menu. Up it pops like a compu-jack-in-the-box, a veritable plume of menu items, options, choices, and commands. If you were a computer archeologist from the future, you could tell by the abundance of its menu items that the Start menu is important. You'd dig further to uncover its deepest, darkest secrets.

The Start menu is the hot spot in Windows. Every program installed on your PC lives there, and just about everything you do on the computer can be done using some gadget or gizmo on the Start menu. Obviously, you're on to something *big* here.

The highlights in this hour include the following:

- Adding programs to the Start menu
- Creating new submenus
- Renaming programs and submenus
- Organizing programs

- Removing programs and submenus
- Starting programs automatically
- Minimizing at the start

A Quick Tour

On the Start menu are eight basic items, as shown in Figure 6.1. You can add more. (This is covered later.) Table 6.1 describes each item.

FIGURE 6.1
The Start menu.

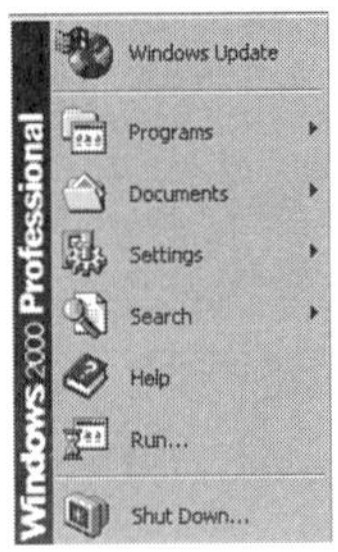

TABLE 6.1 The Start Menu

Menu Item	*What It Does*
Windows Update	An Internet connection that updates your computer with the most current Windows gadgets, bells, and whistles
Programs	Displays a submenu of programs
Documents	Displays a submenu of recent documents you've opened
Settings	Displays a submenu for quick access to the Windows dinking tools
Search	Lists commands that help you find files, folders, and programs on disk
Help	Begins the Windows main help system
Run	Opens a dialog box where you can type the name of a command to run
Shut Down	Offers several options for quitting Windows

The area above the top dimple line (also known as a *menu separator* to the Microsoft suites), where Windows Update lives, is reserved for even more items (as shown in Figure 6.2 in the next section)—a whole totem pole, in fact. These are programs you yourself can stick on the menu. Keep reading, and you will discover how you can achieve such wizardry.

Adding Programs to the Start Menu

The Start menu's key role is to serve as a list from which you can pluck programs to run. The Programs submenu was designed specifically for this purpose. On it, you will find the complete list of every program that comes with Windows, and maybe a few programs preinstalled by your computer dealer.

The menus and submenus in the Programs submenu are yours to command and create. Not only can you add new programs, but you can also create new submenus and rename or rearrange existing menus. However you see fit to organize things is fine with Windows, but two menus are "holy":

- The *Accessories menu* is reserved for Windows programs. (Not that you cannot change that menu, but it's common to all Windows computers, so you shouldn't mess with it.)
- The *StartUp menu* is a special holding place for those programs you want to run when you start your computer.

Everything else in the Start menu is yours to mess with.

Putting Programs "on Top"

You can readily avoid marching through the Start menu by sticking your favorite programs right there on the Start menu itself. That way, you can simply pop up the menu, and you're just one click away from your favorite programs. Figure 6.2 shows an example of what I mean, with two programs I use often—Word and Microsoft Publisher.

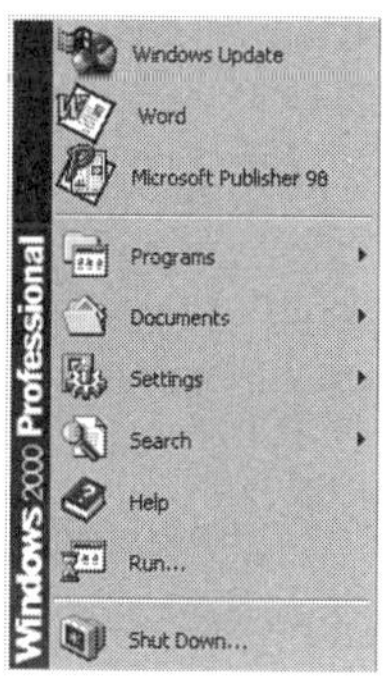

FIGURE 6.2
A customized Start menu.

You're really just adding a shortcut to your program when you add a program to your Start menu. In this first exercise, you will put a program on the top of the Start menu (refer to Figure 6.2).

To Do 6.1: Adding Programs to the Top of the Start Menu

To Do

1. Click the Start button.
2. Point to Settings.
3. Click Taskbar & Start Menu.
4. Click the Start Menu Options tab.
5. Click Add.

   This opens the Create Shortcut Wizard. You're not really moving the whole program; you're just adding what is known as a *shortcut* to the program.
6. Type in the location of your program.

   Uh-huh. If you're wise enough to chant the program name by heart, type it in. Otherwise, join the crowd and use the Browse button instead.
7. Click the Browse button.

   Somewhere in the list is the program you want. The trick is finding it. Most programs will live off your (C:) drive, so you can double-click that option to open it. Also, as luck would have it, Windows 2000 has graciously listed the more popular programs on the bottom of the list.
8. Click the program to add.

   I chose Word because I'm adding Word to my Start menu.
9. Click OK.

   Word's path is put into the text box for you (and thank goodness).
10. Click Next.

    You want Word at the top of your Start menu, so click once on Start Menu to highlight it.
11. Click Next.

    Type in the name you want to call this program. I take the name *Microsoft* off of everything, so I'm editing the title down to just *Word*.
12. Click Finish.
13. Click OK.
14. Click the Start menu button.

Wow, there's your program, sitting there ever so proudly near the top of the menu. Now, you can work through this process again and add a few other programs you use all the time. Be particular about what you add. You don't want to put every program on your list, or your Start menu will get junky.

Creating New Submenus

I like to do graphics and art projects on the computer. My kids also love to use Paint as a way to express their artistic side. So, I've added a submenu to keep my graphics and art programs together. That way, they are all in one place, making it easier for me to decide which program would be best to use.

Before you begin the next task, decide which submenu will best suit you and where it should be placed. I'm going to walk you through the steps I took to add a Graphics submenu. (I use the word *Graphics* because *Art* can be criticized as good or bad and I'm not that good at art.)

To Do 6.2: Adding a Submenu to the Start Menu

▼ To Do

1. Right-click the Start button.
2. Choose Open.
3. Double-click the folder where you want the submenu.

   This is usually the Programs folder. Notice in Figure 6.3 that the two programs I added to the Start menu are listed. This is the secret place on disk where programs added to the Start menu live (or where their shortcuts live).

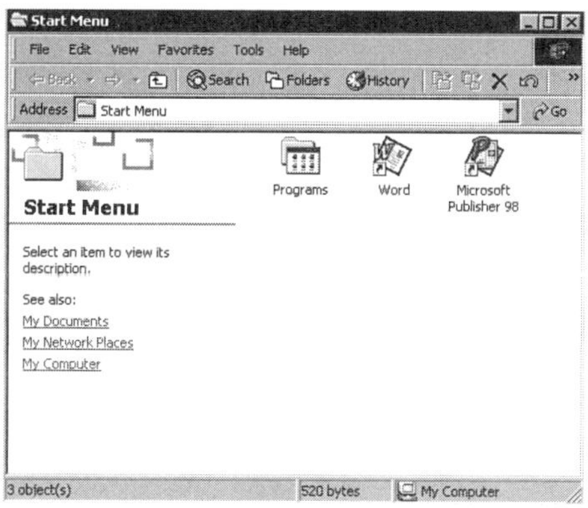

FIGURE 6.3
Things living in the Start menu.

> If you want to make a folder off a submenu of the Programs folder, double-click the Programs folder to find the other options.

4. Choose a folder.

   This is the folder where you want to add a submenu. Click the folder once to select it.

▼

5. Click File.

6

6. Point to New.
7. Click Folder. Figure 6.4 illustrates the steps to reach the new folder option.

FIGURE 6.4
Adding a new folder.

8. Type in a name of the new submenu.

   My new submenu is titled *Graphics*.
9. Press Enter.
10. Click an empty space on desktop.

    This closes and saves your new submenu.

Now, to see whether all this worked, click the Start button and choose Programs, Accessories. There she blows! It's the new Graphics folder, shown in Figure 6.5. Nothing is in it yet, but that will come.

FIGURE 6.5
The new Graphics folder!

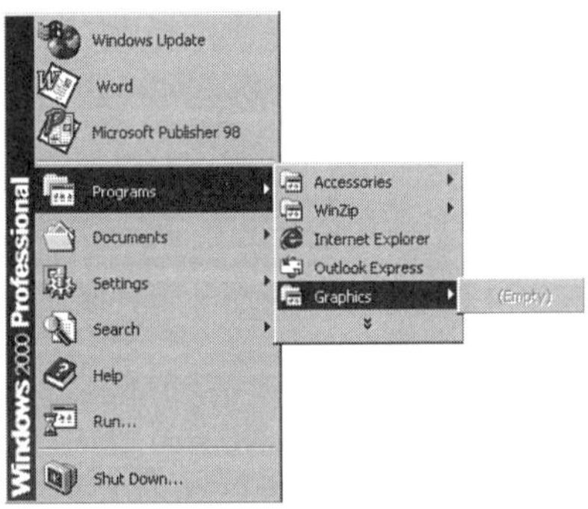

Putting Programs in the Submenus

Now that you have this nifty new submenu, you can add all your graphics programs.

To Do 6.3: Adding Programs to Your New Submenu

▼ To Do

1. Right-click My Computer.
2. Choose Explore.

   Find the program you want to add to your submenu by clicking the plus boxes next to the drives on the Folders side of the window. Keep opening folders until you find your program. I was looking for the Paint program, so I clicked (C:), Documents and Settings, All Users, Start Menu, Programs, Accessories. There's Paint, on the right side of the window, shown in Figure 6.6.

FIGURE 6.6
Items in the Accessories menu.

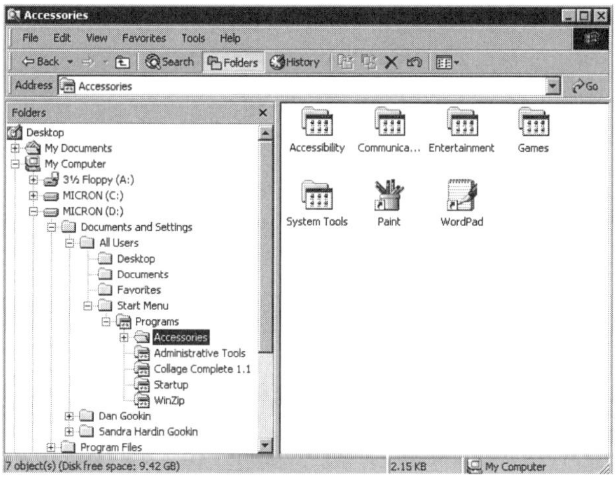

3. Click the icon for the program you want to add.

   While the mouse button is pressed down, drag the icon to Start and then to the submenu. You can release the mouse button when you see that the line and icon (which appears fuzzy but is representing your program) is placed over your submenu folder (see Figure 6.7).

▼

6

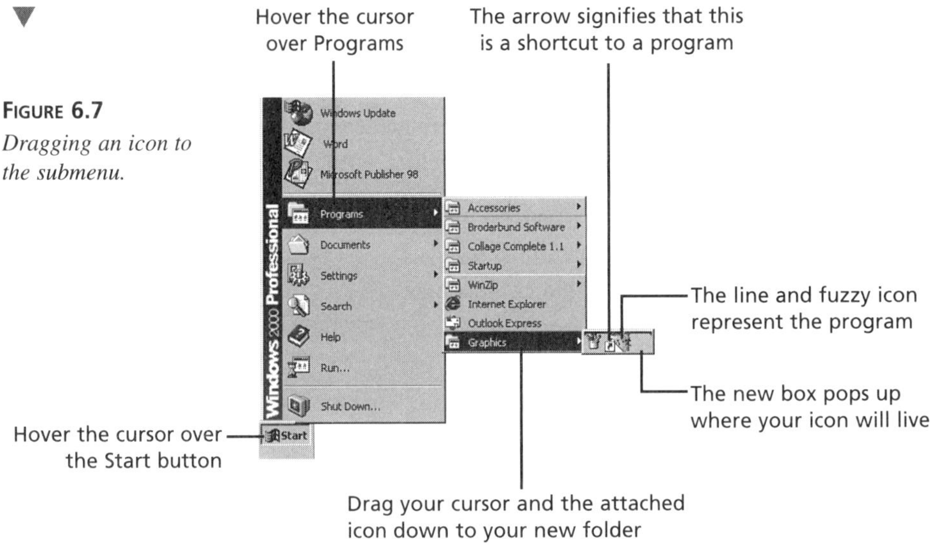

FIGURE 6.7
Dragging an icon to the submenu.

> If you are a network administrator, you can make a new folder for everyone to use on the network by right-clicking the Start button and choosing Open All Users. Then, follow the preceding steps to make a folder that everyone on the network can access.

Renaming Programs and Submenus

You can't expect to be brilliant on your first try at naming a new submenu or program. Giving a title to something is a difficult chore. Take me, for example. Naming my files *Graphics* was really shortsighted. It could mean that I keep pictures in that folder. What I should have titled the new submenu is *Art Tools*. Yeah, that's better.

To Do 6.4: Renaming a Submenu

1. Find your submenu.

   Go through the Start menu until you find the submenu you want to rename.

2. Right-click the submenu.

   Whoa, another menu.

3. Choose Rename (see Figure 6.8).

FIGURE 6.8
The Rename option.

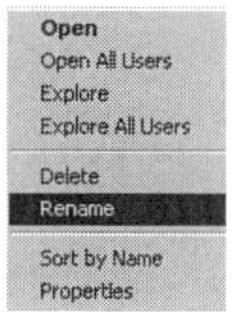

4. Type in the new name (see Figure 6.9).

   The old name is already highlighted. It will be deleted as soon as you start typing.

FIGURE 6.9
The Rename box appears.

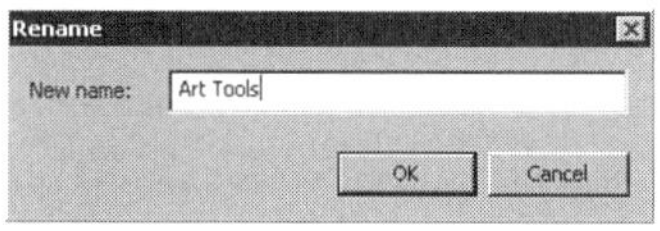

5. Click OK.

> Warning! A dialog box appears telling you that modifying this folder will affect all users who log on. Oops! Better notify the gang (those with whom you share your folders) that you're changing this, so they don't go looking for something that isn't there anymore. Go ahead and click Yes. The name is changed.

Organizing Programs

As time goes by, you will notice that the submenus tend to stack up. Soon, the Programs submenu will rival the Start menu for size. Then, the Programs submenu can even become twin menus, each one sitting beside the other, which makes wading through the programs and sub-submenus a chore.

The solution to avoiding menu bloat is further submenu organization. For that, you use drag and drop with the mouse, to shuffle and reorganize menus and programs on the menus as you see fit.

For example, click any program you want, and simply drag it to a new submenu and then drop it. The dark line (refer to Figure 6.7) is a visual clue to where your program is going to be dropped when you let go of the mouse.

So, with what you've done thus far, you can make your own submenu, title the submenu *Wasting Time*, and click and drop your favorite games and the Windows CD player in it. If you're business minded, you can make a submenu, title it *Embezzlement*, and fill it with Peachtree, Excel, the Calculator, and an Internet link to your bank account in Switzerland.

Removing Programs and Submenus

Nothing you do with these programs and submenus is set in stone. That's because you're not working with the program that's installed in your hard drive, but rather with a shortcut to that program. If you decide that you have made an error in judgement (okay, you goofed) about the placement of a certain program or submenu, delete the darn thing and don't fret over it. See, when you delete the item, you are not deleting the program, merely the menu item—the shortcut. This works in the same way that deleting someone from your phone book does not make him or her physically vanish (although that would be nice sometimes).

Back to the Art Tools submenu. I added Paint to the submenu, and now I've decided that it was silly to do that because the Paint program is sitting in the next submenu. Silly me. Time to remove Paint from the Art Tools submenu.

To Do 6.5: Removing a Program

1. Open the submenu.

   Find the program or submenu you want to remove (delete).

2. Right-click the program.

   A menu pops up, shown in Figure 6.10.

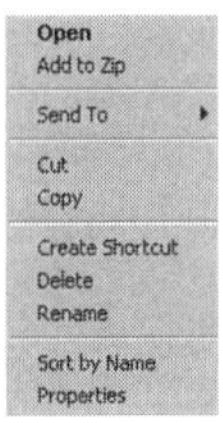

FIGURE 6.10
A list of options for the submenu.

3. Choose Delete.

   A Confirm File Delete box appears. This box appears any time you start to delete something. Windows wants to make sure that you've thought this out (see Figure 6.11).

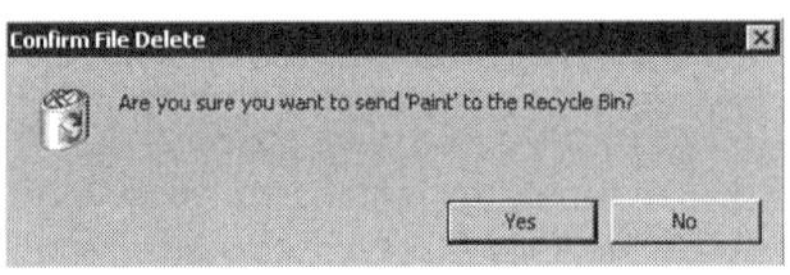

FIGURE 6.11
A confirmation box.

4. Click Yes.

   You've thought it out enough!

The next time you open that same submenu, you will see that your program is gone. Vanished. It's outta there!

Starting Programs "Automagically"

I like to start my computer and have certain things available and ready for me to use, such as my personal organizer. This makes it easy for me to immediately see my schedule for the day (which this program does). You can have your favorite programs start automatically, too, like magic!

To Do 6.6: Starting Programs Automatically

To Do

1. Right-click the Start button.
2. Choose Open.
3. Find your program.

   Double-click the Programs folder and any additional folders until you find the program you want to start automatically.
4. Click and drag your program.

   This requires manual dexterity. Drag the program you've chosen to the Start button, up to Programs, and to StartUp. Drop the icon in the submenu off StartUp. Now, your program will run automatically when you start your computer.

Minimizing on Start

When Windows starts a program, it appears as a window splashed up on the screen. That's fine and dandy for most of your applications. (In fact, you might notice that Windows places your program's window in the exact same spot and at the same size as it appeared the last time you quit that program.)

A special window-size issue can crop up with programs you want to run automatically when the computer starts: the list of programs you have in the StartUp submenu. Some of those programs you might want to start *minimized*, as buttons on the taskbar. If you routinely minimize a window, having Windows tackle that step for you is one of those conveniences promised when you first bought a PC!

To Do 6.7: Starting Programs Minimized

To Do

1. Right-click the Start button.
2. Choose Open.
3. Find the program you want to start minimized.

   You might have to double-click the Programs folder to find what you want. Typically, you will also want to open the StartUp folder because it contains the types of programs you will want to run minimized.
4. Right-click the file you want.
5. Choose Properties from the list.

   Make sure that the Shortcut tab is selected.
6. Look for the word *Run*.

   Click the down arrow to bring up a list of options.
7. Click Minimized.
8. Click OK.

The next time you start your computer, that particular program will run automatically and be immediately banished to the taskbar as a button, right where you want it.

Summary

This hour, you learned how to play with the Start button and navigate its submenus. You also discovered how to blaze your own paths and dredge out shortcuts in the existing ones. The Start menu is your willing slave! Bwaaa-ha-ha-ha-ha! (Excuse me.)

Q&A

Q Can I put other items in the main Start menu?

A You can add programs above the top dimple line, but you cannot delete or move the other Start menu items (Documents, Settings, and so on).

Q What if I can't find the program I want to run automatically?

A You can either use Explorer to find your program or use the Search submenu on the Start menu. When you find your program, you select the icon and click File, Properties. Then, click the Shortcut tab to bring it forward. Follow these same steps to finish making your program start minimized.

Q What's the easiest way to add programs to the Start menu?

A Drag and drop. Find the window containing the program (or use the Search command). Drag that program's icon to the Start button and then to the right menu as the Start Menu and Programs submenus pop up (as you drag over them). Release the mouse button to "drop" the program's shortcut onto the proper menu.

Workshop

The workshop includes quiz questions to help gauge your grasp of the material and exercises to help reinforce your learning. You'll find the answers to the quiz in Appendix A, "Answers."

Quiz

1. What happens to a program when you move it around, rename it, or even delete it from your Start menu?
2. What does the Start button start?
3. What happens to the highlighted *old* name when you begin to type in the Rename dialog box?
4. *Bonus Question*: How many people were in the Air Force during World War I?

Exercises

1. Click the Start menu. Try to find the following items there: the Games submenu, the WordPad program, the My Documents folder, and the option for finding people on the Internet. (Don't actually choose any of these items; just find where they're located.)
2. Put two programs "on top." If you don't need them there, delete them so that you're not cluttering up the Start menu. (And while you're at it, pick up your dirty socks, too.)
3. Create a submenu, give it a funky name, and put at least two programs in it.

Vocabulary

submenu—A menu that lets you know what is tucked neatly behind the items on the Start menu. You can also create submenus of submenus. A wee little arrow next to a menu listing lets you know that a submenu is lurking there.

Windows Update—An item on the Start menu that connects to an Internet site that can update your Windows gadgets.

wizard—No, not as in Merlin, but sometimes as helpful. These are Windows features that hold your hand through a variety of tasks. The Create Shortcut Wizard, for example, will help you through most of the exercises you've learned this hour. And you can call it *Merlin* if you wish.

HOUR 7

The Taskbar Is Your Friend

One of the most important jobs of Windows is to help you manage the programs you run. Windows lets you run more than one program at a time, which could be utter chaos. Fortunately, there is a dose of sanity in how Windows manages more than one thing at a time. That "dose" is called the *taskbar*.

The Windows taskbar is that reassuring gray thing on the bottom of the screen. It's always there and always available so that you can access the Start button or any of the other buttons that might appear. The taskbar is your home plate when you use Windows.

The highlights in this hour include the following:

- Multitasking
- Switching between programs
- Minimizing
- Learning about the Quick Launch bar

- Organizing the taskbar
- Moving the taskbar
- Organizing and rearranging your taskbar
- Finding lost taskbars

Multitasking

A task is a job, something you must accomplish. Doing more than one task at a time is called *multitasking*.

Some people can multitask, and some people can't. It's like being able to walk and chew gum at the same time, which I'm very good at. Other people can't even do that, and these are the same people who try to talk on a cell phone and drive at the same time.

Computers multitask easily. You can sort a database, print graphics, and type a letter all at once. This saves time when you don't have to start and quit programs again and again.

The secret? Just don't quit. Start one program and start another. Only quit a program when you're done. The tricky but important part of this freedom is to know when you have too many programs open. It is wise to eventually close programs. Having too many programs open can really slow down your computer. But I digress.

> Refer to Hour 4, "Working in Windows," for more information on starting programs in Windows.

Switching Tasks with the Taskbar

All programs in Windows run in their own window, which is probably why Microsoft called it *Windows*. And each little (or big) window on the screen has a corresponding button on the taskbar. Open a window, and grow a button. Open lots of windows, and grow lots of buttons. When you close the windows, the buttons go away.

The main reason for connecting a window on the screen with a button is that the taskbar helps you find that window in a hurry. This is necessary under three circumstances:

- When lots of windows are open, so finding and clicking a window takes a long time
- When windows are zoomed to fill the screen and you cannot see anything other than the "top" window
- When windows have been minimized and are not visible on the screen

Figure 7.1 shows several buttons on the taskbar. Each button represents either a window on the desktop or a window that's been minimized.

FIGURE 7.1
Programs in the taskbar (my, but aren't we busy).

The Quick Switch

In addition to clicking buttons to switch between running programs, you can also use the quick-switch key: Alt+Tab.

To work Alt+Tab, you need to press and hold the Alt key. Then, tap the Tab key. The first time you do this, a box appears in the center of the screen. It lists icons for each of your running programs, similar to the buttons on the taskbar.

One of the icons is highlighted, and a description of it appears in the bottom of the tiny window.

As you press the Tab key (keeping the Alt key held down), the highlight moves from one icon to the next, cycling through all running programs. Release the Alt key, and you switch to the highlighted program.

The Alt+Tab key comes in very handy when switching between two windows. You can initially switch by using a button on the taskbar. Then, to switch back quickly, press Alt+Tab (press and release). This switches you between the two tasks without displaying the little window.

Minimizing Windows

In the upper-right corner of the window in most programs are four little buttons. These are the window control buttons, which do four things very quickly.

- *Minimize*—Shrinks the window to a button on the taskbar (hence, the buttons that are found on the taskbar and are mentioned in this hour).

- *Maximize*—Enlarges the window to fill the entire screen, which is the preferred mode of operation when you're using a program.

- *Restore Down*—Shrinks the window to its original size. (Both the Maximize and Restore Down buttons are in the middle of the trio.)

- *Close*—Same as exiting the program, closes the window.

The key button here is Minimize, which shrinks the window to a button on the taskbar. That keeps the program running but gets it out of the way so that you can do other things. It's like almost quitting.

Learning About the Quick Launch Bar

Sometimes you need a program and you need it *now*! This is the reasoning behind the Quick Launch bar.

> If you can't find this Quick Launch bar thingy, it might not be selected to be seen. Read To Do 7.2, "Adding Toolbars." One of the toolbars you can add is the Quick Launch bar.

The Quick Launch bar, located smack on your taskbar, holds icons for your most popular items. You click the icon once (which is much quicker than having to double-click it elsewhere, saving one click of time), and your program immediately appears. Take a peek at Figure 7.2 to see an example of a Quick Launch bar. Notice that the ever-important game of FreeCell has been added to this bar.

FIGURE 7.2
The Quick Launch bar.

To Do 7.1: Adding to the Quick Launch

To Do

1. Find the program you want to add.

   You can use Windows Explorer (covered in Hour 18, "Maintaining and Cleaning Files") or My Computer or right-click the Start button and then choose Open to find the program you want to add.

2. Drag the program to the Quick Launch bar.

   Click once on the program and drag it down to the Quick Launch bar. The dark vertical line, shown in Figure 7.3, represents the program you are dragging. Let go of the icon, and it will "smoosh" over the other programs already there.

FIGURE 7.3
Adding a program to the Quick Launch bar.

> You can make your Quick Launch bar icons small or large. Right-click on an empty spot on the Quick Launch bar and choose View. Then, choose either Large or Small. Play with these for a moment to see how the icons look. Figure 7.3 shows the large icon view.

Additional Toolbars

Windows gives you the ability to add various toolbars to the taskbar, making the taskbar that much more workable for you.

To Do 7.2: Adding Toolbars

1. Right-click on the taskbar.

   There has to be an empty space on the taskbar to get this to work. If you do find an empty spot, a menu pops up after you right-click on the taskbar.

2. Point to Toolbars (see Figure 7.4).

FIGURE 7.4
Adding a toolbar to the taskbar.

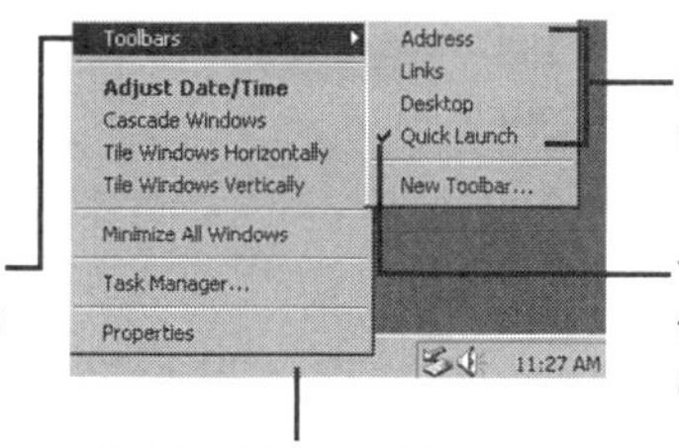

3. Choose a toolbar.

   Clicking one of the toolbars adds a check mark to the list and adds the toolbar to your taskbar.

   - *Quick Launch Bar*—Contains icons that represent programs (or games) or Windows tasks you can start with only one click.
   - *Address Bar*—Displays a text box you can use for typing in Web page addresses.
   - *Desktop Bar*—Places icons representing items from the desktop on your toolbar. This might be overkill.
   - *Links*—Adds various Web links to your toolbar.

4. The toolbar appears.

   Be careful not to add too many of the toolbars. The toolbars were put on this earth to make life easier. A messy one is downright self-defeating.

Organizing the Taskbar

Organization is the key to sanity. Well, that's what organized people say. On the other side of the coin, some say that organization is the key to insanity. Both of these sound like justifying behavior.

With the taskbar, organization is the key to sanity. Too many buttons make the taskbar a nightmare. The icons go away and the names become butchered. Soon, the taskbar is nearly useless because you can't determine what's what anymore. A couple tricks can remedy this problem.

Stretching the Taskbar

One way to fix an overpopulated taskbar is to close a program or two. That's helpful only if you don't need those programs. If you can't bear to close any programs, stretch the taskbar just like a pair of Spandex pants.

To Do 7.3: Stretching the Taskbar

To Do

1. Hover the cursor over the top edge of the taskbar.

   The pointer changes to an up/down-pointing double arrow thing, which means that the mouse is set to drag and move something.
2. Press and hold the mouse's left (main) button.
3. Drag the cursor up.

   The line drags up in given increments, each time widening the taskbar's outline on the screen. If you don't notice the taskbar's outline getting fatter, keep dragging the cursor upward.
4. Release the mouse button.

   Release when the taskbar is twice, or maybe even three times, as large. What you will see when you're finished is a fat taskbar where the buttons are legible.

> You can use the same steps to restore the taskbar to normal size, in case you get carried away. Drag the taskbar's top edge down instead of up.

Rearranging Toolbars on the Taskbar

Each toolbar on the taskbar has a small "handle" on its left side. It's not very obvious, appearing as a vertical, light gray bar. This handle can be used to control the toolbar, rearranging it on the taskbar.

To move a toolbar left or right (or up or down if the taskbar is fat enough), drag its handle. The pointer changes to a double-headed arrow when you have hold of it. This gives you the power to put the toolbars where your heart desires. (In fact, see the next section on floating taskbars.)

Rearranging toolbars by dragging them around can become tricky. You might have to try again and again, using the mouse and the toolbar's handle.

Floating Taskbars

That tiny taskbar can become cluttered very quickly with all those toolbars you can add. If you want to free your toolbar from the confinements of the taskbar, click and drag it to your desktop. You might have to adjust the bottom of the taskbar to make it smaller, but hey, you can do that (see Figure 7.5).

FIGURE 7.5
The floating Quick Launch bar.

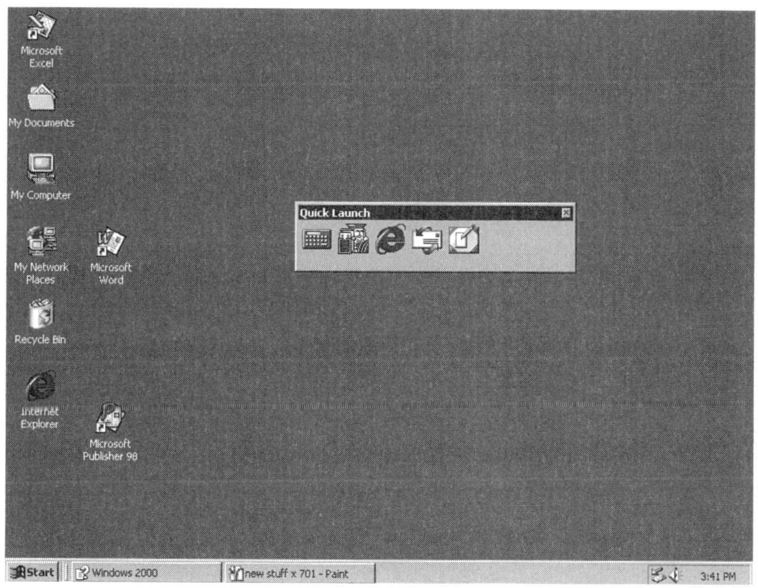

Customizing Your Taskbar

Like everything else in the Windows universe, you can customize the taskbar to your liking.

Right-click a blank area of the taskbar; then click Properties. The Taskbar and Start Menu Properties dialog box appears, shown in Figure 7.6. Make sure that the General tab is forward. These are your options:

- *Always on Top*—Your taskbar is always on top of any other window on your screen. It's never hidden.
- *Auto Hide*—This hides the taskbar when you have a window open, thus giving you just a tad more space to work with. When you close the window, the taskbar is visible again when you point your cursor at the bottom of the screen. Move your cursor and the taskbar slinks down again, out of sight.
- *Show Small Icons in Start Menu*—The Start menu appears smaller.
- *Show Clock*—Shows the clock located on the right side of your screen.
- *Use Personalized Menus*—This keeps the Programs menu neat and tidy by hiding items that you haven't used in a while. You can get to these hidden items by clicking the down arrow at the bottom of the menu.

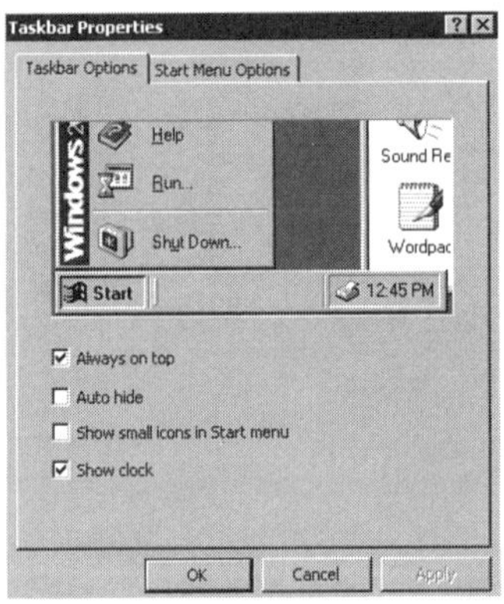

FIGURE 7.6
The Taskbar and Start Menu Properties dialog box.

Feel free to click each box and watch the picture above it. The picture will change according to what you've selected.

Finding Lost Taskbars

A disappearing taskbar is a common problem. Don't worry. It happens. Forget about using the mouse to get it back. Don't bother posting fliers around the neighborhood, either. What you need is a good old-fashioned keyboard. Yes, your keyboard will help you get your taskbar back.

To Do 7.4: Restoring a Lost Taskbar

1. Press Ctrl+Esc.

   This pops up the Start menu. It might make the taskbar appear, but the darn thing doesn't stick around. Don't label it fickle just yet; you can get it back.

2. Press Alt+spacebar.

   This displays the taskbar's control menu, which replaces the Start menu.

3. Press S for size.

   You might not see it, but an up/down arrow appears on the screen where the taskbar lives.

4. Press the up arrow key on the keyboard.

   Each time you press the up arrow key, the taskbar grows in size. Keep pressing the arrow key until you can see the taskbar.

5. Press Enter.

   This restores the taskbar to its normal size on the screen.

Summary

This hour, you learned how to grow buttons on your taskbar, change window sizes, and customize your taskbar by using toolbars and the Quick Launch bar.

Q&A

Q I don't like a fat taskbar, so how can I tell which button is which?

A Point the cursor at the button, and a pop-up message will appear with the button's full name. By the way, the button is named the same as the window it represents.

Q Why don't some icons in the Control Panel have buttons on the taskbar?

A It's probably because the windows those icons open cannot be minimized. I suppose that Microsoft wants you to make adjustments for those windows, close them when you're done, and not switch to another task.

Q I need more screen space. Can I shrink the taskbar to nothing?

A Better than that, just auto-hide the taskbar. From the Start menu, choose Settings and then Taskbar & Start Menu. In the Taskbar Properties dialog box on the Taskbar Options tab, click Auto Hide to put a check mark there. The taskbar then scrolls down whenever you use a program. To make it pop up again, move the cursor to the bottom of the screen.

Workshop

The workshop includes quiz questions to help gauge your grasp of the material and exercises to help reinforce your learning. You'll find the answers to the quiz in Appendix A, "Answers."

Quiz

1. What does each button on the taskbar, with the exception of Start, represent?
2. When your taskbar becomes too cluttered to be of much use, how do you fix it without closing programs you need?
3. How do you ensure that your taskbar is always displayed on top of the windows you have open on your desktop?
4. *Bonus question*: In the movie *Star Wars*, what type of pirate is Han Solo?

Exercises

1. Customize your taskbar by choosing three programs to start with Windows. You can always unbutton them later if you don't want them on your taskbar.
2. Open a few windows and then fatten your taskbar like the Christmas goose. Notice how the buttons respace themselves.
3. Choose a folder to display as a toolbar on the taskbar, such as My Documents. Practice moving that toolbar, the taskbar, and the Quick Launch bar around, rearranging them. (Get rid of the extra toolbar when you're done.)

Vocabulary

icon—A small symbol meant to be a visual representation of an application or command.

minimize—A way of reducing an application to just a button without actually closing the application.

taskbar—One of the most potentially helpful things on your desktop, it sports the Start button and shows you what windows you currently have open.

toolbar—The gray bar at the bottom of the screen with icons showing what programs are open.

HOUR 8

Working with Programs

Some people might disagree, and I *know* that I'll get flack for this, but Windows in itself is fairly "underwhelming." It can't help you do anything. Work is accomplished only in the applications that you add to Windows or that Microsoft has added for you. But Windows itself? Eh....

This hour is dedicated to giving you a quick tour of some programs Microsoft includes with Windows. In addition, you will learn the basics of working in these programs. After you have mastered these, you will be able to work through anything Windows has to offer because all programs typically work the same when it comes to opening, saving, and printing.

The highlights in this hour include the following:

- Start, Save, Print, Close, New, Open (the "Six Command-ments")
- Applets

Just the Basics, Ma'am

Every application you use to get work done has basic commands. Understand those commands, and you're on your way to Power Userhood. Here's the list:

Start	Beginning a new project in the form of a document of some type
Save	Saving something you made to disk, keeping a permanent copy
Print	Making a hard copy of your creation
Close	Closing a program or document window
New	Opening a new document window
Open	Opening a document previously saved to disk

These are the essentials of every application you use.

> Windows is what is called an *operating system*. Its job is simply to make your programs work. However, Microsoft has added several programs, I suppose, as a perk to owning Windows (as if we had a choice). Anyway, if you'd like to see a complete list of these programs, you can find it by doing the following:
>
> Click the Start menu, click Help, click the Index tab, type in `Programs`, scroll down until you see `Included with Windows 2000 Professional`, and then click the Display button. The right side of the screen displays a list of all the programs Windows 2000 offers. Click one of the words to get a definition and, in some cases, step-by-step instructions on how to make it work.
>
> When you finish with one program, click the Back button, located in the upper-left corner of the screen. This takes you back to the original list.

WordPad

To begin, take a peek at WordPad, shown in Figure 8.1. WordPad is a mini–word processor (actually more sophisticated than word processors of 15 years ago). It's a good example because it uses many of the common commands found in all Windows applications. If you learn your way around WordPad, you will be able to rummage around most programs.

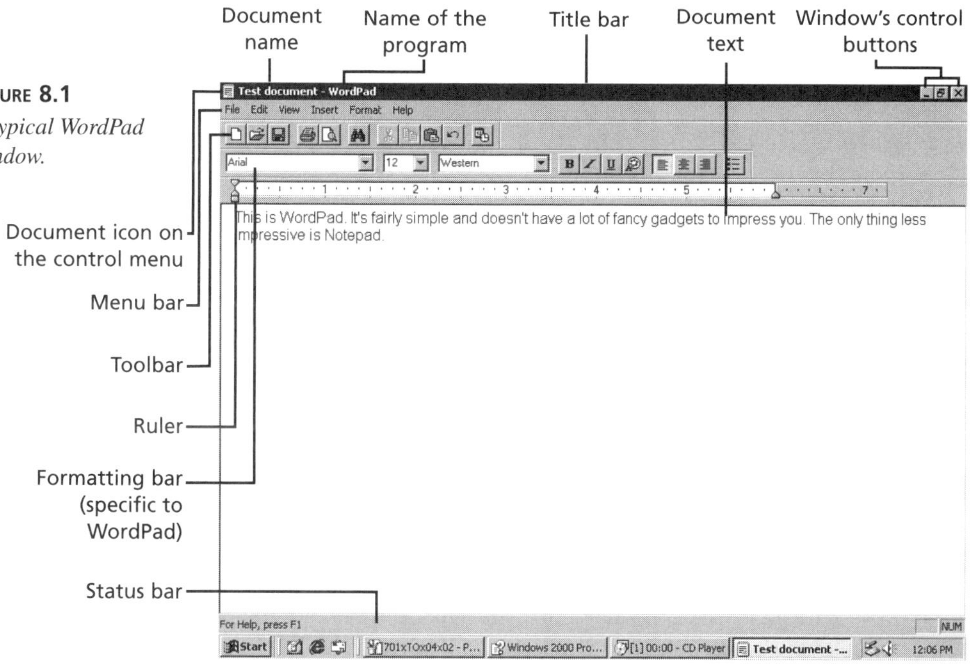

FIGURE 8.1
A typical WordPad window.

In this hour, you will use WordPad to practice working in a typical Windows program. What you learn here can be applied to any program because all Windows applications share the same or similar commands (Save, Print, Close, New, Open, and so on).

To Do 8.1: Starting WordPad

To Do

1. Open the Start menu.

   Do this by clicking the Start button or pressing Ctrl+Esc.
2. Choose Programs.
3. Choose Accessories.

   WordPad should be listed in the Accessories submenu, probably toward the bottom.
4. Click WordPad (see Figure 8.2).

Figure 8.2
The path to WordPad.

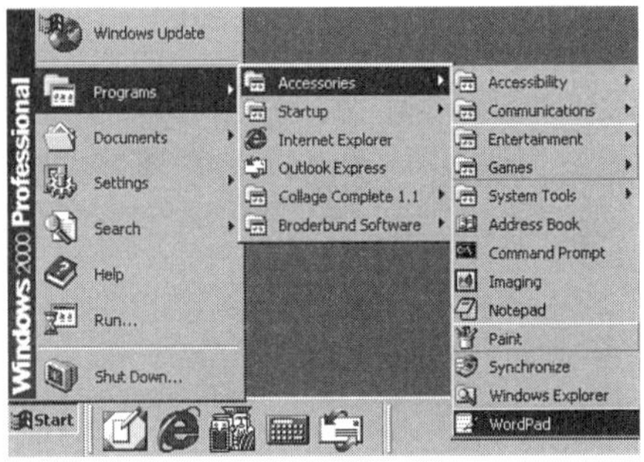

WordPad starts up in its own window on the desktop.

Ordering from the Menu

To get computer programs to work, you must give them commands. These commands are clustered in two places: the menu bar and the toolbar. Generally speaking, all the commands are attached to the menu bar; the toolbar is a bonus goodie that keeps popular commands handy.

The menu bar appears near the top of the program's window. It contains several key words, each of which describes a category of command: File, Edit, View, and so on. Those are the menu names.

To activate a menu, click its name using the mouse. For example, to see what commands are in the File menu, click File with the mouse. The menu contains commands and their quick-key shortcuts, as shown in Figure 8.3. To activate a command, click it or use its quick-key shortcut, if available.

Figure 8.3
The File menu in WordPad.

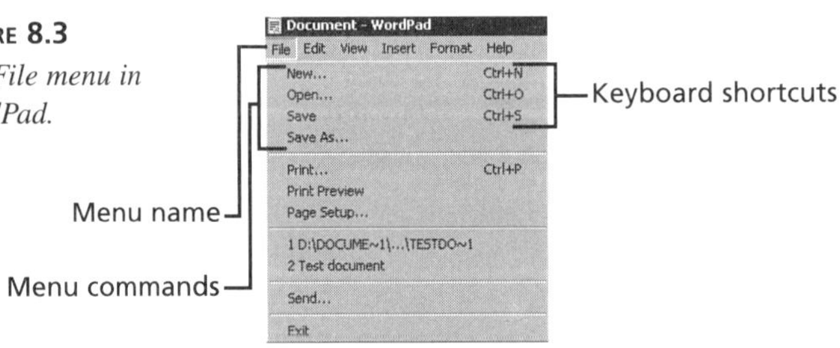

Introducing the Toolbar

Most programs are friendly enough to offer shortcuts to common commands. These shortcuts appear as buttons on a toolbar somewhere below the menu or occasionally on floating *palettes* (tiny windows that hover over your work). The idea here is simple: Click a button with the mouse to quickly get at some command.

If you're a little puzzled about what a button's picture means, point the cursor at the button for a short while. A bubble or balloon-like cartoon dialog will appear over the icon (see Figure 8.4). The bubble is called a *ToolTip*, and it tells what the button does.

FIGURE 8.4
A ToolTip bubble.

Most items have a ToolTip, but on rare occasions, you'll find one that doesn't. So don't feel like you're doing something wrong if you hover your mouse and nothing happens. That particular item might not have a ToolTip associated with it.

The Stuff to Do in Programs

Basically, you can do six things with a program:

- Make something.
- Print something.
- Save something you made.
- Open something else.
- Start some new stuff.
- Close all those things you made.

The order here isn't important. You could open something on disk and print, or you could start something new, save to disk, and then close. However you work the commands, they're the basic operations of every application.

(Yes, there are more commands, mostly those that help you create or modify your stuff. The commands listed here are the basics.)

Making Something

What you create with your program depends on what kind of program you're using. You will use the keyboard, mouse, and various menu commands and tools to get your work done. The end result will be that you will have made things and stuff.

To Do 8.2: Making Something in WordPad

1. Start WordPad.

   See the instructions at the start of the section if you haven't already started WordPad.

2. Type a brief note.

   Use the keyboard as you would a typewriter, except don't press Enter at the end of each line. Keep typing. The computer will do all the work. Here's what I typed:

   `Dear Mom,` (Press Enter twice.)

   `Thank you for those lovely shorts you gave me for my birthday. It was very creative of you to think my hips would look good in stripes. You're always thinking of me.` (Press Enter twice.)

   `My love,` (Press Enter twice.)

   `Sandy`

And there you go. A wonderful little note that you can print in a moment.

Printing Your Stuff

Having your handsome note inside the computer just isn't enough. How is mom supposed to appreciate your sentiments unless she sees your note?

What you want is a *hard copy*, or print-out, of your note. WordPad is going to take your work and make something beautiful of it, something that will come churning out of the printer in only a matter of seconds.

Your printer should be on and ready to print before you use the print command. If it is and everything is set up correctly, the file should print right away.

> Your note should print, but if it doesn't, don't panic. Just jump ahead to Hour 17, "Fussing with the Printer." There's surely something in that chapter to help you out.

To Do 8.3: Printing

1. Click File.

   File is located on the menu bar. You can also press Alt+F if your fingers are glued to the keyboard.

2. Click Print.

   To make things easy, you can also press P. This brings up the Print dialog box with further instructions (see Figure 8.5).

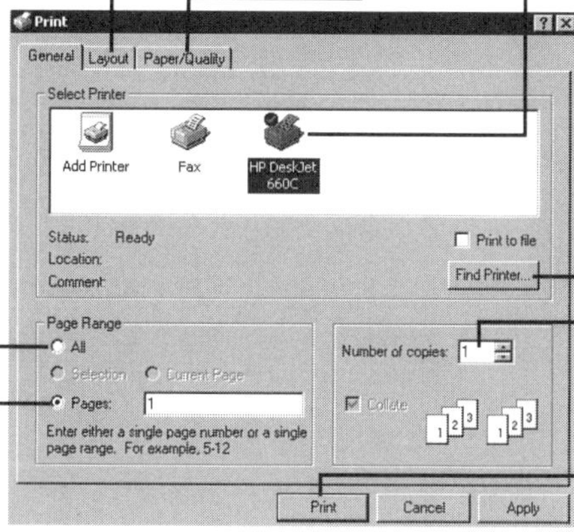

FIGURE 8.5
WordPad's Print dialog box.

3. Click OK to start printing.

   You don't have to mess with the rest of the dialog box. Click OK and your stuff will print.

> Another quick way to print is to click a print button on the toolbar, provided that one is available. This button prints your document instantly without displaying the standard Print dialog box. It just prints.

Saving Your Stuff

Very rarely do I bother typing something that I don't want to save. Yeah, sometimes the grocery list isn't worth saving, but most of the time I want to save what I made. You should, too.

You save your stuff for two reasons. First, you save things so that you don't have to do all that work again. Second, by saving your stuff to disk, you give yourself the freedom to look at it later and edit, modify, and otherwise change everything you did in the beginning.

To Do 8.4: Saving Your Work

To Do

1. Click File, located on the menu bar.
2. Click Save.

   Alternatively, you can click Save As. You can also press Alt+F and then the S key. The Save As dialog box appears, as shown in Figure 8.6. You will be saving your stuff in three steps, so keep Figure 8.6 close at hand to help you find things.

FIGURE 8.6
The Save As dialog box.

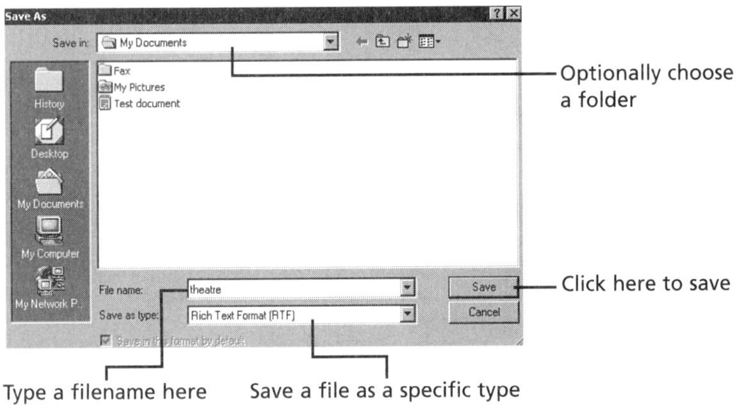

3. Choose a folder for your document.

   The My Documents folder is automatically chosen from the list. If there is a subfolder here, double-click the subfolder to open it.

4. Click once in the File Name box.

   Type in a document name. You might already see the text `Document` in there. Go ahead and type in something else, something descriptive, short, and to the point. Use the backspace key to back up and erase if you make a typing boo-boo.

5. Choose a document type.

   Rich Text Format is used for this example, but Word for Windows 6 is popular, too. (You can always leave this item alone if you're not sure which format is best.)

6. Click the Save button.

   Your stuff is now saved to disk.

Your clue to whether a document has been saved is right on the main title bar of the application's window. Many applications change the window name after a document has been saved.

> The first time you save your stuff to the hard drive, you will see the Save As dialog box (refer to Figure 8.6). After that, choosing the Save command merely saves your stuff to the hard drive again.

Opening Stuff

You will find that working in Windows is a process of opening and closing files. The more programs you work with, the more things you have to open.

8

After you open a file, the program sits there on the screen, ready for you to play with it, edit, print, and then save again when you're happy with what you've accomplished (or in some cases, not really happy with the results but too tired to mess with it any more).

To Do 8.5: Opening a File

▼ To Do

1. Choose File from the menu.
2. Choose Open.

   This summons the Open dialog box. You can also press the handy Ctrl+O shortcut. There is also the option of using the Open button on the toolbar. It has an icon on it that looks like a folder being opened.

   The Open dialog box, shown in Figure 8.7, is a common part of almost every Windows program. You use it to forage your hard drive and folders, hunting down a file on the disk you want to work with.

FIGURE 8.7
The Open dialog box.

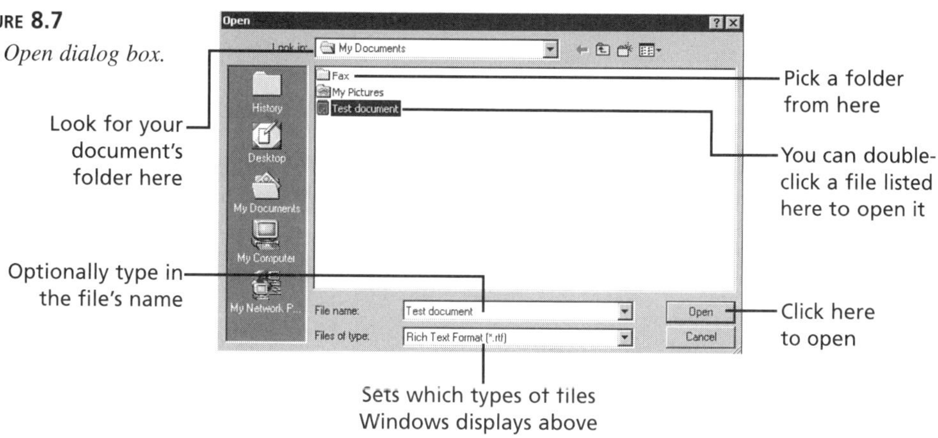

3. Locate the folder or disk drive where the file is located.
4. Double-click the file.

   There it is! The file you wanted. You can also click the file once and then click Open.

▲

> Some applications keep track of the last few things you've been working on. These are kept in a list located near the bottom of the File menu. You can open these files by clicking them once from the File menu.

Starting Some New Stuff

Starting a new document is as simple as turning a page in a book. There is no need to exit your program and start all over, although I'm sure that there are those who would choose this method.

To Do 8.6: Starting a New Document

1. Click the File Menu.
2. Choose New from the File menu.

   You can also use the Ctrl+N shortcut keys to start a new document.

   Also, there's always that New icon on the toolbar, which looks like a blank sheet of paper.

Some applications might ask you to save your current work when you select the New command. Select the Yes button when asked. Then, see "Saving Your Stuff" earlier in this chapter for information on how to use the Save dialog box.

Closing Stuff

When you're done with your toys, you should put them away. That way, they don't get lost and you know where to find them. I just had this conversation with my boys after a morning hysterical breakdown brought on by the disappearance of a precious *Star Wars* action figure.

Same thing goes for your documents. You should put them away when you're finished with them.

The Close command closes a window (or document), but does not close the program. Close commands typically appear in programs that have a Window menu, which allows you to use several windows to work on several things at once. Unfortunately, WordPad lacks a Close command because you can work on only one document at a time. Bummer!

To close your document, choose File and then Close from the menu. The window closes, the document is gone, but you haven't quit your program. For a refresher on quitting your program, flip back to Hour 4, "Working in Windows."

> The File and Close route is my favorite way to close, but there's no rule saying that you have to do what I like. You can also get fancy by using Ctrl+F4 to close a window and Alt+F4 to close both the document and the program.

Close is not the same as Save. You save when you think that what you have is good. You close when you're done messing with it. As a side effect, closing something that hasn't been saved will prompt Windows to ask you whether you want to save it.

Fun with Applets

Windows comes with a dozen or so applets, or mini applications. Nearly all of them can be found in the Start menu by choosing Programs and then Accessories.

Paint: The Picture Program

Windows comes with its own drawing program, called *Paint*. You can use it to create images, make art for documents and new desktop wallpaper patterns, edit graphic images, or even doodle if that's what makes you happy. Paint is quite handy and will suit most of your needs most of the time. In fact, the screen shots for this book were created using Paint.

General Painting Instructions

Whenever you paint an image, you must choose three things in this order:

1. *The tool*—Choose one of the 16 tools that appear on the left side of the screen (see Figure 8.8).

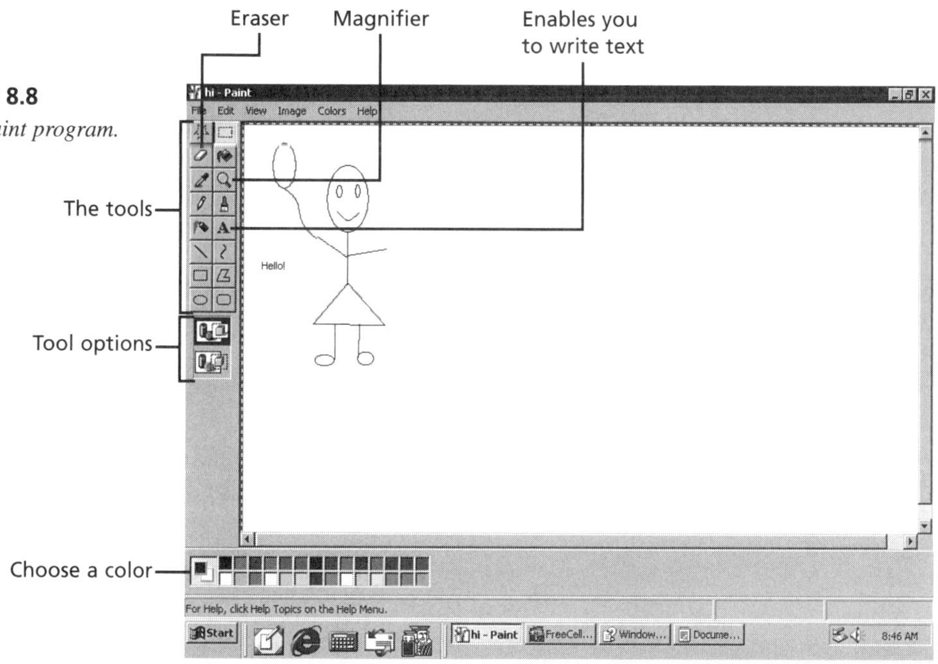

FIGURE 8.8
The Paint program.

2. *The tool's options*—Choose the line style, width, and other options from the options area.
3. *The colors*—Set the line and fill colors, which determine how your object will be colored when it's drawn.

There's not enough time in this hour to show you all the tools in Paint, but it's a fairly easy program. You can have a lot of fun goofing around with the tools to see how they work.

More Fun with WordPad

WordPad's main purpose is to write. It's the freebie program that comes with Windows. With WordPad, you can format your text and add a few fancy effects such as bullet points, automatic insertion of the date and time, and maybe even a picture. You can't get too creative with WordPad because it does lack features such as a spell-checker, page numbering, footnotes, and so on.

Notepad

Notepad is the Windows text editor. It's not a word processor at all and offers no tricks, bells, or whistles. No, with Notepad, you can only work on and create plain, boring text documents. (You might end up using it a lot because computers are fond of boring text documents.)

To start Notepad, click the Start button and choose Programs, Accessories, Notepad. Figure 8.9 lets you peek into the exciting world of Notepad. Kinda boring, really.

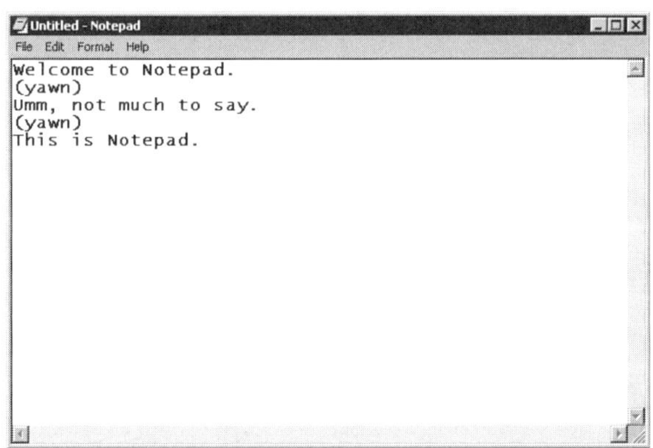

FIGURE 8.9
Notepad.

Calculator

Windows has a calculator, but don't throw away that solar-powered one you received as a freebie from your title company. The Windows Calculator enables you to make all sorts of calculations. You can even copy and paste the results between Calculator and other applications.

To start the Calculator, click the Start button. Then choose Programs, Accessories, Calculator. The Calculator pops up, looking like Figure 8.10.

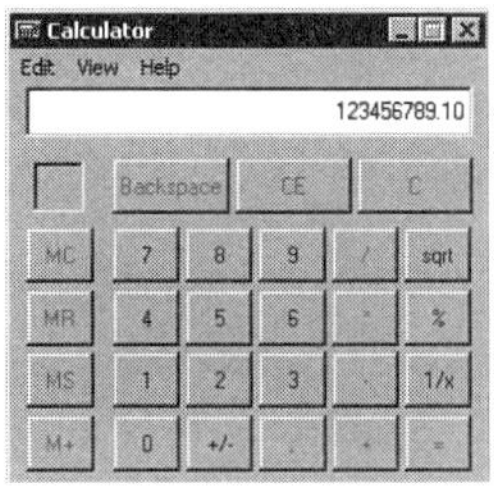

FIGURE 8.10
Punchin' numbers with the Calculator.

A bigger, "I've gotta use this in my Chemistry class" version of the Calculator is also available. Choose View and then Scientific from the menu. Now, you see the impressive calculator keys for doing complex, scientific-like things. I don't know what all those buttons mean! Click the View menu button again, and there's a really long list of options. I'm guessing this has to do with those mysterious buttons on the calculator. Can you tell I wasn't a science major?

Address Book

The Address Book is a nifty gadget. It's much like the one in your Day Timer or the little black book in your back pocket. Unlike your little black book, though, the Address Book stores information you can use in Outlook and Internet Explorer. You can search for people, send and receive electronic business cards, and even create groups of contacts for mailing lists.

You can find the Address Book by clicking the Start button and then choosing Programs, Accessories, Address Book.

Summary

This lesson teaches you the basic skills that enable you to use the programs already generously installed by the Windows gods. You should now be able to create files, print and save them, open them, close them, and then create a new one to start the process all over again. You were also briefly introduced to some applets you will find in Windows 2000.

Q&A

Q How can you claim Windows 2000 doesn't do anything? It's the PC's operating system, right?

A Windows is the program that controls the computer, managing all the hardware and software for you, but it's not what's known as "productivity software." The real reason you bought a computer was to use software to get something done. A computer with only Windows on it would be a boring place.

Q Does Windows 2000 offer any software that deals with images?

A Yes, it's an applet called *Imaging*. Its purpose is to view and perform basic tasks with image documents. You can find Imaging by clicking the Start button and then choosing Programs and then Accessories.

Q Why would I ever use the Of Type drop-down list in the Save As dialog box?

A Each application saves its documents as a specific type. Sometimes you need to share your documents with others. In that case (and in other circumstances), you must save the file as a different type, usually to be compatible with someone or something else—such as saving a graphic image as a GIF file type for posting on the Internet.

Workshop

The workshop includes quiz questions to help gauge your grasp of the material and exercises to help reinforce your learning. You'll find the answers to the quiz in Appendix A, "Answers."

Quiz

1. What are the three ways to open the Print dialog box?
2. What three things must you choose before you can doodle in Paint?
3. What is the advantage of adding a word processor (Word, for example) when Windows 2000 already comes with WordPad?
4. *Bonus question*: What is the full name of Rhode Island?

Exercises

1. Using the Start menu, check out all the programs that have been installed in Windows 2000. Choose two to poke around in.
2. Write a love note (or for you romantically impaired types, a shopping list) using WordPad. Print it.
3. Find the Windows applet that can help you determine the cosine of 863.

Vocabulary

hard copy—The actual, physical, ink-and-paper "proof," or printout, of the work you have spirited away in your computer.

operating system—This is what Windows is. Put simply, an operating system is something that provides a method to the madness of running your programs.

ToolTip—A bubble that describes what a button on the toolbar does.

Hour 9

What's in Them Folders and Files?

A disk drive may have a gazillion files (well, maybe not that many, but a lot). If all of them were in one place, it would be a mess. Imagine having to look through some massive window in My Computer for one teensy file. It would be just as if your closet was one big box and everything was tossed in with no rhyme or reason. It would be chaos.

To avoid chaos, you can put your computer files into folders. These folders are used to store files and to help keep you organized—just as shelves and hanging racks help keep your clothes organized.

The highlights in this hour include the following:

- My Documents
- Making a folder
- Deleting files
- Undeleting files
- Renaming files
- Copying files
- Moving files

Understanding Folders

Folders contain files, usually files of a related type. For example, all the documents used to create this book live in a folder called *Windows 2000*. Each chapter is a file. The folder that keeps all my letters to this publisher is called *Macmillan*. Each one of those letters is saved as a separate file. These folders keep those specific files separate from other files and folders on the hard drive.

My Documents

Your PC's hard drive has lots of space where you can make a folder—and then forget where you put it. So Windows 2000 makes it easy for you by giving you your own personal folder, called *My Documents* (meaning *your* documents, not *my* documents). It's the primary location for all the stuff you'll create and toy with while you see Windows 2000.

Take a peek at your desktop and you'll see the My Documents icon sitting there. Clicking that icon opens a folder that's *the* holding place for everything you do. It's your own personal filing cabinet for everything you create in Windows. In fact, Windows is so adamant about you keeping your files in the My Documents folder that it will automatically put them there unless you save the files elsewhere.

There are no rules about deleting files and folders until you talk about My Documents. You cannot delete the My Documents folder. Microsoft wants you to have it and you're going to keep it. So there! If you right-click the My Documents folder on your desktop, you'll notice that there is a Delete option. That option is for deleting the shortcut, which is actually what you see on the desktop, but you're not getting rid of the My Documents folder itself.

You can rename My Documents if you want. Right-click the folder and choose Rename. Type the new name. I don't recommend this, though, because this book, and others, assumes that you have a My Documents folder and not a folder named *Larry*.

You can share My Documents with others—those who are networked to your computer and those who are set up as a different user on your computer. Just follow along with the steps.

To Do

To Do 9.1: Sharing My Documents

1. Right-click the My Documents folder.
2. Choose Properties.
3. Click the Sharing tab.

   This brings the Sharing tab forward—where you decide who gets to share, who doesn't, and how much control they have over your folder. Ah, ha! Power!

4. Choose the Share This folder.

   Everything now comes alive and you have all kinds of options:

   - *Share Name*—You can change the name of My Documents.
   - *Comment*—Feel free to add a comment about the use of My Documents. Something such as, "Don't access between 1 and 2 p.m. for update purposes."
   - *User Limit*—Either everyone possible or maybe just some random number.
   - *Permissions*—Click the Permissions tab to see the restrictions you can place on those using your folder.
   - *Caching*—Allows you to set how the file server (if you have one, of course) provides access to the files in a folder if your computer isn't currently on the network. (Obviously, this isn't an option for mere mortals to set; confer with your location's network manager for help if you need it.)

9

Making a Folder

The My Documents folder can easily get messy if you don't think ahead and make additional folders to further organize your stuff. Remember, My Documents is just like a big filing cabinet. When you need a new file, say for a new subject, you make a folder for it. As you continue to work, you'll fill each folder with different files.

To Do 9.2: Making a Folder

To Do

1. Double-click My Documents.

   What you see should be similar to Figure 9.1, except that you won't have all the files I have.

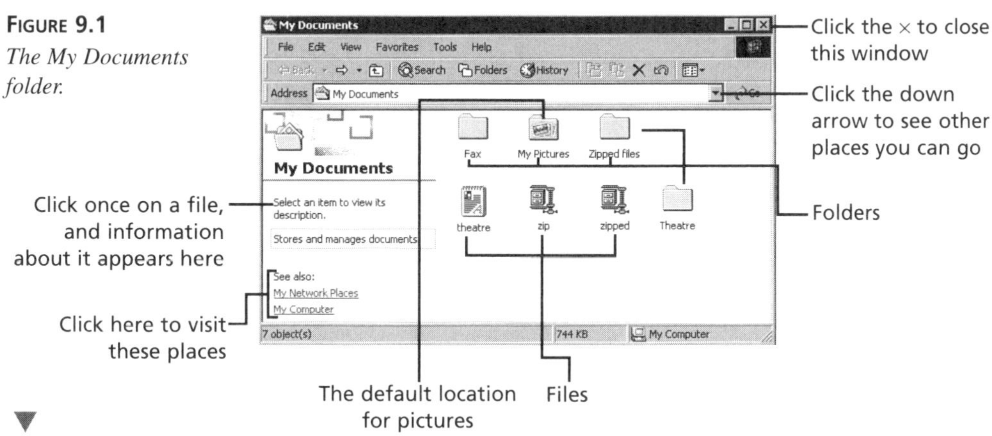

FIGURE 9.1
The My Documents folder.

2. Click File.
3. Choose New.
4. Choose Folder.

   A folder is added with the name *New Folder* highlighted. Windows is ready for you to type in a new name (because *New Folder* isn't very creative or descriptive of what the new folder will be used for).
5. Type a new folder name.

   Make the name descriptive. Perhaps the name of a project or event. Some ideas for folders you can create: *Downloads*, *Temp*, *Video*, *Audio*, and *Work*.
6. Press Enter after typing the new name.

   This "locks in" the new name. The folder is now ready for use.

Getting files into the folder is accomplished in two ways: You can copy or move existing files there, or you can simply save files into the new folder using the Save As dialog box.

My Pictures

My Pictures, shown in Figure 9.2, is the holding place for pictures you save when you use a digital camera and then transfer them to the computer. You can also use My Pictures as the folder for any graphics you want to keep. The pictures you get from the Internet or from e-mail would be saved in My Pictures.

FIGURE 9.2
The My Pictures folder.

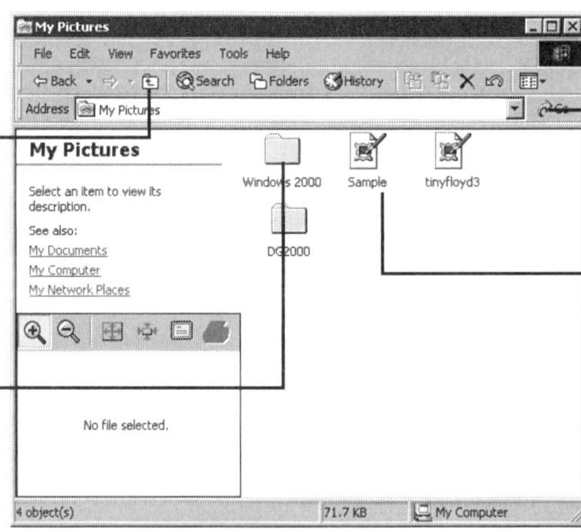

Frivolous Fun for Files

The most basic element you'll find in any My Computer window is a file. The file is represented by an icon on the screen, with a name floating beneath the icon. What it represents is a file, a program, a document, or any chunk of information stored on the hard drive.

The icon's image should clue you in about what the file is and does. For example, WordPad documents all have files with similar icons, as shown in Figure 9.3.

FIGURE 9.3
WordPad documents.

How to Open Files and Folders

Everything in Windows opens with a double click of the mouse. Open a folder to display the files (and maybe even other folders) held within that folder. Open a file to start a program, or open a document for editing (see Hour 4, "Working in Windows").

Some types of files are stubborn and refuse to be opened. In that instance, you're faced with an Open With dialog box. Press the Esc key when that happens.

To Do 9.3: Opening a File or Folder

To Do

1. Double-click on a disk drive icon.

   Your drive (C:) icon is a good one to choose. There's always stuff in there. Double-clicking the icon opens drive (C:) and enables you to see what files and folders live there.

2. Mosey around.

   Double-click on a folder. This opens a folder, and you see another window full of files and maybe even more folders.

3. To open another folder, double-click on its icon.

   Just for fun, double-click on the Program Files folder to open it. This displays another window, with even more files and folders inside.

4. Close the folder when you're done.

   Click the folder window's close (×) button, located in the upper-right corner of the window.

> Just to remind you where you are with all these files and folders open, the name of the current folder you're looking at appears at the top of the window, in the title bar.

Deleting Files

I like to purge—you know, get rid of things that just aren't useful anymore or things I don't like—such as clothes your mother-in-law gave you, shoes that you thought would eventually get comfortable, baby clothes, former husbands. You can also get rid of files that you deem no longer necessary.

To Do 9.4: Deleting a File

1. Select the file destined for destruction.

   Click the file once with the mouse to select it.

2. Choose Delete from the File menu.

   Danger! Danger, Will Robinson. Are you sure that you want to send the file to the Recycle Bin (the Recycle Bin is where all deleted items go)? See Figure 9.4 for a glimpse of the warning box.

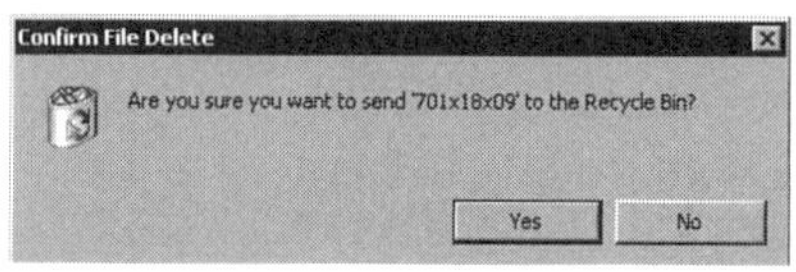

FIGURE 9.4
A warning before you delete.

3. Click Yes.

   If you change your mind, you can always click No. If you choose Yes, you might get a brief glimpse of a graphic depicting papers flying into a can. This means that your file is being thrown away and all is well with the world.

Undeleting Files

Windows gives you ample time to change your mind about deleting an item. When you select an item and pick Delete (or press the Delete key), you get a warning, asking you whether you are absolutely sure that you want to delete. Do you want to think about this for a moment? Is this what you really, really want to do? It's like your dad asking you whether you really want to marry that boy who's been hanging out on your doorstep for the past couple of months.

Okay, you delete the file.

Oops! You're not so sure after all. Not to worry. There's an icon on your desktop called the *Recycle Bin*.

To Do 9.5: Undeleting a File

1. Double-click on the Recycle Bin icon.
2. Find the file you deleted.
3. Click once on the file.
4. Click File.
5. Choose Restore.

   Your file disappears from the list and is magically placed where it originally started.

> The Recycle Bin is an interesting place to visit. Hour 18, "Maintaining and Cleaning Files," talks more about the place where deleted files go when they're no longer wanted.

Renaming Files

I find that I have to rename files all the time. Why? Maybe because I'm not bright enough to do it right the first time. You know, an impulsive save? For whatever reason, Windows lets you rename files, should you choose to do so.

To Do 9.6: Renaming a File

1. Find the file you want to rename.

   You can use Explorer, or even if you're starting to open a file and you see this misnamed file sitting there, you can go through the following steps to change the file's name.

2. Press the F2 key.

   There are several ways to get at the Rename command. Although the F2 key isn't the most memorable, it is the handiest; because you need to type to enter the new name, your hands are on the keyboard anyway. F2 is just handy!

   After you press the F2 key, the file's name is highlighted with a box. Windows is ready for you to type something more creative.

3. Type a new name.
4. Press Enter.

   And there you have a new, more creative name.

Copying Files

In Windows 2000, copying a file is done like copying information in a program: You select the file and then choose Copy from the Edit menu. To make the copy, you find a new folder or disk drive for the file and then choose the Paste command from the Edit menu. It's copy and paste!

To Do 9.7: Copying a File

To Do

1. Find the file you want to copy.
2. Right-click on the file.
3. Select Copy.
4. Find the place where you want to paste this new copy.
5. Select Edit from the menu bar.
6. Choose Paste from the list.

   And there plops the new file.

To be really efficient, you should do this from the Windows Explorer. All your files are listed and available to be maneuvered. Just select the file you want to copy, select Edit from the menu, and then click Copy. Now, go to the file's new location, click Edit again from the menu, and click Paste. It's fairly simple stuff.

Send To

The Send To option enables you to send a copy of a file or a folder to one of many locations: a floppy disk (usually in drive A:), your desktop, a mail recipient (sending it by email), or My Documents.

To Do 9.8: Using Send To

To Do

1. Find your file (or folder).
2. Right-click on the file.
3. Choose Send To.
4. Click one of the four options:
   - *Floppy Disk*—You must have a disk in drive A: (or your floppy disk drive).
   - *Desktop*—This sends a shortcut to your file or folder and puts it on the desktop.
   - *Mail Recipient*—This opens Outlook Express's Internet mail. Type in the address in the To: box, or click on the address book next to the word *To* for

an Internet address. Click the Send button when you're finished. And you really should read Hour 10, "Doing the Internet," and Hour 12, "The Joys and Sorrows of E-mail."

- *My Documents*—Makes a copy of the file or folder and sits it in the My Documents window.

Moving Files

Moving files is like copying files, although the original is deleted; only the copy (the "moved" file) remains. It's like cut and paste in any program. Remember that the whole point behind this moving and copying and deleting files is to keep things organized so that your files are easy to find.

You can move files a couple of ways: by cutting and pasting or by dragging.

Cutting and Pasting

Cutting and pasting a file or a folder is just like the cut and paste option in any of the Office programs, such as Word or Excel. You find, you cut, you paste.

To Do 9.9: Cutting and Pasting a File

To Do

1. Find the file you want to use.

   Again, this file can be found anywhere. Open My Documents, use Explorer, whatever.
2. Right-click on the file.
3. Choose Cut.
4. Find the folder where you want to paste the file.

   How you get to this folder doesn't matter, but you do have to actually open the folder (by double-clicking it).
5. Select Edit from the menu.
6. Select Paste.

   And it's done!

Dragging Files

Dragging files is the quick and dirty way to move a file. It's especially good for those quick jaunts when you've left files to be somewhat flailing about without a folder to sit in. For example, look at Figure 9.1. Notice that there is a theatre file and a theatre folder? That theatre file needs to be put into the theatre folder. And, because the folder is so close, it'd be pretty darn easy to drag it over there.

To Do 9.10: Dragging a File

1. Select the file and drag.

   Don't let go of the file after you click on it. You're literally picking up the file, and you're going to drag it.

2. Hover the icon over the folder.

   This is the folder where you want the file to go.

3. Let go of the icon.

   Now your file sits safely in its new home.

Finding Files and Folders

As much as you try to keep organized, there will be times when you can't remember where you put a file or a folder. Although Windows tries to keep you organized with the My Documents folder, things can get messy.

Luckily, Windows supplies a Search feature. It searches for files and folders based on a variety of criteria.

To Do 9.11: Starting Search

1. Click the Start button.
2. Choose Search.
3. Choose For Files or Folders.

   You'll notice in Figure 9.5 that the Search option can also search for people or for information on the Internet.

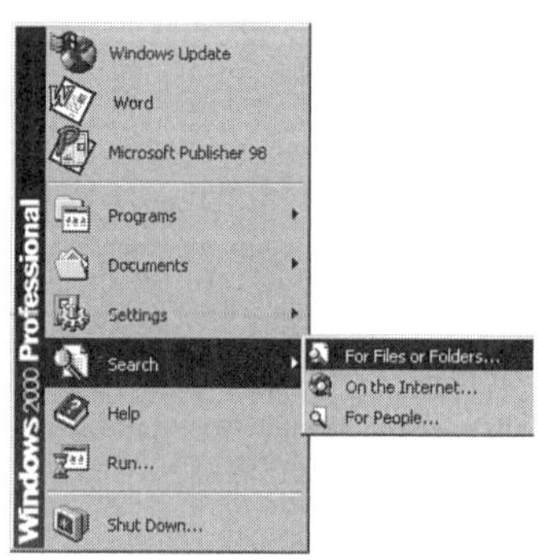

FIGURE 9.5
The Search feature.

Examine Figure 9.6. This is the box where you can put as many or as few search options as you need.

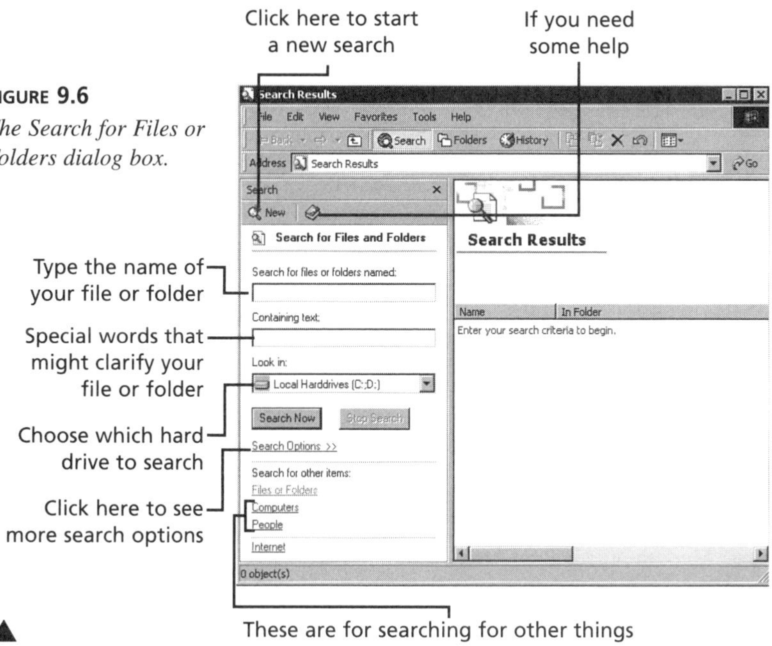

FIGURE 9.6
The Search for Files or Folders dialog box.

To Do 9.12: Searching for a File

1. Type in the name of the file.

   This needs to be accurate. You can't hope that Windows knows what you are trying to spell. You have to type it correctly.

2. Add text.

   The Containing Text box is optional. If you know the text, you might want to type in a few words. But again, this is optional.

3. Choose the hard drive.

   Click the down arrow to find your list of options.

4. Click Search Now.

   Your computer hums and the bottom line shows a very quick process of running through all the files for everything that contains the name of the file you want.

5. Review the Search Results.

   The right side of your Search box now displays a list of files and folders that contain the name you typed into the Search field (see Figure 9.7). There's a description of where these files and folders are located. You choose what you want by double-clicking on the file and folder, and you're immediately swept to that location.

FIGURE 9.7
File and folder search results.

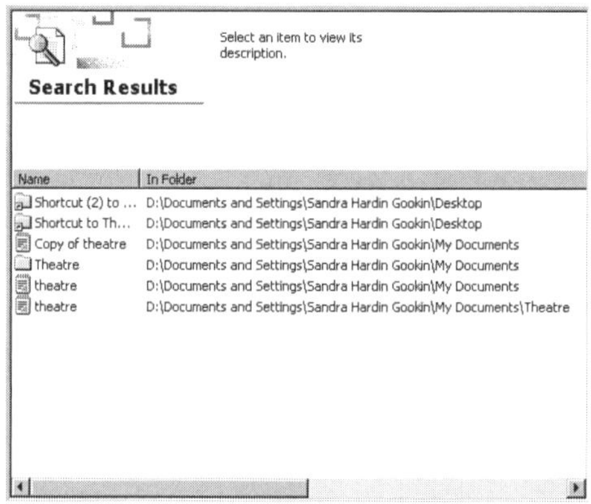

The Last Word on Folders

Everything you just read about files—deleting, undeleting, moving, and copying—also applies to folders. Every process is the same except that you apply it to a folder instead of a file.

As a rule, never rename, move, copy, or delete any folder you yourself did not create. Especially in the Program Files folder or WinNT folders. Don't mess around in there!

Summary

This hour is dedicated to helping you stay organized through the process of copying, cutting, pasting, and moving. It's the understanding that sometimes we need change and sometimes we put things in places without seeing the big picture. It's nothing to be ashamed of. Really. So don't be shy about looking at and analyzing what you've done with your My Documents and moving those files and folders.

Q&A

Q Is there anything wrong with deleting a folder?

A Nope, but keep in mind that deleting a folder removes all the files in that folder, as well as any subfolders and all their files and folders! It's mass destruction! Always be careful that the folder is empty or contains only trivial stuff before you drag it off to its death.

Q Why won't Windows let me rename an icon?

A The new name might not be permitted for more than one reason. Files cannot be given the same name as similar files in the folder, nor can files contain certain characters, such as \, /, :, *, ?, ", <, >, or ¦.

Q Can I change my mind in the middle of a Cut or Copy operation?

A Yes. Any time after cutting or copying a file, you can stop, choosing not to paste the icons. A "cut" icon remains dimmed on the screen until it is pasted. To un-dim the icon, select it again and choose Copy from the Edit menu.

Workshop

The workshop includes quiz questions to help gauge your grasp of the material and exercises to help reinforce your learning. You'll find the answers to the quiz in Appendix A, "Answers."

Quiz

1. In which folder will Windows 2000 automatically save a file if you yourself don't designate one?
2. What do you do if you want a file saved within two different folders or even on more than one drive?
3. *Bonus question*: The red triangle on every bottle of Guinness Stout has what kind of reputation?

Exercises

1. Choose a couple of folks to allow access to your files in My Documents. Now, give them that access, but with a few whimsical restrictions thrown in for good measure. You can always undo this if you need to.
2. Create a special folder to hold all those inspired haikus you've taken to recently (just play along with me here). Name it for your favorite obscure poet.
3. Delete a file and then rescue it from the Recycle Bin. You probably want to choose something not too critical, just in case your first attempt at this is clumsy.

Vocabulary

My Pictures—The folder Windows 2000 has so graciously provided for your photo and other graphic files.

parent directory—The directory the next level up from the one you are currently looking at. For example, the parent directory shows you the contents of the folder in which the folder you are looking in is contained. Depending on the complexity of your filing system, you might also have grandparent directories and great-grandparent directories and even itsy-bitsy seventh-generation baby directories.

paste—The handy tool used for moving or copying selected material or even whole files or folders. Also, one of several sticky substances central to a toddler's diet.

undeleting—The process by which you get back a file or folder that you thought you had no more use for. Significantly more simple than making up with the beloved you all too hastily dumped last spring.

TIME OUT 2

Solitaire: Being Alone in a Game

I'm not going to take the cheap and easy way out and tell you that Solitaire is a great game to play for those who need to practice using the mouse. Sure, it's great for that pointing and clicking exercise that newbie computer users need. Instead, I'm going for the honest approach: Solitaire is like a drug. It's addictive and you can't stop. You will crave the game like some people crave chocolate or cigarettes, or worse yet, a Diet Coke first thing in the morning. You can't hide from this addiction.

Oh, it's also good for practicing your mouse techniques.

And now, for your first glimpse into Solitaire land, check out Figure TO2.1.

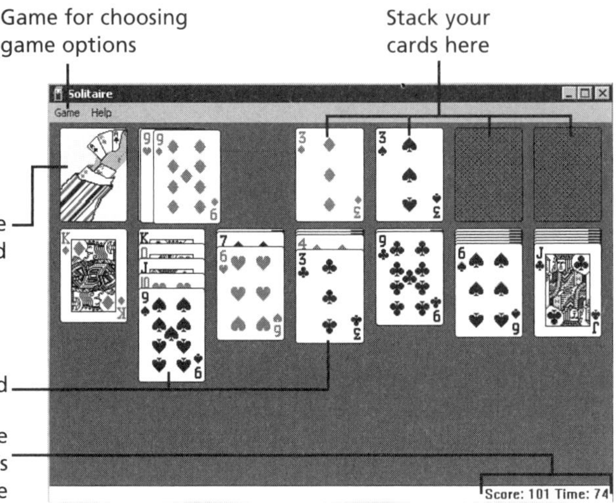

FIGURE TO2.1
Ahhhh, Solitaire!

Follow these steps to find the games:

1. Open the Start menu.

   Click the Start button on the taskbar, press Ctrl+Esc, or press the Windows button on your keyboard (if you have the enhanced type of keyboard).

2. Choose Programs.

   The Programs submenu appears.

3. Choose Accessories.

   The Accessories submenu appears.

4. Choose Games.
5. Click Solitaire.

Learning to Play

Solitaire is the anti-FreeCell game. If I had to guess, I'd say that Solitaire is 10% skill and 90% luck of the deck. There is a good chance that you could put a lot of time and energy into a game and still not win because, honestly, you didn't have much of a chance in the first place. Ha! See why it's addicting? But nevertheless, it's still a lot of fun.

The Object

The object of Solitaire is to use all the cards in the deck to build up the four suit stacks (called the *base*) in the top-right part of the window. You have to build them in ascending order (starting with the ace, then 2, 3, 4, and so on, ending with the king) and you have to use all the cards. Can't have any leftovers (like when you build your six-year-old's bicycle and end up with a few extra bushings).

Playing the Game

When you first open Solitaire, you should have a game waiting for you. If for some reason that isn't the case, click the Game menu and then click Deal. (Old hands know to use the F2 shortcut key.) This step is also used if you want to start a new game.

First, double-click any of the aces. This moves them to the stacks in the upper-right corner of the screen (provided they are the bottom card), and the game begins. Now it's just a matter of rearranging cards by dragging cards from one column to another and putting red cards on black (and black on red) in descending order. You do this so that you can start building these stacks in the corner. And because you are addicted.

There will be a point in time when you can't move. Then, you go to the upper-left corner and click a facedown card to turn it over to see whether you can play it somewhere. Either put this new card on the suit stack in the corner, or add it to the columns below (black on red in descending order).

You can drag whole columns or just parts of columns if you want, but they have to be in order already and black on red. The bottom card you want to move has to be in order already with the card stack. Figure TO2.2 demonstrates moving a short stack of cards (the 8 and 7).

FIGURE TO2.2
A game in progress.

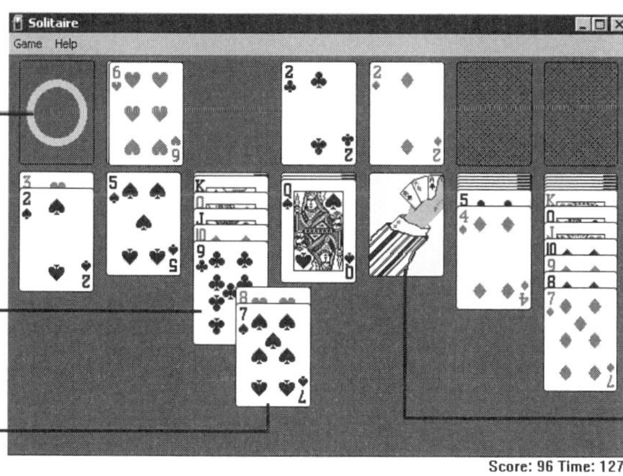

If you have an empty column, you can move a king to that column. This helps to start building this stack of cards.

Options

You have a few alternative ways to play this game. Click Game and then Options to view your choices in the Options box, shown in Figure TO2.3.

FIGURE TO2.3
The Options box.

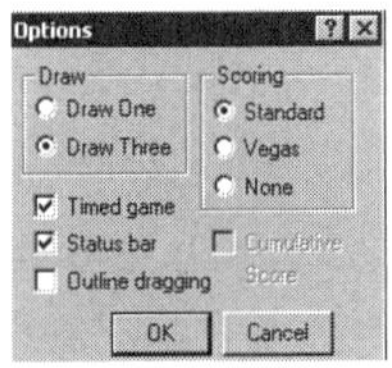

As you can see in Figure TO2.3, you can change how many cards are drawn from the draw pile or how the scoring goes (look at the bottom of your screen for the score and the time). These scores are good if you like to try beating your best time.

Tips and Tricks

Click the empty stack to turn over the deck, and start your draw pile again.

You can put only a king on a blank spot. Try putting any other card there and it just won't work. Even if you think the true hierarchy of the universe would value the female over the male, the rules of Solitaire still have the king reigning above all.

Click Game and then Deck to change the pattern on your deck of cards. Truly a cool feature!

You can drag a card off the suit stack and put it back into the column of numbers. I don't know whether that is a terribly smart move (sometimes it works in my behalf and sometimes it doesn't), but you can try.

Hunting Down Other Games

Another favorite place to get games is `http://www.download.com`

> No need to quit a game if you're not finished with it. You can simply minimize the game and continue it later, like when the boss leaves your office. Refer to Hour 6, "Everything About the Start Menu," and read the section about minimizing windows.

Hour 10

Doing the Internet

For many folks, the Internet is *the* reason to own a computer; Windows 2000 merely gets in the way, like an ugly doormat at the gates of heaven. The Internet is perhaps the biggest thing ever to happen to PCs. And people are more nuts about it now than ever.

Whether you're an Information Superhighway wannabe or an online auctioneer, Windows 2000 will usher you to a nice spot on the Internet and get you going. This hour tells you how to make the Internet connection using Windows 2000. The following two hours give you examples of what you can do on the Internet.

The highlights in this hour include the following:

- Setting up to use the Internet
- The Internet service provider (ISP)
- Installing your Internet software
- Connecting
- Disconnecting when you're done

Connecting to the Internet

There is Internet truth and Internet fiction. Internet truth is that Windows 2000 is not the Internet, nor is it related in any way. The Internet is a collection of computers, all networked together, which exchange and store information.

Internet fiction is that Microsoft is some great empire bringing you this new fad called the *Internet*. Oh, how they want that to be true. But it isn't.

To use the Internet, you need these:

- A computer, modem, and phone line
- An Internet program (software like Internet Explorer)
- An Internet service provider (ISP)
- Money

Setting Up Your Modem

The first thing you need in order to "do" the Internet is a modem and a phone line so that your computer can dial in to the Internet. (There is a possibility, however, that you might have direct Internet access at your company or access through a local area network.)

If you have a new computer, chances are good that you already have a modem installed (known as an *internal* modem). If you don't, then go out now and buy the fastest modem you can afford.

You also need a phone line. The best situation is to have a separate phone line for the computer. If you're using Windows 2000 at work, all this is probably not even an issue. If Windows is for your home, having only one phone line can be a real bother. For example, if you have a separate phone line for your modem, you don't have to worry about someone else picking up an extension and disconnecting you. Also, you can't receive any calls while your computer is using the phone, so having a second line means that people can still call your house while you're on the Internet. A dedicated line for the modem makes your life easy, although there aren't any rules that say you can't use your main line.

> You don't pay any extra for using a computer on your phone lines. No toll or extra tax is involved. You still pay for long distance, and if you pay per call, then each call the computer makes is racked up like any other call.

Internet Software

After the modem, you need Internet software. There are two parts to Internet software. There is a dialing program (a *dialer*), which dials the modem and connects to the Internet. Then there are programs you use to access information on the Internet.

Windows 2000 already comes with the dialer program. It's called *Dial-Up Networking* and can be found in the Control Panel (the Network and Dial-Up Connections icon).

The other software—the programs you actually use on the Internet—generally include a Web browser for surfing the Web and an e-mail program for reading messages. Both these programs come with Windows 2000 in the form of Internet Explorer (the Web browser) and Outlook Express (the e-mail program).

Other Internet programs are available as well, although the main two are the Web browser and e-mail.

Finding an Internet Service Provider

Internet access is provided by various companies, some big and national and some small and local, that connect you to the Internet. These companies are referred to as *ISPs,* or *Internet service providers.*

The Internet provider offers access to the Internet and additional services. Among the services an ISP should offer are

- An e-mail account, for sending and receiving Internet mail
- Access to newsgroups, the more the better
- A Web page, Web space, or disk storage (which are all about the same anymore)

You can find an Internet provider in the phone book under *Internet.* Even my own little hometown has several listed. When you call a provider, make sure that it offers these services, in addition to having customer service people available to help you with questions. Perhaps, maybe, even offering classes to help you get started.

> The best thing an Internet provider can offer you is a handy booklet, and maybe a startup disk or CD. That's better than just taking your money and giving you a cryptic photocopy.

Gathering Information from Your Provider

What your Internet provider absolutely must provide you with is technical information about connecting to the Internet. I believe that the hardest part of getting on the Internet is the gathering of numbers and other bits of information you're required to have before you enter the world of the Internet. You cannot access the Internet without this information. And if your Internet provider is really with it, it will provide these numbers and information in a handy booklet.

The Money Issue

Access to the Internet is usually paid monthly. It runs anywhere from $5 to more than $50, depending on what you're getting from your provider.

In some circumstances, the Internet can be free (and I'm not referring to limited free-time offers, which are a ruse to sign up long-term for more-than-free). If you work at a large company or for the government or are associated with a university or college, you might have free Internet access.

In these cases, you can get on the Internet just as you would at home. Ask your administrator, boss, head honcho, or whoever is in charge for more information about what your Internet access may be.

Configuring the Internet

After you get Internet information from your ISP, you set up your computer for Internet access. In Windows, this is done by starting the Internet Explorer (the Web browser).

Because you have not yet accessed the Internet, running the Internet Explorer in Windows 2000 automatically configures your PC for the Internet by running the Internet Connection Wizard. How does it know? I suppose it's like how your mom knows that you really didn't clean your room. Somehow it knows.

Have the information from your Internet provider handy so that you can fill in the various numbers and other information as required.

Here is a short list of some of the more important tidbits of information you might be asked. Go ahead and use this to copy the information from your Internet provider.

The phone number you dial to connect to your ISP: ______________________________

Incoming mail (POP) server: ______________________________

An SMTP server: ______________________________

POP3 name: ______________________________

(or POP3 number: ______ . ______ . ______ . ______)

Your host's domain name: ______________________________ (For example, `microsoft.com` or `mcp.com`)

Your login (user) name: ______________________________

Your login password (You don't have to write this down.)

Your e-mail name: ______________________________ (Just the name, not the @ and whatever follows it)

Your e-mail password (You don't have to write this down.)

Your full e-mail address: ______________________________ (For example, `dang@wambooli.com` is Dan's e-mail name; Sandy's is `sandyg@wambooli.com`).

10

Your login name and e-mail name might be different, as may your two passwords. The Dial-Up Networking dialog box will ask for your login name and password (see the next section). Your e-mail program will want to know your e-mail login and password, which can be different.

You might be asked other, specific questions. Your Internet provider, or its handy booklet, should give you all the answers. If not, phone them up and ask. That's why you pay them money.

Installation is done!

The end result of installation will be an icon in the Dial-Up Networking folder that connects you to the Internet. How that works is covered in the next section.

To Do

To Do 10.1: Working Through the Internet Connection Wizard

1. Double-click the Internet Explorer icon.

   You can also click the Connect to the Internet icon. The Internet Connection Wizard welcomes you (see Figure 10.1). Feel free to click the Tutorial button to learn a tad more about the Internet (see Figure 10.2).

> After you work through the Internet Connection Wizard, this first step doesn't retrieve the wizard. If for some reason you want to work through this wizard again, you'll find it by clicking the Start button and then choosing Programs, Accessories, Communication, and then Internet Connection Wizard.

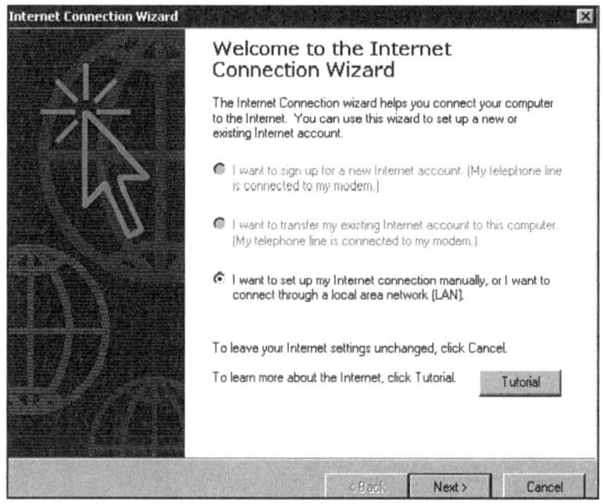

FIGURE 10.1
The Internet Connection Wizard welcome page.

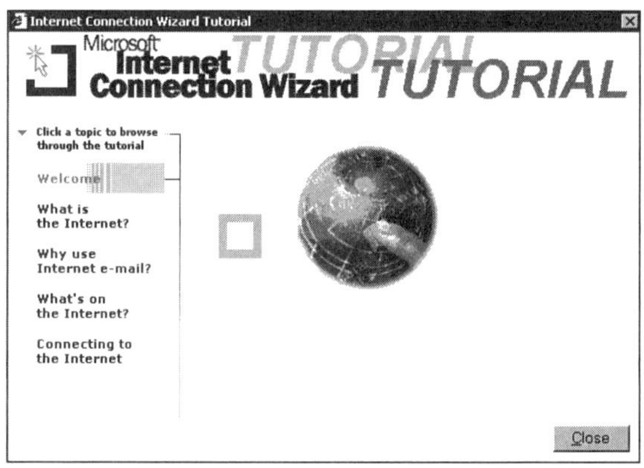

FIGURE 10.2
The Internet tutorial.

2. Click Next.

   You must know whether you are connecting to the Internet directly with the phone line or your connection is going through a network. If you're on a network, ask your administrator what the answer is here. If you're not on a network, no problem! Choose the top option.

3. Click Next.

   This is where those numbers come in handy. This phone number is the one your ISP gave you. It's the phone number your modem is going to call.

4. Type in the ISP phone number.

Click the down arrow if you're not in the United States. Click in the box to either add or remove the check mark for the area and country code. If you're dialing a local number, click in the box to remove the check mark.

You'll need to click on the Advanced setting only if your ISP has said to do so because of technical information you'll have to add. Otherwise, ignore it. Click Next.

5. Type in your password.

   You had to give your ISP a password. This isn't the time to change it. Type in the password you gave to your provider. You won't see the actual word, only ***. That's to keep it secure for any snoopy eyes that may be peeking over your shoulder.

6. Click Next.

   The connection name can be the name of your ISP.

7. Click Next.

   The Connection Wizard asks you about an Internet mail program. Click Yes. Then click Next.

8. Type in your name.

   This is how your name will appear in outgoing messages.

9. Click Next.

10. Type in your e-mail address.

    Don't get this wrong if you ever want e-mail. Don't put any spaces where they don't belong. Don't add any additional periods. Every space and dot accounts for something. Click Next.

11. Type in e-mail information.

    This is part of that information your ISP should provide. Click Next.

12. Type in the account name and password.

    Also, click in the Remember password box. This just saves you the step of always having to type in your password. Click Next.

    You've just completed the Internet Connection Wizard. If you're eager to go right to the Internet (a true test to see whether this worked), leave the check mark in the box next to To Connect to the Internet Immediately, Select This Box and Click Finish. If going to the Land of Internet Glory just isn't in your plans right now, click the box to remove the check mark.

13. Click Finish.

Connecting: Is Anyone There?

After running the Internet Connection Wizard, you're ready to connect your computer to the Internet. This is done by having your computer dial up your Internet provider's computer. This is the easy part: Just start any Internet program on your PC, and Windows 2000 connects to the Internet automatically.

> Windows 2000 already has the Internet Explorer icon pasted not only on the desktop, but also in the Quick Launch bar. They're pretty determined to make it easy for you. If you have installed (or plan to install) different Internet software, and the software program didn't automatically put an icon on the desktop for you, refer to Hour 16, "Organizing the Desktop." This walks you through the steps of putting your Internet software someplace where you can quickly get to it.

To Do 10.2: Connect to the Internet

1. Double-click the Internet Explorer icon.

   You should already have an Internet Explorer icon on the desktop. And, if your Quick Launch bar is visible, you might have one there as well.

2. Choose connect.

   The Dial-Up Connection dialog box is visible. Some of the information you already provided is available, such as your ISP and username. You might have to type your password. If you do, choose the Save Password option so that you don't have to do this all the time. Figure 10.3 shows what happens when you type in the wrong password (which I accidentally did, but thought I'd use it as an example of what not to do!).

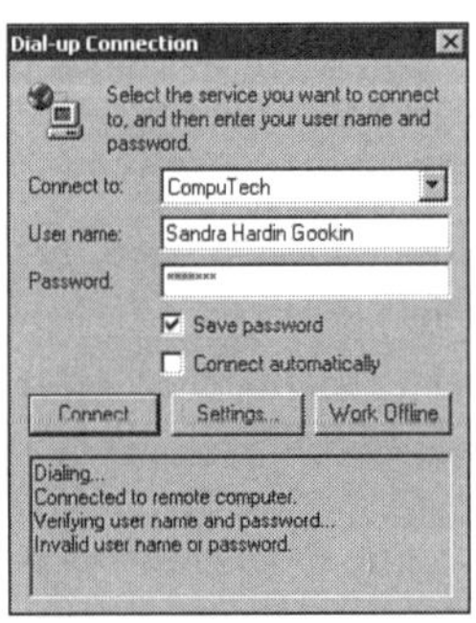

FIGURE 10.3
The Dial-Up Connection dialog box—notice the warning at the bottom. Oops!

3. Listen for your modem.

   You'll hear your modem beep and buzz and make some noise. This is actually a comforting sound because it means that you've done everything right and should be connected right away.

4. Enjoy the Internet.

   Microsoft, in its self-promoting glory, has already set your *home page* (the page you automatically go to when you first jump onto the Internet). You can change your home page to whatever you want, which is covered in Hour 11, "It's A Wild World Wide Web We Weave."

> Most Internet software is smart. When you go to start a program like Netscape Navigator or Microsoft's Internet Explorer, your Internet program automatically switches on the Connect To dialog box. All you have to do is click the Connect button and you're online, ready to do whatever.
>
> If, however, your Internet software doesn't automatically bring up the Connect To dialog box, you yourself can retrieve it. Open your Control Panel and double-click the Network and Dial-Up Connection icon. Double-click the icon that represents your Internet server. There you'll find a connection dialog box where you can click the Dial button, and you'll be connected.

> The next time you see the Dial-Up Connection dialog box (refer to Figure 10.3), click the box next to Connect Automatically. This saves you the step of clicking the Connect button and has your modem automatically dial the Internet.

Disconnecting from the Internet

The Internet is fun, but there will be a time when you've had enough and you'll want to get away from it.

To Do 10.3: Quitting the Internet

To Do

1. Click File.

   All Internet software programs have some kind of menu on the top of the screen. Find the File menu.

2. Click Close.

Or, depending on your program, it might say *Exit*. The point is that you want to close your program, just as you learned how to close a program in Hour 8, "Working with Programs."

3. Click Disconnect Now.

   A disconnect dialog box will appear (shown in Figure 10.4). Clicking the Disconnect Now button officially hangs up your connection to the Internet, ending your Internet session. However, if you've manually connected to the Internet, the auto-disconnect won't work and you'll have to manually disconnect.

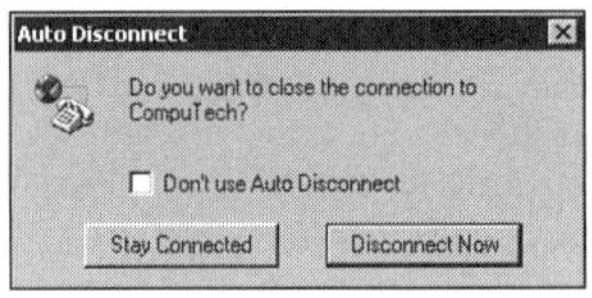

FIGURE 10.4
The Auto Disconnect dialog box.

Some Internet providers might hang up on you if you sit idle for too long. Typically, they'll wait for 15 minutes before assuming that you've walked away or fallen asleep at the keyboard. Other Internet providers—primarily the ones who charge you by the hour—don't mind if you stay on all day!

> If you plan on calling the Internet a lot, it helps to make the connection icon handy. Hour 16 talks about organizing and adding icons to your desktop. You might think about adding your Internet software icon to the desktop to make things just that much easier for yourself.

Summary

To recap, before you can get on the Internet, you need an Internet service provider (ISP), so go look for one in the phone book. You'll need a computer, a modem (you might already have one in the computer), and something like Internet Explorer, which is Internet software. Research the ISPs because you want one that is going to be helpful and provide you with everything you need in an easy-to-understand process. Now, go and conquer the Internet!

Q&A

Q What about getting online with AOL?

A I don't recommend it. The best way to access the Internet is with an ISP. When you go through AOL, you're limited by the speed of AOL's modems and whether the AOL computers are "up." Although you can use AOL all over the country, an ISP is simply the most direct way to get on the Internet from your home or office.

Q My modem was working, but now Windows refuses to recognize my modem. What should I do?

A If it's an external modem, turn it off and on again to reset. For internal modems, shut down Windows and turn off your PC. Then turn on your PC again (after a few seconds). That should reset the internal modem.

Workshop

The workshop includes quiz questions to help gauge your grasp of the material and exercises to help reinforce your learning. You'll find the answers to the quiz and exercises in Appendix A, "Answers."

Quiz

1. How can you avoid having to retype your password each time you want to access the Internet?
2. Can you use a different password for your e-mail than you use for your dial-up connection?
3. If you think you need the Internet Connection Wizard after your computer has already been configured, can you bring him back to life?

Exercises

1. If you have not yet signed on with an ISP, research at least three of those offering service in your area. If you already have an ISP, shop around a bit, considering monthly charges, hourly fees, and the amount of customer service provided.
2. If you are using a browser other than Internet Explorer, follow the steps outlined in Hour 7, "The Taskbar Is Your Friend" to put its icon on your desktop or Quick Launch bar.
3. Find someone in a position to know, and ask him or her what your Internet access from work is.

   Or, from the Internet Connection Wizard, click the Tutorial button and try to find any Internet factoids you were unaware of.

Vocabulary

dial-up networking—Provides a connection between your computer and the Internet, a network, or another computer.

home page—The Web site that your computer will automatically go to each time you connect to the Internet. You may also return to this site automatically just by clicking the Home button atop your screen.

modem—The little contraption that allows you and your computer to access the Internet, as well as send and receive information from other computers over a phone line. The "speed" of a modem refers to its capability to quickly transmit this information. It may sit on your desk (*external*) or come already implanted in your computer (*internal*).

HOUR 11

It's a Wild World Wide Web We Weave

The World Wide Web (*the Web*) is the most exciting part of the Internet. It's where you go to visit fun or informative places, do some shopping, research something, order airplane tickets—you name it. It's vast, an ocean of information right there at your fingertips.

The highlights in this hour include the following:

- Connecting to the Internet
- Touring a Web page
- Choosing a home page
- Visiting Web sites
- Using search engines
- Downloading files
- Shopping on the Web

Connecting to the Internet (An Overview)

Hour 10 is all about connecting to the Internet. As a brief overview, follow these steps.

▼ To Do

To Do 11.1: Connecting to the Internet

1. Click the Start button.
2. Choose Programs.
3. Choose Internet Explorer.

Another option to get connected is to double-click the Internet Explorer icon that is sitting on your desktop.

You're not going to go very far if you haven't worked through the steps in Hour 10, "Doing the Internet." Getting your modem hooked up and finding an Internet service provider (ISP) are absolutely necessary. So, for those of you who are skipping an hour to get through this book in 23 hours (instead of the required 24), go back and read Hour 10. Thanks.

The Quickie Tour of a Web Page

Internet Explorer is Windows's very own *Web browser*, the software that lets you view information on a Web page. The following features are there to help you. You can find most of these features in Figure 11.1.

- M*enu bar*—The place to go for choosing various commands and setting options on your computer.
- *Back*—Takes you back to the page you just viewed (like flipping back a page in a magazine).
- *Forward*—Takes you forward one page, which works only after you've clicked the Back button. You can go back and forth—which doesn't sound exciting now but comes in handy as you view information on the Web.
- *Stop*—Stops the Internet from loading the current Web page. This is handy if you ever click something accidentally or if you're impatient and just want to get on with your life. (More things in real life should have a Stop button.)
- *Refresh*—Reloads the the current Web page. This is useful for viewing Web pages with changing content, such as a newsy Web page or bulletin board. Refreshing the page displays any new information.
- *Home*—Displays your Web browser's home page.
- *Search*—A shortcut to Microsoft's approved method of searching the Web (although there are others, covered later this hour).

- *Favorites*—A list of Web pages you've visited and bookmarked for quick access later. You can add any Web page to a list of your favorite sites. When you want to return to that favorite page, click on the Favorites tab and then choose one of the sites you've added.
- *History*—Keeps a log of where you've been today, yesterday, a few days ago, last week, two weeks ago, and three weeks ago. Great if you want to keep track of where your kids are going on the Web—or your spouse!
- *Mail*—You can read your mail and send messages.
- *Print*—Prints can the page you see on your screen. Great for getting hardcopy of your online orders.

FIGURE 11.1
Microsoft's home page.

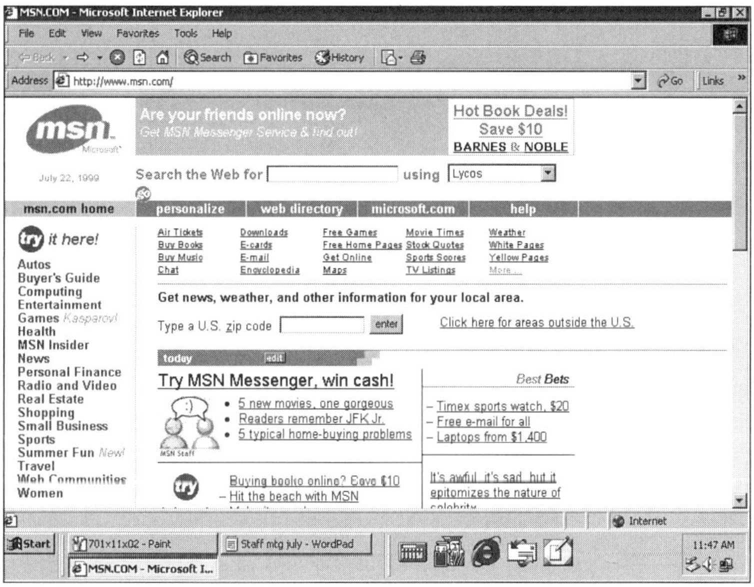

Choosing a Home Page

The first thing you see when you connect to the Internet is the Microsoft Internet Explorer Web page. "Welcome," it says.

That first page you see when you start your Web browser is what is called the *home page*. It's your starting point in the World Wide Web. You have to have a home page. It's required by some native culture somewhere.

Even if your home page is blank, it's still considered a home page. Your home page can be anything, any page anywhere on the Web. Some people prefer a *search engine* as their home page. Others prefer news pages or so-called "portal" sites that offer a little bit of everything, such as Yahoo!.

The following task walks you through the steps of setting a new home page. (Because, really, this Microsoft hoopla can get tiresome pretty darn fast.)

To Do 11.2: Setting a Home Page

1. Connect to the Internet.
2. Click on Tools from the menu.

   This is set up very much like any window you've seen thus far. The top line of your screen contains a menu bar. Find *Tools* in this bar.
3. Choose Internet Options.

   Figure 11.2 gives you some clue as to what you're looking for.

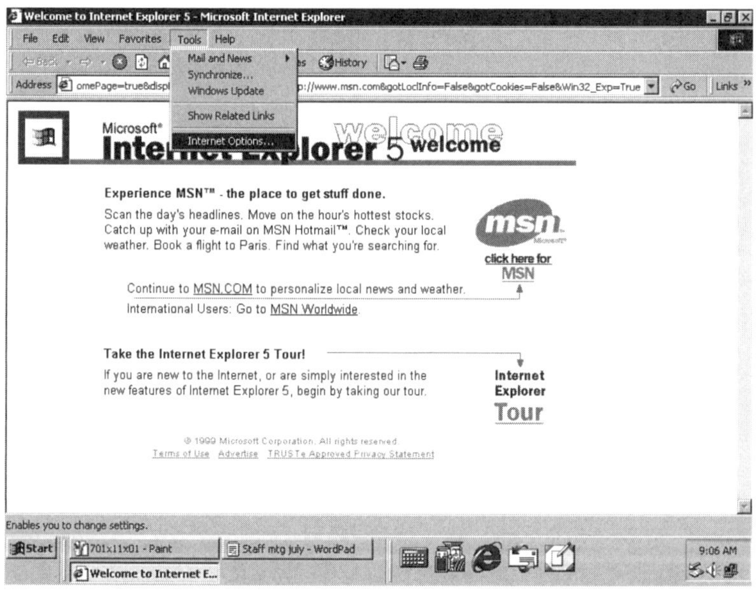

FIGURE 11.2
The Tools drop-down menu.

4. Click the General tab to bring it forward.

   Look for the Home page box, which is at the top. You have four options for getting your home page:

   - Type in the name of the Web page you want to use.
   - Use the current page (assuming that you're already viewing the page you want to make your home page).

- Use the default home page (which is Microsoft's self-obsessed page).
- Use a blank page.

5. Choose one of the options.

   Me? I choose Yahoo!: `http://www.yahoo.com`. Choosing a home page is very personal. I know those who don't like Yahoo. So be it! But it works well for me.

6. Click OK.

This is one of those tasks you might want to visit again later. As you start exploring the territory of the Web, you'll find some interesting places and might want to change your home page.

Yes, changing home pages is perfectly okey-doke. It's not a sign that you're fickle if you do it too much.

Visiting Web Sites

To go anywhere on the Web, you have to know a Web page's address, or *URL* (pronounced *you-are-el*). Type that address into the Web browser's address box and press the Enter key. That Web page loads into your browser for viewing. Figure 11.3 shows the address line with a URL to one of my favorite spots. Looking at Figure 11.3, you can see that Windows remembered my Amazon Web page and offers me the option of one of these Web pages I've already visited. The first line, `http://www.amazon.com`, is the actual URL (or Web page address).

11

Notice that as I started typing, a whole list of `amazon` listings appeared. Choose the one option you want. I'm going for the first option, which will take me to my favorite online bookstore, Amazon.com.

These are the basics for finding Web pages. Here are some Web pages you can visit if you're looking for something different to do on the Internet:

`http://www.whitehouse.gov`	The White House's Internet page
`http://www.yahoo.com`	A good Internet portal site
`http://www.sullistudios.com`	The online art gallery of a great artist I know
`http://www.about.com`	News and information
`http://www.msn.com`	News, search, information
`http://www.microsoft.com`	Microsoft's home page

`http://www.jokes.com`	List of jokes
`http://www.moviedatabase.com`	The Internet movie database
`http://www.amazon.com`	An online book store
`http://www.wambooli.com/titles`	A list of books we've published

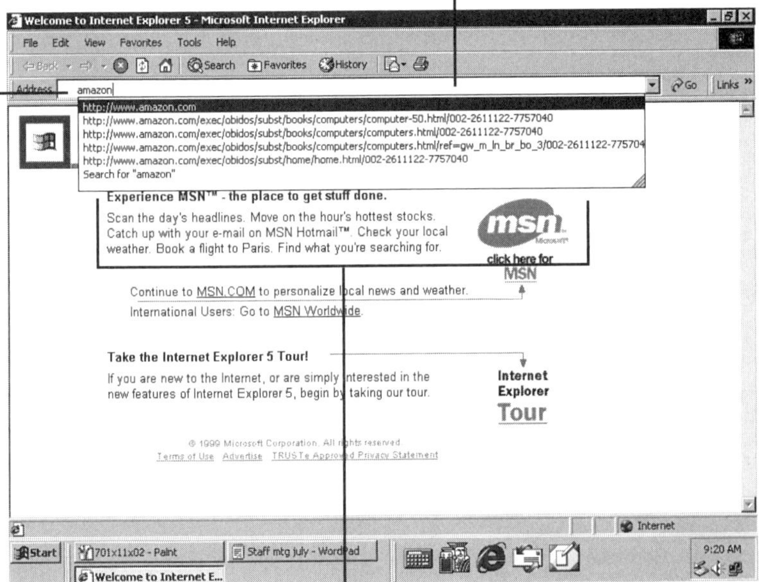

FIGURE 11.3
The URL to amazon.com.

Windows has been kind enough to offer you more links, and they are already listed for you.

Choose Favorites from your menu bar. Choose media, and whoa, there's a long list of options. Everything from ABC News to Windows Media Showcase. Can you imagine what some of these folks had to pay to get Microsoft to list their Web page? It boggles the mind!

> As you toodle around the Web, you might be asked whether you want to install a product like Microsoft audio filter. A special dialog box appears to discuss the issue. It's your choice whether you say yes or no. If this question is asked and you choose No, chances are, you won't be connected to what you're looking for.

Using Search Engines

The Web is a bottomless sea of information, and there are no charts or maps to point you this way or that. Well, nothing official anyway.

To help you get around the Web, certain Web pages are known as *search engines*. These pages contain lists of other Web pages, which help you find or search for information—like an Internet "Yellow Pages." The search engine then lists Web sites that have anything to do with Shakespeare.

Here is a list of some popular Internet search engines:

Dogpile	`http://www.dogpile.com`
Ask Jeeves	`http://www.dogpile.com`
Goto	`http://www.goto.com`
C|Net Search	`http://search.cnet.com/`
Lycos	`http://www.lycos.com`
AltaVista	`http://www.altavista.com`
Excite	`http://www.excite.com`

Use the links in the table to go to each of these search engines, and take a peek at each one.

To Do 11.3: Using a Search Engine

To Do

1. Choose the search engine you want.

   Use any of the engines just mentioned, because they all work about the same.

2. Find the Search box.

   This is an empty box somewhere on the screen.

3. Type your request.

Type the *thing* you're wanting to search. For example, I just looked for monologues, so I typed in the word *monologue*. I got a great list of different kinds of monologues.

4. Click Search.

   You have to click Search or whatever the search engine of your choice has as an option—which might be different from Search. There may be a slight delay when the search engine starts looking for your topic. The more Web pages to look for, the longer it may take. Also, the older your computer, the longer it takes.

5. Scan through the list.

   Usually, there is a list of matching Web pages with maybe a brief description of what each is about.

6. Click on one of the links.

   This will take you to a Web page. Read it. If this isn't what you were looking for, click the Back button and click on another link from the list.

> Going to Web pages requires time. You have to do a lot of research and reading to find what you want. Be prepared—get comfortable and start reading.

Shopping on the Web

Great news! You can shop on the Web! Bad news. You can shop on the Web.

Yes, Internet shopping is both good and bad news. It makes shopping for anything easier in some cases and just not worth it in others. For example, you can go to Amazon.com and shop for books, music CDs, sheet music, videos, DVDs—any kind of electronics—and they've just added toys, games, and electronic greeting cards. After you set up your account, you can click one button to buy what you're looking for, and everything is done (see Figure 11.4). Now all you have to do is sit and wait for your new toys to come in the mail…

Amazon, as well as other online retailers, really understands Internet shopping. Not all shopping on the Internet is quick and easy.

For example, I've found that anything to do with buying clothing is slow because it takes a while for the pictures to upload. You also don't have that element of trying on things or feeling fabrics. Of course, I suppose the same could be said about catalog shopping.

FIGURE 11.4
Amazon.com's easy one-click shopping.

And sometimes relying on a description can be frustrating. I went to an online office supply store to order a three-ring binder. Do you know how many kinds of three-ring binders there are? I was offered a whole list of options, none of which sounded familiar because I'm used to walking into my favorite office store and grabbing what *looks* like what I want. Oh, frustrating. Very frustrating.

> To find anything on the Internet—whether it be a blouse or information on *Blue Book* values for a car—means doing a lot of searching. If you get involved with the constant clicking and searching, but then remember that you forgot to print a copy of the page with that great salmon recipe, click the History tab located at the top of your screen. Then choose the Today option. You'll find a list of all the places you've visited that day. Search for the place that offers the recipe, and click it. You're instantly taken back to that spot. Amazing, eh?

Places to Shop

There are lots of places to go shopping. Rather than be unfair to those places I'm unaware of, the best thing I can suggest is that you start your shopping spree somewhere like the Microsoft home page, `http://home.microsoft.com/`. Look for the category *Shopping* (or the shopping tab that is across the top). Click once there and you're whisked off to categories of shops. Keep picking categories until you find the store you want. Now shop!

You can also go to Web sites that are related to your favorite stores. You can try typing the store name directly into the address line. Or go to one of the search engines and search for the name of your store. Try searching for *shopping* or even *online shopping*. Those both bring up some interesting results.

Another option is to let the Internet do the shopping for you. Online *agents* can scour all available Internet stores for the best bargains in just about anything. One such agent is MySimon (`http://www.mysimon.com/`), where you can compare prices on just about anything sold on the Internet. (It's my favorite comparison price site because I have a son named *Simon*.)

Security

Shopping on the Internet is safe. So safe, in fact, that zero cases of credit card theft on an Internet purchase have been reported. That's good. Although you might be safe, be aware that Internet Explorer does try to scare you with various warning messages whenever you send information on the Internet. Don't fret; there will never be information such as "Tom Sullivan is searching for information on buying drag race cars" stored anywhere. Don't worry about it. Figure 11.5 shows such a warning box.

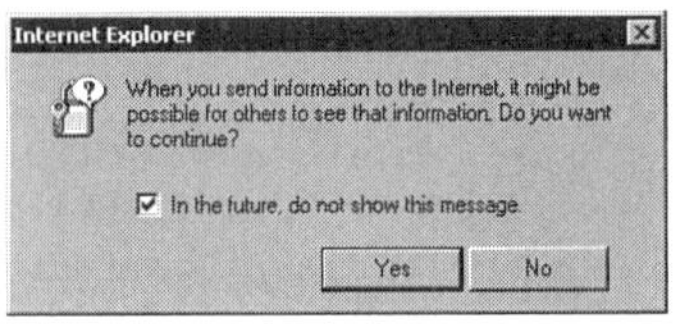

FIGURE 11.5
A simple warning from Internet Explorer.

So what *could* go wrong by ordering items off the Internet?

- Something you order doesn't fit, and you have to send it back.
- The color of the item doesn't quite match that the lovely rosebud in your wallpaper, and you have to send it back.
- You go overboard and buy too much, and your spouse takes away your computer.

Summary

The wild, wild Web. It can be a real time-waster or very helpful. Just learn to turn the thing off and get on with your life.

You should walk away from this hour knowing how to get information by using search engines and how to choose a new home page. For those adventurous ones, try doing a little shopping. This hour also offers several links to a variety of places. Get comfortable using the Web by visiting these places.

Q&A

Q How can I go back three Web pages at once?

A Click the down arrow by the Back button. That displays a list of the past several Web pages you've visited. To return to one, just choose it from the drop-down list.

Q Can people see what I'm doing on the Internet?

A No. Theoretically, they can, which is why there are warnings about sending information on the Internet. But in reality, it just doesn't happen.

Q I've used all the search engines you mentioned but still cannot find what I'm looking for. Help!

A The Web doesn't contain everything. Also, some older Web pages tend to dry up and disappear, meaning that a link mentioned by a search engine might be gone! Just try again, rephrasing what you're searching for. But be aware that sometimes the information might not be out there.

Q What's a 404 error?

A It means that the Web page isn't available. Check your typing and try again. If the error continues, there just isn't any such Web page.

Q Internet Explorer says that there is no "DNS" something or other. What's up?

A A common error. This typically means that the Web is busy. Try again. If the error persists, some computer somewhere on the Internet might be down. Try again later.

Workshop

The workshop includes quiz questions to help gauge your grasp of the material and exercises to help reinforce your learning. You'll find the answers to the quiz in Appendix A, "Answers."

Quiz

1. What is a quick and easy way to retry a hefty download that has stalled out partway through?
2. What is perhaps the best reason to take an exit ramp off the Information Superhighway?
3. *Bonus Question*: What did the great Buddha die of?

Exercises

1. Change your home page. Even if you really want the one you have now, change it and take pride in the extra practice you will get by changing it back at the end of this hour.
2. Use a search engine to research a relatively obscure interest, for example, perhaps Ultimate Frisbee. Practice a discerning perusal of the Web sites offered. Enjoy.
3. Window-shop through a few online retail sites. Get a feel for navigating both the user-friendly ones and those more awkward. Make a few mental notes of what makes the likable sites better and easier than the frustrating ones.

Vocabulary

online—Another way of saying that you are connected to the Internet. Surfing, researching, chatting, shopping, checking e-mail, and so on, for each of these you must be on the Internet, or *online*.

search engine—A category of numerous Web pages that allows you to search endlessly for information on countless topics (like telling your encyclopedia what you need to know, and it opens to the right page). Unfortunately, your search engine will open every virtual encyclo-whatever, no matter how useful (or not). So, when using search engines, specificity and patience are the keys.

URL—Although it literally stands for *uniform resource locator*, all you need to know is that it usually refers to the address of a Web site, as in `www.dogpile.com`.

HOUR 12

The Joys and Sorrows of E-Mail

Every so often, high school teachers and college professors feel the need to ask their students this mind-boggling question: What has been the biggest change to our society this century?

In years past, television and computers were the popular answers. If I were back in school (thank God, I'm not), my answer would have to be electronic mail, lovingly called *e-mail*.

There are those who complain that e-mail has replaced formal written letters. Yep, it sure has, to some degree. But I can't help wondering whether it has also reduced phone bills and increased communication at the same time. People are finding that they communicate more with family members, and grandmothers are keeping better in touch with their grandchildren. It's a family unity revolution! Okay, so I'm getting a little carried away, but I have to admit that I enjoy e-mail because I don't like talking on the phone.

The highlights in this hour include the following:

- Touring of Outlook Express
- Sending e-mail
- Receiving e-mail
- Sending attachments
- Receiving attachments

Touring Outlook Express

Sending e-mail starts with the software program Outlook Express, which is the program Microsoft already provided for you when Windows 2000 was installed. Granted, you can send e-mail with a variety of other programs, but hey, this is a Windows 2000 book, so I'm not going to talk about those other programs. Instead, I'm just going to focus on Outlook Express.

To Do 12.1: Starting Outlook Express

1. Click the Start button.
2. Choose Programs.
3. Choose Outlook Express.

> Outlook Express is one of those programs that's great to have on your Quick Launch bar or as an icon on your desktop. That way, you can quickly click on the icon.

4. Listen to the modem.

   The Dial-up Connection box appears and the modem takes off. When you're connected to the Internet (see Hour 10, "Doing the Internet," for more information about that), you're ready to send mail, read mail, and do all kinds of things.

Take a gander at Figure 12.1 for a tour of Outlook Express.

FIGURE 12.1
Outlook Express.

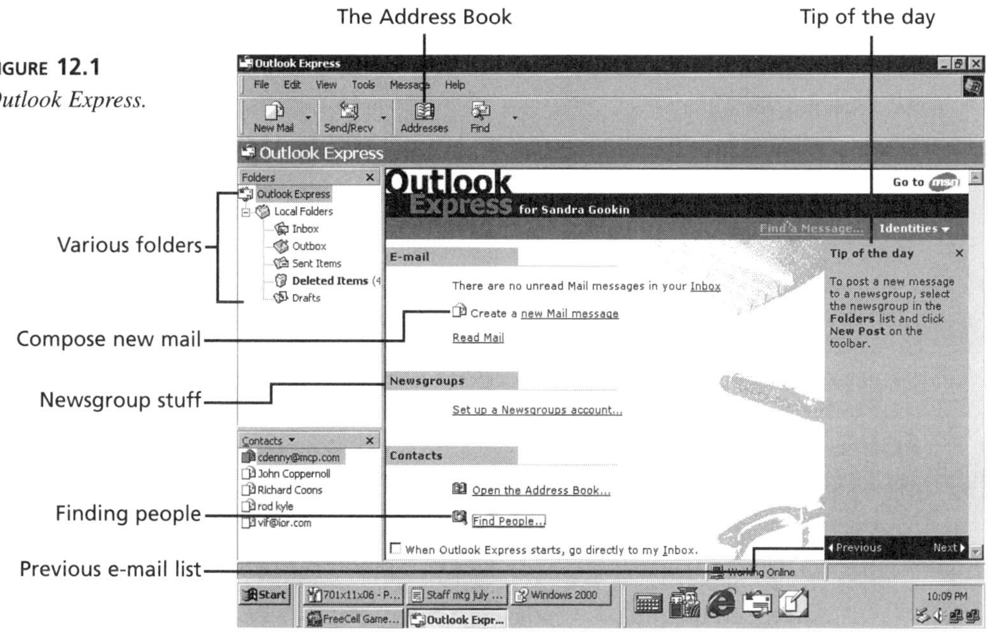

12

Tip of the Day

You can't learn enough about this e-mail stuff, and the tip of the day is going to make sure you get bits and pieces of information every day. Click the Previous arrow to see yesterday's tip. Click the Next arrow to see tomorrow's tip. Click the × at the top corner of the Tip box to get rid of the tip of the day. Click Tips, located in the upper-right corner, to bring back the tip of the day.

E-Mail

You can check your inbox, mail a new message, or simply read your mail from this area. Just hover your cursor over one of these underlined areas and click. You're then taken to the spot where you need to be to accomplish these tasks.

Newsgroups

Newsgroups are a whole other world and a topic for some specific Internet book. Walking through the steps of Set Up a Newsgroups Account basically gets things ready for when you do start a newsgroup. (In a nutshell, newsgroups are like public e-mail messages—and like nutshells, there are lots of nuts insides the newsgroups.)

Contacts

This is the private eye of Outlook Express. Your options are to open the Address Book or use Find People.

The Address Book, like the address book on your desk or in your purse, is where you store all your e-mail buddies. This helps greatly when you want to type in `mom`, for example, instead of listing her full e-mail address, which is probably `wogga-wogga-zip-blat@diggedy-dank.com`.

Find People is a search function for locating people you might have in your Address Book or, if you click the down arrow next to Look In:, other areas on the Internet. Click the down arrow just for fun to take a peek.

Folders

The Folders section contains none other than folders. It's a way to keep your e-mail sections organized. Click once on Local Folders to show the folders and their contents.

To Do 12.2: Making a New Folder

1. Click File in the menu.
2. Choose New.
3. Choose Folder.
4. Type in the name of your new file.
5. Click OK.

Figure 12.2 shows you what to look for.

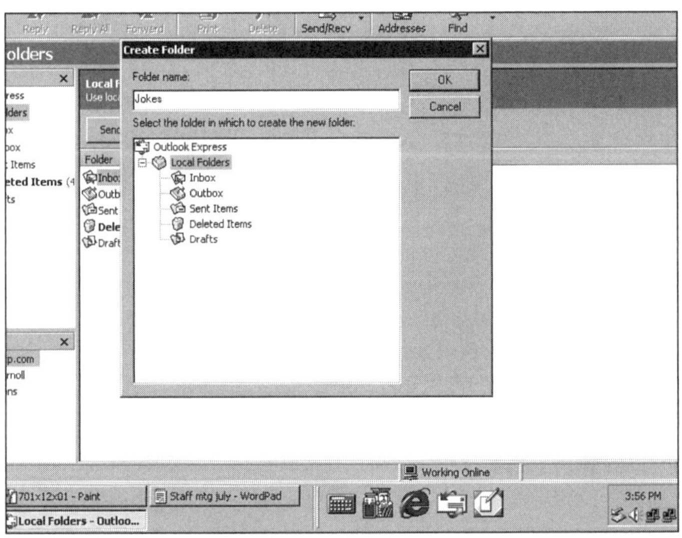

FIGURE 12.2
A nifty new folder.

Be creative with your new folders. Have one for business, one for family, one for online order receipts, and especially one for jokes—because now that you have e-mail, you will receive more jokes than necessary.

After you read e-mail messages, you can click and drag them to a folder. For example, you would drag a good joke into your Jokes folder.

Messages you don't like, such as the popular junk e-mail or SPAM, you can delete. To delete a message drag it to the Trash folder.

> Deleted messages are held in the deleted file until you decide to completely empty that file. Deleting files is a part of keeping your messages organized and well maintained. So when you're finished with a message, you should either drag it to a new folder for keeping or simply click the Delete button to get rid of it.

Send

You can send an e-mail in a variety of ways. The To Do 12.3 covers one of the ways to send an e-mail.

To Do 12.3: Sending E-Mail

1. Click the New Mail button.
2. Find an address.

   Click the book next to the To: line to select an address from a list of people in your e-mail Address Book. Otherwise, you can manually type in an e-mail address.
3. Type a subject.

   This is a brief description of what the message is about. It could be simple like `Hi!` or something more detailed like `Breaking up with you!`. (Detailed is obviously better; short and to the point are ideal.)

> You can use the Tab key to move from one box to the next or use your mouse to click the areas you want.

4. Type your message.

```
Hey Jerkhead! I'm breaking up with you...!
```

If you feel flowery, you can use the Font box, along with the other formatting features. You can make your message just as attractive as a word processing document.

> No longer do you have to settle with sending a boring e-mail. Now you can select stationery. Yippee! Now the fun begins. Click the down arrow next to New Mail; then click Select Stationery. You're provided with a whole list of different kinds of stationery in which to write your e-mail. Make sure that there is a check mark in the box next to Show Preview. Now, click once on each type of stationery to see what it looks like. When you find the one you like, click on it and then click OK. The Send Message box appears with your new stationery, and you're ready to write your e-mail.

5. Click Send.

Your message is whisked off on the Information Superhighway, delivered to the proper e-mail recipient for her viewing. Delivery is instant, and there is no way to recall sent e-mail.

If the e-mail address was improperly typed or does not exist, your e-mail will "bounce" back to you. When that happens, check the address and try sending the message again. (Forward it to the proper recipient, or copy the message text and paste it into a new message.)

Other Ways to Send E-Mail

There are several ways to send an e-mail. I suppose that Microsoft wanted to make it really easy when the urge to e-mail comes over you. The following are a few of those options.

- Option 1—On the bottom left of Outlook Express is a Contacts list. Find the name of the person to whom you want to send an e-mail. Double-click on his name, and there is your new message box, waiting for you to compose something brilliant.
- Option 2—In the E-mail section on the first page of Outlook, there is a line that reads `Create a new Mail message`. Just click on the underlined words, and there again is your new message box. Write a message to dad, asking for money so that you can upgrade your printer!
- Option 3—Click File from the menu. Choose New and then Mail Message. A new message box appears.

- Option 4—Click the Address icon located at the top of your screen. Your Address Book appears. Click once on one of the names. Now, click the Action button and then choose Send Mail. Whoa! There is your new message box again.
- Option 5—Click the Message option in the menu. Choose New Message. Boy, oh boy, another new message box.
- Option 6—Press Ctrl+N. This opens the new message box.

This makes seven different ways to start to send a message—don't forget the one in To Do 12.3. Can anyone say "overkill?"

> If you open the new message box and then decide not to send the message or write it, click the × in the upper right of the box. This is the Close button. You may be asked whether you want to save the changes to your message. Just choose No. If you've been opening up all those new message boxes, you'll need to close them all now. Or start writing notes because you have them open.

Now with all this e-mail you're sending, you should start to get some back. Read the next section on receiving mail.

Receive

Sending mail is really where all the work is. Receiving mail means that you do nothing much more than connect to the Internet and wait for the beeps and buzzes to stop. Then, you can warm up with that sweet glow that happens when you know someone cares enough to send you e-mail.

Task 12.4: Receiving Mail

To Do

1. Start Outlook Express.

   Click the Start button, choose Programs, and then choose Outlook Express.
2. Click Connect.

   (This is only if your computer isn't set to automatically connect.)
3. The computer checks for messages.

There isn't anything you have to push or click. The computer does it automatically when you first open Outlook Express. You'll get a notice at the bottom of your screen that lists the number of new messages you receive—or the sad `No new messages` notice.

You don't have to restart Outlook Express to check for messages. There are easier ways:

- Option 1—Click the Send/Recv button located at the top of your screen.
- Option 2—Click the down arrow next to the Send/Recv button. This gives you the options of sending and receiving all your messages, just receiving messages, or just sending messages.
- Option 3—Click the Tools button, and choose Send and Receive. Again, you can send and receive all your messages, just receive your messages, or just send all your messages.

Sending Attachments

E-mail became popular when people realized that they could correspond in a fast and relatively inexpensive way. But then things really became exciting when it was understood that you can do more than write cute notes: You can also send people pictures or documents. For example, I sent all the pictures and text for this book to my wonderful editor, Chris. He reviewed them, typed in a bunch of notes on the documents, and then sent them back to me—all via e-mail.

To attach any file to an e-mail message, start by writing that message just as you normally would. Then, "paper-clip" the file to your message. The file you attach can be anything—a Word document, a graphic, it doesn't matter.

To Do 12.5: Attaching a Document

To Do

1. Create the file you want to send.

   This should be done ahead of time. After all, you need something to attach.
2. Fire up Outlook Express.
3. Compose your message.

   Decide where you're sending your stuff, have the TO: box complete and the subject line filled in, and write a little note explaining what you're sending.

4. Click the paper clip.

   It's easy to find. It has the word `Attach` under it, and it looks like a big ol' paper clip. Hover your cursor over this button, and the message `Attach File` appears. Go ahead and click the paper clip.
5. Find your file.

   My Documents opens, and you are welcome to hunt through the folders until you find the file you want to attach.

6. Select the file you want to send.

   Click on the file once to select it.

7. Click Attach.

   You now have an Attach line added to your message, with your file placed there, ready to be sent.

> Do you want to keep your friends? If so, then be careful about sending large files. Many of the jokes and cartoons that people regularly find and send via the Internet are large files. Meaning, they take up valuable disk space and can take a lot of time to download them. If you have something that you absolutely must send, you may want to send a quick e-mail that is alerting your friend of the big file that is coming.

8. Click the Send button.

   Your e-mail message and the attachment are now being whisked off through the Internet.

> If you want to see the progress of your message being sent, click the Send/Recv button. This brings up the message box, and you can watch your message being sent. Notice that your message takes longer to send when you attach files; the larger the file, the longer it takes to send.

Receiving Attachments

The flip side to sending attachments is receiving them. Fun, fun, fun. Now, not only will you get loads and loads of jokes, funny pictures, and singing poetry, but there's also that risk that you'll get work.

To Do 12.6: Receiving an Attachment

To Do

1. Run Outlook Express.
2. Browse through your list of new mail messages.

   The clue that you have an attachment to your message is the paper clip symbol. There are actually two places to find this: One is next to the From line in your list of new messages. The second is in the right corner of your new message box. In Figure 12.3, you can see both these paper clip areas.

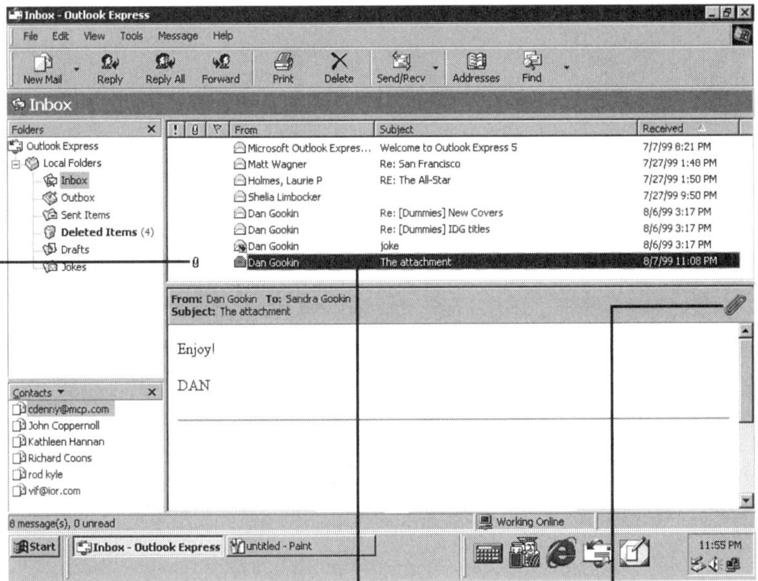

FIGURE 12.3
The attachment paper clips.

3. Open your message.

   You open a message by clicking on it.

4. Click on the paper clip.

   Some attachments, like photographs, may already be visible in the message. If not, click on the paper clip to open your attachment.

5. Possible warning.

   You may get a warning asking you how you want to open the attachment. Always open to disk.

6. Choose the Open to Disk option.

   This displays a Save As dialog box you can use to save the attachment somewhere on your hard disk (such as in the My Documents folder or maybe a special Attachments folder you created). You can then deal with the attachment after you're done reading your e-mail.

E-mail attachments *can* contain viruses that could damage your computer. The viruses cannot be sent through an e-mail message; that's not possible. But infected files can and are attached to e-mail messages. If you open such a file, you could infect your computer. The best way to avoid this is *never* to open a file attachment you receive from someone unknown to you or a file you weren't expecting. Picture files (GIFs and JPEGs) are okay and cannot be infected. Program files, Word and Excel files *might* be infected, so use caution when opening them. If you know the sender, confirm that the file was meant for you. Otherwise, if it is unexpected or from an unknown source, do not save the file to disk or delete it.

When you're finished with reading or viewing your attachment, just close the document.

Summary

This hour is dedicated to e-mail. E-mail. Ah, the sound of it. Getting mail, every day, all day long. You should be comfortable with sending, receiving, and deleting e-mail, in addition to working with your e-mail attachments.

Q&A

Q How can I forward a message to someone else?

A Click the Forward button located on the toolbar. The message reappears in a message box (as if you are sending the message) so that you can now add the address of the person to whom you're forwarding the message.

Q How can I create an e-mail nickname, such as *wife* for my wife's e-mail address?

A This happens when you are adding names to your Address Book. As in any address book, you type in the name of the person you're adding; then, you type in her e-mail address. (You cut and paste it, which is safer, so you don't make a typing error.) You can give the person any name you want, whether it be *wife-unit* or *Babe*.

Workshop

The workshop includes quiz questions to help gauge your grasp of the material and exercises to help reinforce your learning. You'll find the answers to the quiz in Appendix A, "Answers."

Quiz

1. Why should you save an e-mail attachment to disk?
2. What kind of files can you clip on to a piece of e-mail as an attachment?
3. What are two ways to check for e-mail without restarting Outlook Express?
4. *Bonus question*: What were the last words of the famous composer Ludwig van Beethoven?

Exercises

1. Use the Contacts function to poke around the Internet for long-lost friends. Write a note (electronically) to a couple of the folks you locate.
2. Make at least two separate folders for your incoming messages, one for communiqués from the boss and one for the sweet notes you just can't bring yourself to delete.
3. Add some names to your Address Book in the Contacts list.

Vocabulary

Address Book—A list of e-mail names and addresses kept by Outlook Express. It makes composing new e-mail messages a snap.

attachments—A file sent along with the e-mail message.

newsgroups—A whole bunch of people you can e-mail at once. When you send an e-mail to your newsgroup, a copy of it is sent to every member in that newsgroup.

HOUR 13

Getting Stuff from the Internet

Golly, but there certainly is a lot of stuff on the Internet. Stuff to do. Stuff to see. And stuff to take.

Now, I'm not encouraging any form of theft here, but in addition to being a great resource for information, the Internet is also a great source for files and programs, images, and information, all of which you can copy or download directly from any computer on the Internet into your own PC.

The highlights in this hour include the following:

- Saving a Web page to disk
- Saving an image to disk
- Finding files on the Internet
- Downloading a file
- UnZipping a file
- Using an FTP window

Saving a Web Page to Disk

Perusing Web pages and reading interesting, albeit trivial information on anything is a passion I hope you share. Alas, it consumes a great deal of computer time, which means, although the mind is stimulated, the clock winds on, withering your work time down to almost nothing.

Rather than waste time dawdling at some long-winded Web page, save it to disk instead. That way you can read it later. (Yes, you can just print the Web page and read it later *anywhere*. But printing Web pages isn't the topic.)

To Do 13.1: Saving a Web Page

To Do

1. Find the Web page of your choice.

   Hour 11, "It's a Wild World Wide Web We Weave," will help you find the Web page of your choice.

2. Choose File from the menu.
3. Choose Save As from the list of options.

   A common Save As dialog box appears (see Figure 13.1), although it's called "Save HTML Document," and it has a few more features.

FIGURE 13.1
Saving a Web page.

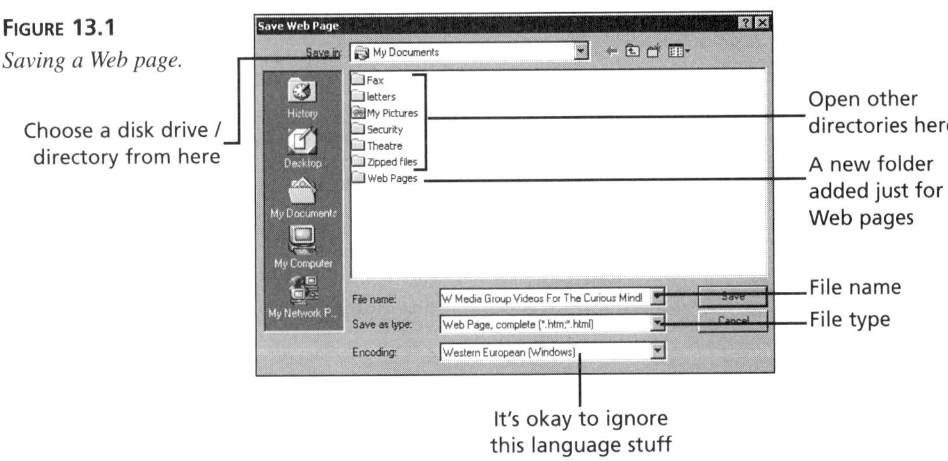

Work the Save As dialog box as you would any Save As dialog box. Find a location for the file; then click the Save button.

> If you're going to get in the habit of saving Web pages, you might want to make a separate Web page folder. Refer to Hour 9, "What's in Them Folders and Files?" to remind yourself how you make your own folders.

The Save As type drop-down list enables you to save the file as either an HTML File (which is the native tongue of Web pages) or as a plain text file. For off-line reading, choose Web Page—complete. To save the document's text, for example, to paste into another document, use the Text File type.

4. Find a folder to put the Web page in.
5. Click the Save button to save the Web page to disk.

   With the Web page saved on disk you can read it later, at your leisure, anytime, whether or not you're connected to the Internet.
6. Close your Web page and disconnect from the Internet.

   Now that you have a nifty little Web page to read at your leisure, you can find your Web page and start reading.

To Do 13.2: Reading Your Saved Web Page

1. Open Windows Explorer.

   Hour 18, "Maintaining and Cleaning Files," discusses Windows Explorer, if you need a reminder.
2. Locate the Web page file.
3. Double-click the icon to open the Web page (HTML) document.

   All the text will be there, plus maybe a few graphic images. Figure 13.2 illustrates the Web page file saved in the new Web Pages folder. Alas, saving a Web page to disk does not save the graphic images, but in most cases it's just the text that interests you anyway.

Saving an Image to Disk

Sometimes it's not the text but the images you want from a Web page. Think of it: Not only can you write your relatives about the Big Storm, but you can send them a satellite photo as well! Wish you were here? Probably not!

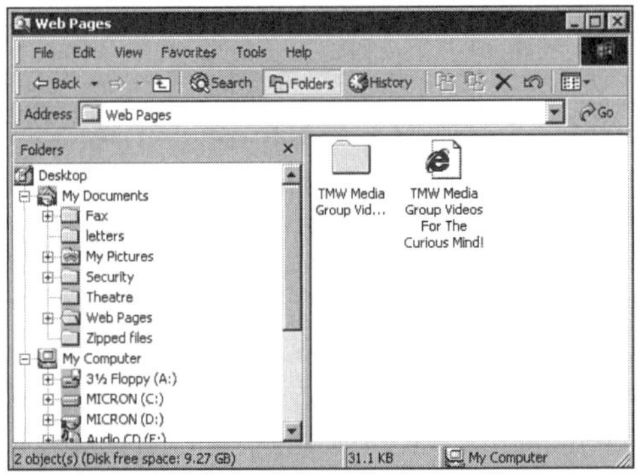

FIGURE 13.2
The Windows Explorer view of the saved Web page.

To Do 13.3: Grabbing an Image from a Web Page

1. Find an image on the Internet.
2. Right-click on the image.

   This displays a pop-up menu listing several interesting items.
3. Choose Save Picture As.

   A Save Picture dialog box appears, which works like the standard Save As dialog box, but is designed to save pictures on Web pages. The My Pictures folder is ready and waiting for you. Again, if you're going to be saving a lot of pictures from the Internet, you might want to make a Web Pages folder in which to save all your pictures (see Figure 13.3).

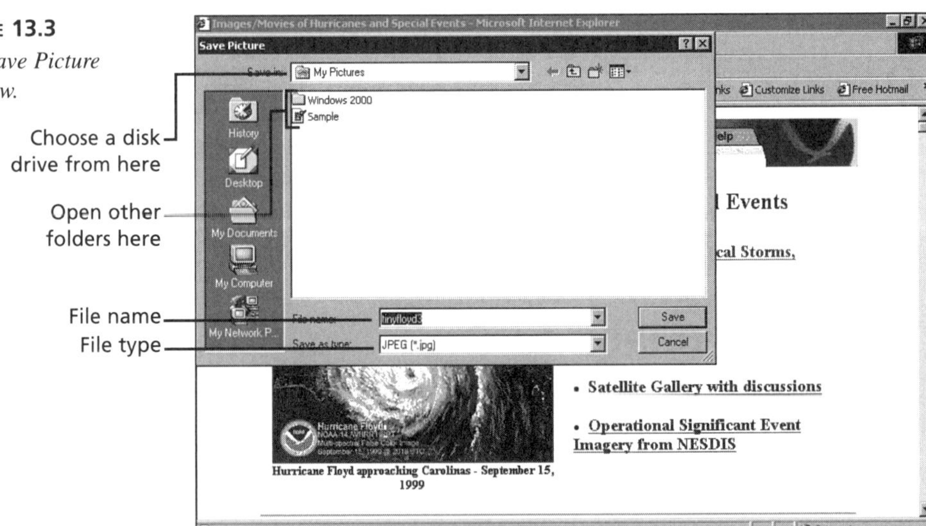

FIGURE 13.3
The Save Picture window.

4. Click the Save button.

   The image is then saved on disk for later use or abuse.

Is this theft? Probably not. Many images on the Web are copyrighted, and their use is restricted. You can, however, download (save) images from a Web site to your hard drive for your own personal use. Reusing an image in a commercial or public manner without permission, however, is usually not allowed.

> Most images on the Web are of two flavors: GIF and JPG or JPEG. These are graphic image file types, both of which can be opened and read (displayed) using the Internet Explorer program. Other programs on your computer, such as Windows Imaging, might also be available to view or manipulate the images.

Finding Files on the Internet

Another item you can grab from the Internet and store safely in your computer is software. There are tons and tons of files available on the Internet, all free for the taking. There are games, utilities, applications, and even full operating systems available. All you need is the location of the file on the Internet and the time to download it into your computer.

Finding the Files

As with finding anything on the Internet, to find files for downloading you need a search engine. In this case, what you need is a file-finding search engine. There are many of them.

My favorite places to look for files are the following sites:

```
www.filemine.com  File Mine

www.download.com  CNet's Download.com

www.jumbo.com  Jumbo!
```

There are more sites as well, most of which can be found using Yahoo!: Visit the Computers and Internet section, then go to Software, and then the Shareware page.

Most file-finding engines have a main page that contains the following elements (also shown in Figure 13.4, which details FileMine's Web page):

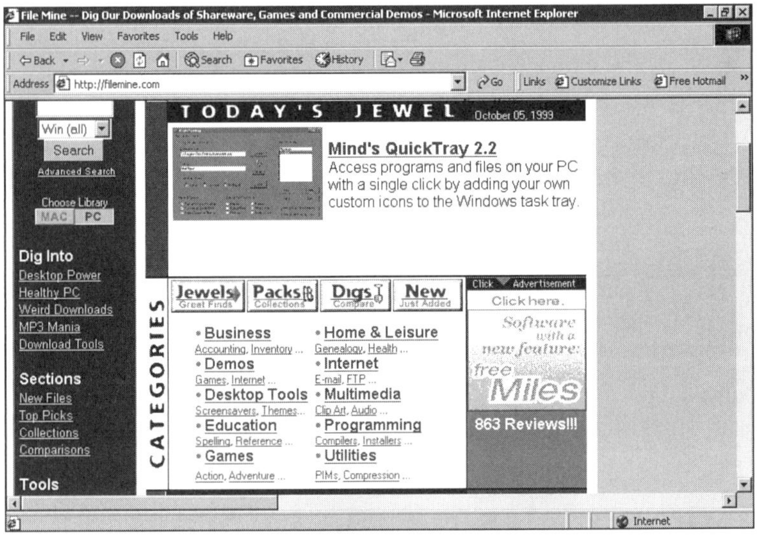

FIGURE 13.4
FileMine's Web page.

A simple search engine You type in the name of the program you're looking for or a topic, such as `card games`. Optionally, choose an operating system, then click the button.

A list of topics You can also browse for software by various categories listed on the page.

A list of top downloads See what everyone else is downloading!

Featured items Sometimes these are suggestions for neat and overlooked stuff, although I often have my suspicions that these are really paid advertisements. You judge.

Necessary items A good downloading Web page can also highlight some common tools every computer user should have, such as an unZip utility, Web browser, chat client, or a host of other interesting must-haves.

To Do 13.4: Downloading a File

1. Go to the Address line on Internet Explorer and type `FileMine.com`. Press Enter.
2. Type `Canasta` into the search dialog box.

   Make sure that the proper operating system is chosen. If there is a Windows 2000 (or even Windows NT) option, choose it. Note that some games and programs that work for DOS or other versions of Windows will not work under Windows 2000. Keep your eyes peeled. Also, if you're a true Canasta fan, go to `www.canasta.net` for another fun game.
3. Click the Search button.

▼ In a few Internet instances, the results of your search are displayed. If you're lucky, you'll see a list of files with further instructions. If you're not lucky, you'll see the dreadfully disappointing "Sorry, no matches were found" message. Try again; this time type card games.

When an item is found, information is displayed, as shown in Figure 13.5. The information tells you a little about the file: how large it is (which affects download time), the date it was first posted, which operating system it works for, plus other requirements—including the price (if any). FileMine really shines for the quality of information it displays, as shown in the figure.

> In Figure 13.5, you'll see the shareware cost. The price of this game is paid on somewhat of an honor system. If you don't pay, you're reminded. When you do pay, you're given a registration number, and the program no longer reminds you to pay.

FIGURE 13.5
Information about Rummy Drop.

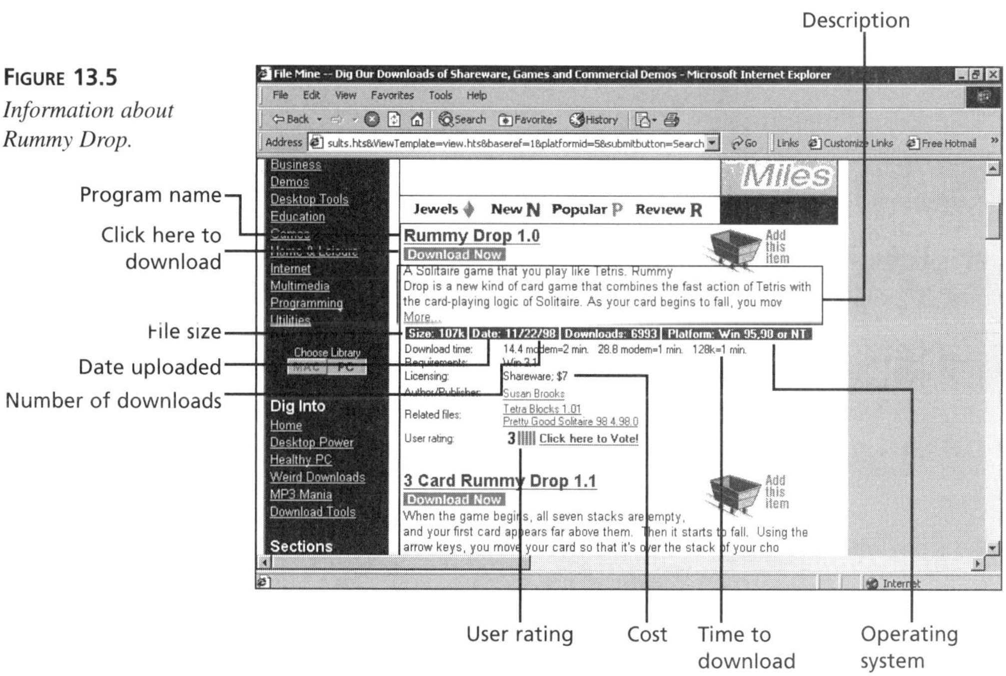

4. To download the file, click the proper download button.

   With FileMine, you have the option of adding the file to an In-Basket, which enables you to collect files and download them all later or at once. ▼

13

After clicking the Download (or similar) button you might instantly be faced with the Downloading dialog box. In FileMine, you might have to scroll to the bottom of the page to see the download list, as shown in Figure 13.6. If so, skip to the next step. Otherwise, you might see another Web page offering more information and perhaps a choice of download links.

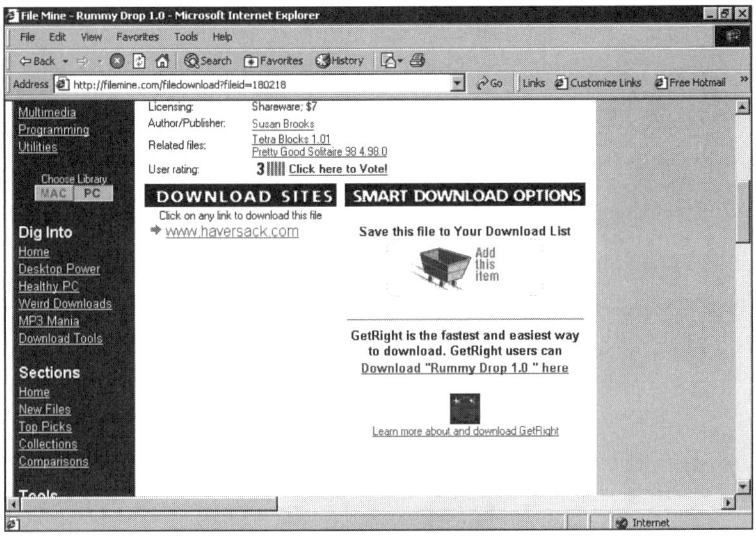

FIGURE 13.6
The Download list from FileMine.

5. Heed the Web page's information; then click a download site.

   The File Download dialog box appears, as shown in Figure 13.7.

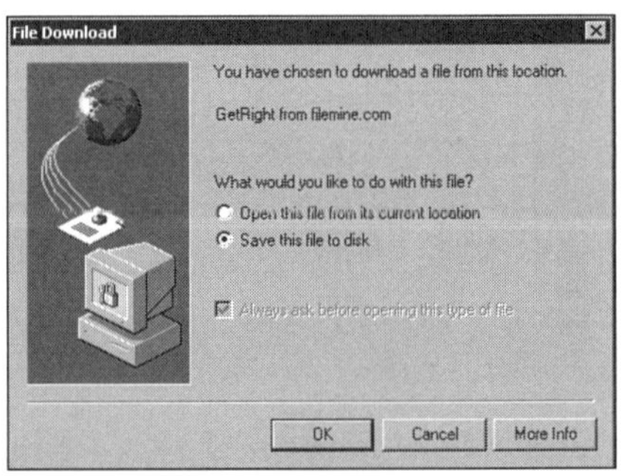

FIGURE 13.7
The File Download dialog box.

6. Choose Save this program to disk.

   You do not want to run the program; you want to save it. Click OK.
7. Save the downloaded file into the proper folder on your hard drive.
8. Click OK after choosing the proper disk drive and folder.

A dialog box appears, amusing you while you wait for the file to download. This could take some time, or it could be lickety-split, depending on your modem's speed. While you wait you can

- Get a cup of coffee.
- Continue to browse the Web. (Windows can both download and browse at the same time.)
- Read or compose e-mail.
- Get some exercise or fresh air.

The only thing you cannot do is disconnect from the Internet. That interrupts the download.

When downloading is complete, you'll see the Download Complete dialog box similar to what you see in Figure 13.8. Click Close. You're done! Well, you're done with the first part.

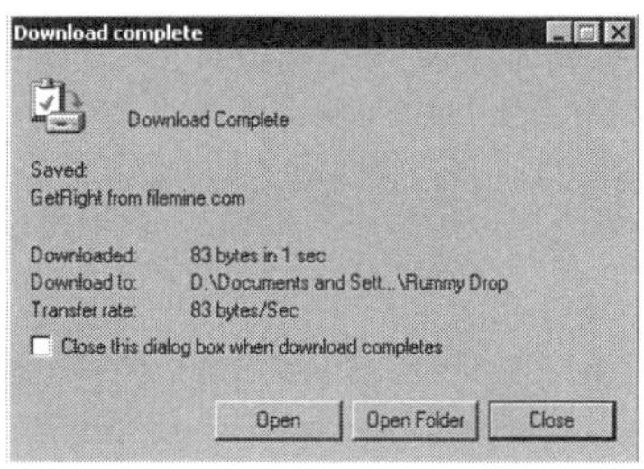

FIGURE 13.8
A friendly notice—the Download is complete.

The file is now saved to disk, most likely in your Download folder or whatever folder you chose from the Save As dialog box when you downloaded the file.

The file you downloaded is probably an *archive*, or a collection of many files, stuffed into a single, smaller file for expediency in downloading. Your next task is to unarchive the file and install the software.

Unarchiving the file is done by opening the downloaded file's icon. (This can be done whether or not you're connected to the Internet, though be advised that some installation or setup programs demand you quit other programs running on your computer.)

To Do 13.5: Unarchiving a File

1. Locate the downloaded file's icon.
2. Open the icon.

If you're lucky, the downloaded file will be a program, which automatically unarchives itself and then runs a setup program.

If you're not lucky, the downloaded file is a Zip file and you'll need an unZip program to remove the contents (see the next section).

After opening the file, the SETUP program should run. If not, locate the Setup icon and run it to install the program.

From this point, you're on your own; each program has its own installation procedure, most of which are easy enough to follow if you've been using a computer for awhile.

Try to install the new program in its own folder in the Program Files folder.

Files to Consider Downloading

To get you started, I can recommend several files you should consider downloading, not only for practice, but because you will need these files if you plan on using the Internet much.

In each of the following cases, ensure that the version of the program you get is fully Windows 2000 compatible.

Adobe Acrobat Reader This free program is available from Adobe Systems and is used to view all sorts of documents on the Internet. For example, you can download this year's tax forms from the `www.irs.gov` Web site in Acrobat (or PDF) format. But you need the Acrobat Reader to display and print the files.

You can download the Acrobat Reader from

`http://www.adobe.com/products/acrobat/readstep.html`

WinZIP There are many popular programs available for archiving, though my favorite is WinZIP. It can be used to create archives or remove files from archives. The ZIP archive is the most popular format available for Windows.

WinZIP is a "real" program, though you can download an evaluation version — or pay on-line and then download the commercial version. Either way, visit

`http://www.winzip.com`

McAfee anti-virus Finally, everyone needs antivirus software. The most popular source for it is the McAfee Web page, where you can get an evaluation version of its famous antivirus software. Or, as with WinZip, you can surrender your credit card number and download a paid-for version right there on the spot. The address is

`http://www.mcafee.com`

By the way, paying for and downloading software instantly is one of the true benefits of downloading software. As an example, I routinely order fancy fonts on-line at `http://www.eyewire.com`—a commercial Web page. They sell fonts and then, after you buy them, allow you to download the fonts right into your computer. No shipping! Now, if only the printer could make clothes and food, I'd never have to leave the house!

UnZipping a File

One of the horrors of downloading is discovering that you have on your computer a ZIP file archive. Unless you have the proper unZip program, you're kinda stuck. This happens quite a bit, which is why I've added this section to help you with your ZIP file woes.

Suppose you download a file, and Windows doesn't know what to make of it. In that case, the Generic file icon is used.

To discover what type of file it is, right-click on the icon and choose Properties from the menu. The icon's Properties dialog box lists the file's name and the type of file (in addition to size of file, when it was created, that sort of trivia).

ZIP files are archives. They are a single file that can contain several other files, all of which are compacted into the single file. The archive makes downloading the files easier; instead of spending more time downloading several dozen files, you need to download only a single ZIP file. But to get the files out of the ZIP file, you need an unZip extraction utility.

The unZip utility I recommend is WinZIP, which you can download from the Internet as described in the previous section.

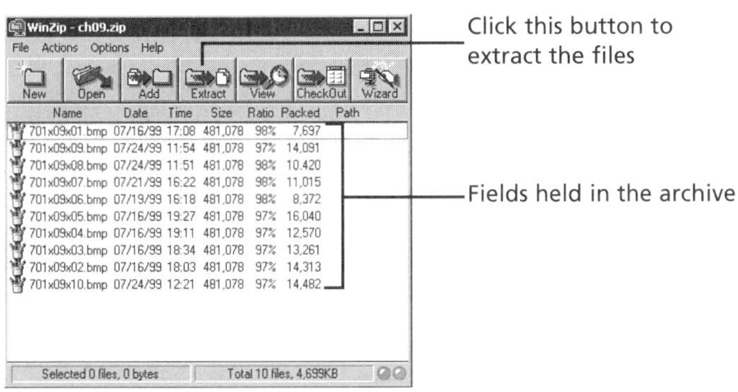

FIGURE 13.9
WinZIP is open.

To Do 13.5: UnZipping Files

1. Open the WinZIP program.
2. Double-click on any ZIP file archive to open it, as shown in Figure 13.9.
3. Click the Extract button or press Ctrl+E.

   An Extract dialog box appears, as shown in Figure 13.10.

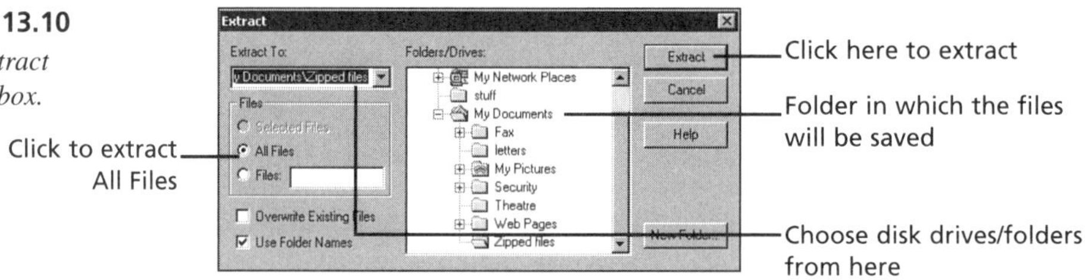

Figure 13.10
The Extract dialog box.

4. Locate a folder for the extracted files.

   If you're unZipping a program archive, create a new folder in the Program Files folder (use the New Folder button in the Extract dialog box). Otherwise, choose a proper folder in which to extract the files.
5. Ensure that All Files is selected.
6. Click the Extract button.

   The files are pulled from the ZIP archive and saved to disk in the folder you specified.

You can close WinZIP by clicking the X button in the upper-right corner of its window.

From this point on, you install the program as you normally would: Run the SETUP program or read the README documentation to discover what to do next.

You can save the original ZIP file if you want to. However, ZIP files do tend to accumulate. It's okay to delete them.

Using an FTP Window

Back in the olden days, before the Web made using the Internet as easy as reading a magazine, files were grabbed from places called FTP sites.

FTP stands for File Transfer Protocol, and it's the means and method by which files are sent to and from on the Internet. And even though the Web is the easiest way to download a file, there can be times when you'll need to point your Web browser in the direction of an FTP site.

For example, type in the following address (actually it's a URL, but I'm not one to pick nits) into your Web browser:

```
ftp://ftp.simtel.com
```

If that site is busy, try

```
ftp://ftp.microsoft.com
```

What you see on your screen is an FTP site as viewed through the Web browser. In this mode, the Web browser acts more like a file viewer—more like Windows Explorer than Internet Explorer. Figure 13.11 shows you what's interesting.

FIGURE 13.11
ftp://simtel.com.

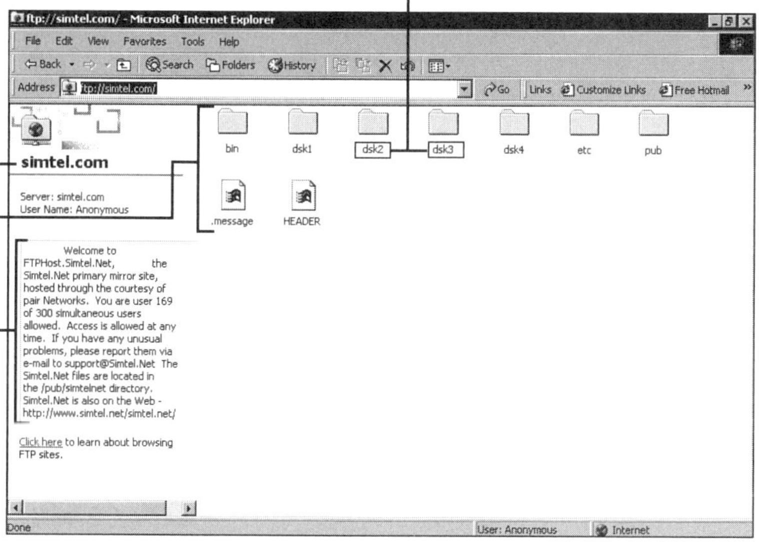

You browse through the folders by clicking on their links. For example, on `ftp.simtel.com`, you can click the pub link to open that folder and see what folders lurk beneath it.

The /pub/simtelnet/win95 folder contains several additional folders of software available for Windows 95/98—though not much for Windows 2000.

This is merely a tutorial, though. In practice, you'll probably be given a specific location on an FTP server to visit, along with the name of a file. Clicking on that filename either displays the file in your browser (for text and graphics) or displays the File Download dialog box, in which case downloading works exactly as described earlier in this hour.

Summary

This has been a busy hour. You have learned how to save a Web page to disk, save an image to disk, how to find files on the Internet, how to download a file, how to unZip a file, and last but not least, how to use an FTP window.

Q&A

Q What if I don't want to save a whole Web page, just a bit of text *from* the Web page. How can I do that?

A Easy: Select and copy. For example, select a swath of text in a Web page, then choose Edit, Copy from the menu (or press Ctrl+C). You can then paste the text into any document or program that accepts text input. If you want to print only that bit of selected text, choose File, Print from the menu and click the Selection button in the Print dialog box. Click the Print button to print only the selected text.

Q Do I have to pay for the programs I download?

A It depends. Some programs are free and state so (either they're "public domain" or "freeware"). Some programs require you to pay a fee for registration, usually a few dollars. Others require you to pay in order to activate features. It should tell you what the payments are when you install the program, or the information might be available in a README text file that accompanies the program.

Q I downloaded a file and Windows can't figure out what it is. How can I tell?

A Generally speaking, unknown file types are most likely PDF or Adobe Acrobat files, ZIP or archive files, or some type of graphics file format your computer cannot read. Your options are limited as to what you can do with an unknown file type. If possible, you can try to fetch another file, one that your computer recognizes. Or you can discover what type of file it is and download or buy the proper application to read it.

Q Can I get a virus from a program I download?

A Absolutely, which is why you must be careful. Downloading a file from a reliable source, such as FileMine or any of the other public download Web pages, is generally safe. Those places base their reputations on not having infected programs. But other locations for files should be suspect. It's always a good idea to have a virus scanner and scan any program file you download before you run that program.

Workshop

The workshop includes quiz questions to help gauge your grasp of the material and exercises to help reinforce your learning. You'll find the answers to the quiz and exercises in Appendix A, "Answers."

Quiz

1. What is WinZIP?
2. Is it possible to save just an image from a Web page and not the text?
3. What does FTP stands for?
4. *Bonus question*: One in three Taiwanese funeral processionals has one of these. What is it?

Exercises

1. Find a Web page and save to disk.
2. Find an image and save to disk.
3. Find a game to download.

Vocabulary

archive—A collection of files, compressed and stored into a single file for easy transfer. The most common archive format is the ZIP file.

download— To transfer a file from another computer into your own computer. The opposite is "upload," which is where you send a file from your computer to another computer.

FTP —Acronym for *File Transfer Protocol,* a primitive way to send files back and forth between UNIX computers. The method of sending files back and forth on the Internet.

GIF—Acronym for *Graphics Interchange Format*, a special file format developed by CompuServe to store graphics that all computers can use.

image— A picture or graphic on a Web page.

JPEG—Acronym for *Joint Photographic Experts Group*, a universal graphic standard designed to replace the old GIF graphic standard. GIF files can contain up to 256 colors where as JPEG files can display up to 16 million colors in a single graphic image.

PART III
Networking

Hour

HOUR 14

Using the Local Network

Networks enable you to do what your kindergarten teacher taught that you should always do: share. You can share information with colleagues on the computer network by using each other's files, folders, and printers. Sharing files and folders makes sense; if you're working at a location where there are several computers, exchange of files and information happens daily. The network makes that easy. And by sharing printers, you enable several computers to use a handful of diverse and interesting printers. (This turns out to be especially nice if it's the guy down the hall who has the ultra-nifty, color laser printer, and you're the one stuck with the dot matrix printer.)

The highlights in this hour include the following:

- Adding network hardware
- Accessing other systems on the network
- Allowing others to access your stuff
- Accessing Win95/98 systems

The Necessity of a Network

If you are a single computer user—no office or people to share things with—you don't need a Local Area Network (LAN). You can stop reading now and go have a nap for an hour! But if you're in an office with more than one computer; a home with multiple computers where you would like to share information with your family; or a larger company where you all use common files, programs, or a big whopping database of information, you may need a network.

Setting Up the Computer

Setting up the network requires a little bit more physical work than I like. But you'll only be doing it once (for each computer), so it's not that painful. And there are inexpensive network starter kits available to help you on your path to networking nirvana.

If you're starting out small, with just two computers, it's easy to set up both of them individually. From that point on, you can add other computers to the network, one at a time. Just make sure that everything works along each step of the way.

Here are the steps to add any computer to the network:

1. Install the network interface card (NIC or "nick").
2. Install the network interface card's software.
3. Set up the network interface in Windows (if necessary).
4. Configure Windows for networking.
5. Configure the network.

Yeah, there seem to be a lot of redundant steps, but that's the way it goes. Configure, configure, configure. Go figure. Remember, you do this only once.

Installing the Network Interface Card

Setting up a network interface card is a snap. It's the software setup after that when you start to go a little crazy. But don't worry. Just getting through the following deserves some type of award.

The Hardware Setup

Installing a NIC into your computer is like installing any other expansion card. Specific instructions come with the card, informing you what must take place before, during, or after installing. The instructions offered here are general.

> Always read through *all* the installation instructions before you do a thing. It's important to be familiar with the overall installation and to have a general idea of what the next step entails. This recommendation also applies to assembling backyard barbecues and children's toys at Christmastime. (See? This book is full of added value.)

Pay careful attention to those handy pictures that are in the manual. They are pretty helpful if you've never done this before.

To Do 14.1: Setting Up the Network Card

To Do

1. Turn off the computer.

   There's something about electricity that terrifies most people, which is a good thing. Turning off *and* unplugging the computer is a good idea.

2. Open the computer box (console).

   This is where you might need to look at your computer's owner's manual. You're looking for the picture that shows you where and how you open the boxy part of your computer. Sometimes the front comes off or the side panel slides off with a push of a couple of buttons. You may need a screwdriver for this.

3. Install the network interface card into one of your PC's expansion slots.

   You'll need to remove the slot cover from the back of the computer. A screwdriver does the job (and you can toss the slot cover out). Plug the card firmly into the expansion slot. Screw the back of the card into the slot cover's hole. (See the NIC's installation manual for handy illustrations.)

4. Close the computer box.

5. Connect the network hose.

   Some network hoses (which is my term; they're really wires) plug into the NIC, just as the phone cord plugs into the wall.

   Older style hoses might require a T connector to be twisted to the NIC first. The network hose then connects to both ends of the T connector, or you connect the network hose to one end and a doohickey called a *terminator* (not Arnold) to the other end.

6. Turn on the computer.

   Windows should recognize the NIC right away. You'll see the New Hardware Found dialog box display as the computer sets itself up to recognize the network interface.

If you're asked to insert the Windows CD, do so.

You also might try searching for any missing files on the floppy disk that came with your expansion card.

If you see a Version Conflict dialog box, always go with the current or newer file.

7. Restart your computer if you're prompted to do so.
8. Log in.

Because you now have a network, you'll be required to log in. Refer to Hour 15, "Juggling Multiple Users," for more information about logging into your computer.

> If you're using thin Ethernet (the coaxial cable type of connector), that cable connects all the computers. If you're using the RJ-45 (phone jack-like) connectors, all the computers must be plugged into a network hub. Each computer plugs directly into the hub using the network hose; do not plug each computer's NIC into the other computer's NIC. It just doesn't work that way.

Installing the Software Disk

Most network interface cards come with an installation disk. The steps are easy to follow. They basically ask you for the make and model of the network card you just installed.

Configuring the Windows Networking Software

Don't think you're done just because the network interface is installed, connected, and Windows has installed software for it. That's merely the hardware part of the installation. Next you must tell Windows what type of network you're connecting to and how you want to share your computer's goodies with others on the network.

Essentially you need to do four things:

1. Confirm that your network interface software has been properly installed.
2. Confirm that the Client for Microsoft Networks is installed.
3. Add file and printer sharing.
4. Describe your computer and network.

Checking Configuration

You must confirm that your network hardware is properly installed.

To Do

To Do 14.2: Confirming Network Configuration

1. Open the Control Panel.
2. Open the Network and Dial-up Connections icon.
3. Open the Local Area Connection.

FIGURE 14.1
The network and dial-up connections box.

The Local Area Connection Status box is displayed.

4. Click the Properties button.

   The Local Area Connection Properties box Configuration panel appears, similar to that in Figure 14.2.

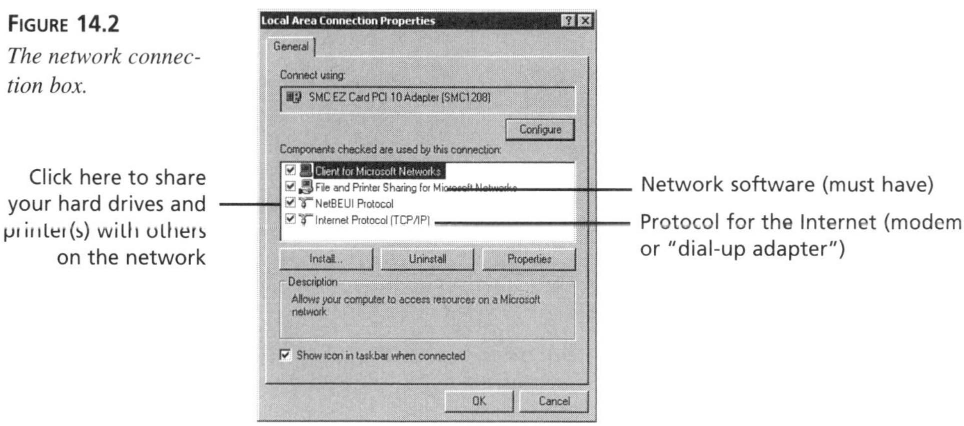

FIGURE 14.2
The network connection box.

Three different types of components appear in the Configuration panel:

- **Client for Microsoft Networks:** This enables your computer to retrieve information on the network. Your computer is the *client* on the network. (The big momma computers that run Windows 2000 Server are the *servers*.)
- **File and Printer Sharing for Microsoft Networks:** This enables you to allow other users on the network to access your PC's hard drive and printers.

14

- **Internet Protocol:** The Internet transmission information (the technical babble stuff we mortals don't care about).

Reach Out and Touch Other Computers

Now that your computer is set up on a network, you have to tell your computer to which computer (or computers) you want to connect. This happens in two ways: stealing or surrendering. (Those are my terms, but they work better than any technical terms I could dream up right now.)

Note that the following information applies only to peer-to-peer networking—the simple sharing of files between Windows 2000 (and Windows 95/98) computers. This type of networking does not involve central file server systems. If you have such a system, your location's network administrator can brief you (or probably has already—dozens of times) on what can be done with the network.

Stealing from Others

There are two things you can steal from other computers on the network: disk drives (or folders on these drives) and printers. Printers are easy, so I'll cover them first.

Adding a Network Printer

Any printer that has been made available on the network is up for grabs as far as your computer is concerned. That nifty color printer Ed has down the hall? It's yours for the taking! Ha-ha! Stock up on the nice paper, Ed!

To Do 14.3: Installing a Network Printer

To Do

1. Double-click My Documents.
2. Double-click the Control Panel.
3. Open the Printers Folder.
4. Double-click the Add Printer icon.

   This starts the Add Printer Wizard. More about this Wizard can be found in Hour 17, "Fussing with the Printer."
5. Click Next.
6. Click the dot next to Network Printer and click Next.
7. Type the printer name.

The name must be typed in this way:

```
\\computer\printer
```

For example, to connect to Dan's computer, I typed `\\BIGGEEK\colorsprite`. `BIGGEEK` is the name of his computer. `colorsprite` is the name of his printer.

If you don't know the name, go down the hall and ask your neighbor his printer's name. Or, you can always skip the typing and click Next so you can browse for the printer you want.

If you do want to browse for a list of printers, don't type anything into the printer name box. Instead, click the Next button, and all the available printers are listed. Figure 14.3 shows you the list of the Gookin computers that are available.

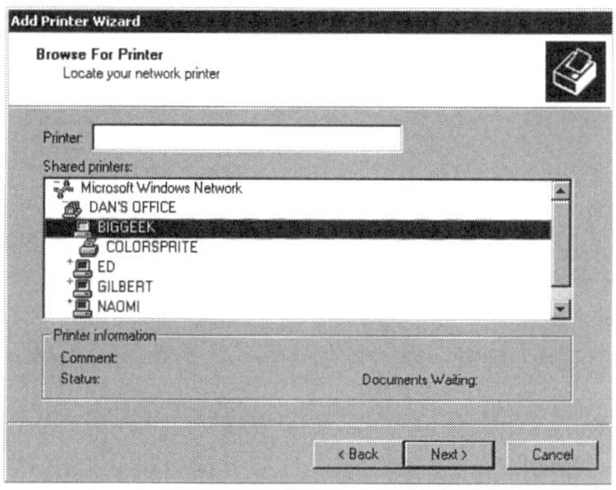

FIGURE 14.3
Browsing for a printer to share.

> You may get a notice telling you that you don't have the correct printer information. You also will be asked, "Do you want Windows to install that for you?" Click Yes. You need that information for the particular printer you're trying to connect to.

8. Do you want to use this new printer as your default printer?

   You should probably click NO. Choosing the default printer means that this printer is the one your computer automatically prints on. You can read more about picking default printers in Hour 17.

9. Click Next.

   If all has gone well, you'll see the Completing the Add Printer Wizard sign as shown in Figure 14.4.

FIGURE 14.4
Completing the Add Printer Wizard.

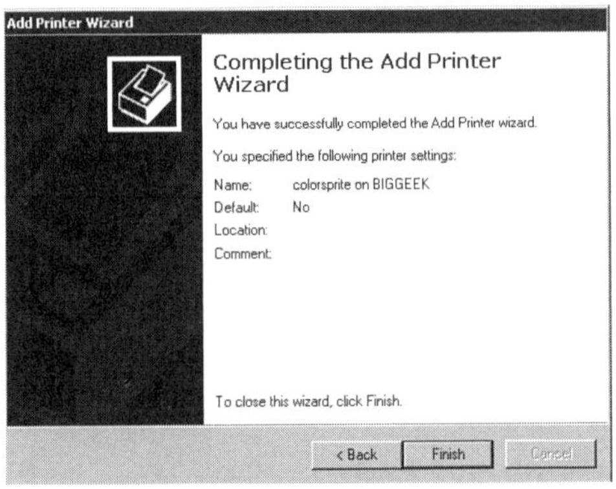

10. Click finished.

You can now see your new printer in the Printers window, which is where you started.

Accessing Another Computer

To access information (files) on another computer you can do two things:

1. You can browse the various computers on the network to see what's available.
2. You can specifically *map* (their term, not mine) another computer's hard drive to behave as if it's a hard drive on your own system. Either way, you can access files elsewhere on the network.

Browsing with My Network Places

To browse other computers and see what's available, use the My Network Places icon on the desktop.

FIGURE 14.5
Opening the My Network Places displays a list of other computers in your workgroup or on the entire network.

To Do

To Do 14.4: Finding Computers on the Network

1. Double-click the My Network Places icon.

   Figure 14.6 show you what you'll see when you open My Network Places.

FIGURE 14.6
The inside of My Network Places.

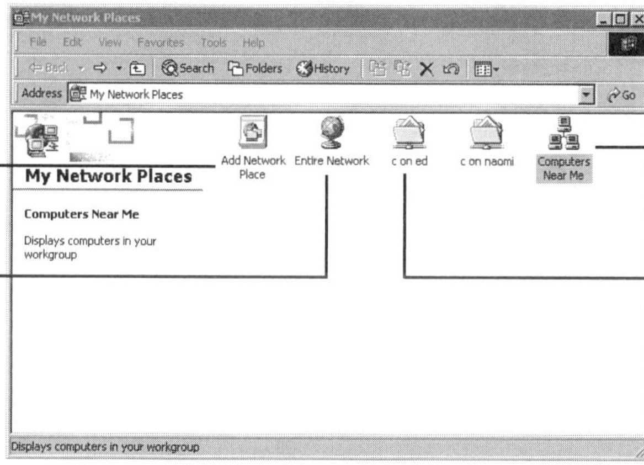

2. Double-click Computers Near Me.

What you see is different than what I see because we're not hooked up to the same network. Well, at least I don't think yours is hooked up to mine. That being said, check out Figure 14.7 so that you have an idea of what you should be seeing.

FIGURE 14.7
The computers on the Gookin network—great names, eh?

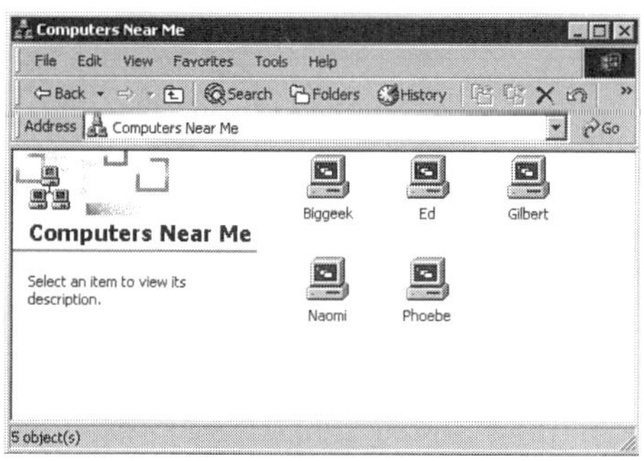

Mapping a Hard Drive to Your System

14

Browsing is fine, but there might be another hard drive on another computer to which you need constant access. For example, a disk drive (or folder) shared on Ed's computer might be full of great audio clips. You can make access to that folder easy and permanent by mapping it to your hard drive.

Mapping is merely a strange term for taking any hard drive or folder up for grabs on the network and fooling Windows into thinking that drive is on your own computer. So, for example, the network may call Dan's audio folder \\ED\C\My Documents\Audio (Ed is actually the name of the computer, not the name of the person using it). But you can map all that junk to be, say, drive S: on your computer. Here's how:

To Do 14.5: Mapping to a Network Computer

1. Right-click My Computer.
2. Choose Explore.

   You work in the Windows Exploring window to get all this done.
3. Click on Tools from the menu bar.
4. Click Map Network Drive.

   Figure 14.8 shows the box you use to find the folder you want to access.

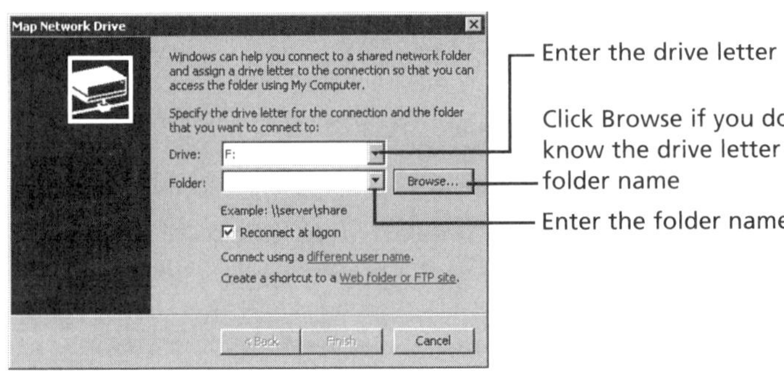

FIGURE 14.8
Starting the Map Network Drive process.

5. Enter the drive letter and folder name.

   Click Finish if you're able to summon the drive letter and folder name.

   If you don't know the letter and name off the top of your head, click the Browse button and look for the folder from the list of computers. (This, to me, is a far easier method than using the previous steps.)
6. If you've clicked the Browse button, find the computer you want to use.
7. Click the plus signs to continually open the folders.

   This process is similar to using Windows Explorer, which is covered in Hour 18, "Maintaining and Cleaning Files." Figure 14.9 shows the process on my computer. Your files and computer names won't be the same, but you get an idea of how things look.

▼

FIGURE 14.9
Browsing for the folder you want.

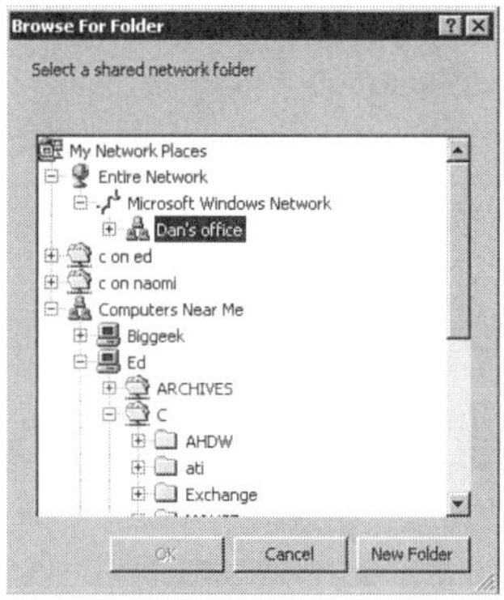

8. Find the folder you want to use.

   Click on the folder you want to use. Then click the OK button. The complete pathname is put into the folder box (as shown in Figure 14.6).

▲ 9. Click Finish.

The folder you selected is now plopped in your My Computer window. And as a special bonus, Windows automatically opens it for you. Wow, Dan has some interesting sounds on his audio folder. Is it really necessary to have saved the theme music to *Gilligan's Island*?

Surrendering Your Stuff to the Network

Sharing is a two-way street. It's both give and take. Sure it's fun to borrow information from other hard drives and to steal Ed's beautiful color printer. But what about you? What are you giving back?

There are two things you can share on a network: disk drives and printers. You can make them available to others on the network.

Sharing a Disk Drive

When you offer your disk drive to be shared by others, you are literally allowing them to reach a long hand through the network wires, grab a folder out of your disk drive, and read through the files in that folder. For people who share information, as Dan and I do when we are writing a book, it is extremely handy for both of us to pluck files out of each other's disk drives and work on them.

To Do 14.6: Sharing a Disk Drive

1. Double-click the My Computer icon sitting on your desktop.
2. Right-click the drive you want to share.

   Figure 14.10 shows the disk drive's property box. For this example, it's drive (D:) on my computer.

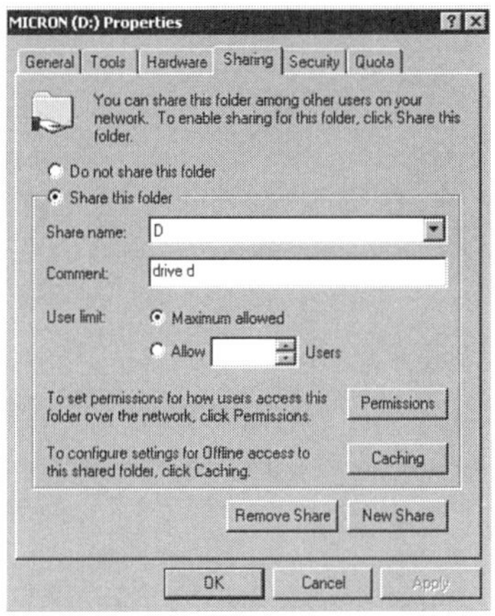

FIGURE 14.10
Sharing Drive (D:).

3. Click next to Share This Folder.
4. Click the Permissions box.

   This box gives you control over how people access your drive. You can give them full control (meaning they can read and alter the information on your drive), change, or read (all they can do is read the information). Click OK when you're finished.

   You also have a few other options as to the number of people allowed to dip into your drive at one time.
5. Click OK.

> You must be logged on as an Administrator, Server Operator, or Power User to share folders and drives. All others need not even bother.

Sharing a Printer

Setting up a printer to share requires very similar steps to sharing a disk drive.

To Do 14.7: Sharing a Printer

▼ To Do

1. Double-click My Computer.
2. Double-click the Control Panel.
3. Double-click the Printer icon.
4. Find the printer you want to share.

   If you have only one printer listed, this should be an easy task.
5. Right-click on the printer.
6. Choose Sharing.
7. Click the button next to Shared As.
8. Type a name for your printer.

   When you click the Shared as button, the printer name appears—for example, HPDeskJet (actually, you're limited to the number of characters, so you only see HPDeskJe). You can rename your printer to something clever. Type in the clever name.
9. Click OK. ▲

Now you'll see the sharing hand under your printer, which is your indication that others are able to use your printer. Be a pal; keep paper in your printer at all times!

Summary

This hour was dedicated to getting you hooked up to a local network. You should be able to install a network card and configure your computer to use the network.

Q&A

Q How do I select a network printer when printing?

A You choose the printer in any Print dialog box. This is covered in Hour 17. The network printers appear in the drop-down list.

Q What if I don't want others messing with my hard drive?

A Simple: Don't share that hard drive. Or, if the hard drive has information on it you want to share, but you don't want others to change, share the drive as a read-only device. You can also restrict access by simply sharing a folder instead of the whole drive. Just right-click on the folder and choose the Sharing command from the shortcut menu.

Q I cannot access another disk drive on the network! Why?

A There could be a multitude of reasons, the first being that the network might be down or that other computers might be disconnected or currently turned off. Generally speaking, networking problems should be brought to the attention of your location's network manager for correction.

Workshop

The workshop includes quiz questions to help gauge your grasp of the material and exercises to help reinforce your learning. You'll find the answers to the quiz and exercises in Appendix A, "Answers."

Quiz

1. What is the first step in setting up a network?
2. What is My Network Places?
3. How can you tell you have a shared or mapped hard drive?
4. *Bonus question*: What is the funny bone?

Exercises

1. Go through the steps to share your disk drives.
2. Go through the steps to share your printer.
3. Try to access a folder on some other computer.

Vocabulary

hub—The central hardware of the network. All computers connect to the hub using special network cable, which I call the "network hose."

map/mapping/mapped—The process of adding a network hard drive to your system, as if the network hard drive were a disk drive on your computer. The network hard drive is *mapped* to your computer—given a drive letter and icon in the My Computer window. *Mapping* is the process of creating a mapped drive.

network—Hardware and software that enables multiple computers to share resources.

NIC—A Network Information Card, the expansion card or circuitry inside your computer that lets your PC access a network. The network "hose" connects to your computer's NIC and, through the hose, to other computers on the network.

permissions—The rights and privileges of other computer users on your computer. Permissions are set for every device shared on the network. They tell Windows 2000 who can access which devices and how much access they have to each device.

shared—A resource on your computer—disk drive or printer—that is made available for use by other computers on the network.

Hour 15

Juggling Multiple Users

One of the powers of Windows 2000 is the capability for many people to use one computer. If you're just one person with one computer, there's no point in reading this chapter. But if you're in any situation where more than one person has access to the computer, such as at home or in an office, then letting several people use the computer is often a necessity—one that Windows 2000 makes easy.

Computers can be a very personal item, so sharing one requires each user to organize and work with his computer in the way that best fits him. That is what this hour is about—personalizing something that, for whatever reason, must be shared.

The highlights in this hour include the following:

- Configuring for multiple users
- Logging on
- Logging off
- Changing passwords

Configuring for Multiple Users

These are the players in the game of multiple computer users:

Administrator: The administrator is like the head honcho, boss, the big cheese. This is the person who sets up sharing of a computer. Only an administrator or someone in the special elite administrator's group has the power to add or delete a user, change a password, modify any of the system settings that deal with users, and perform basic maintenance of the system.

If you're a home computer user, Windows 2000 automatically sets you up as an administrator. If you're in a business setting, you'll probably be told if you're an administrator.

Microsoft recommends that you run your computer as a nonadministrator or normal user. You should reserve Administrator mode only for administrative tasks. (This is because running Windows as an administrator makes the network system somewhat vulnerable to viruses and people trying to steal information from computers.)

User: The person using the computer—basically a nonadministrator. The administrator adds users to the system and determines which users can do what with the computer.

If you're an administrator, you should add yourself as a user. Then log back into the computer as an administrator when you need to do your administrative work.

> Administrators have the ability to tweak and manipulate quite a few things when it comes to the computer. Adding users is just one of those tasks.

User Groups: A group of users that share the same computer system settings.

The following is an example of using the user and administrator groups in a typical home or single-user setting.

Administrator	*User Group 1 (older family)*	*User Group 2 (children)*
Mom	Mom	Son, Simon
	Dad	Son, Jonah
	Son, Jordan	Son, Jeremiah

Okay, so Mom has the power to decide what kind of user Group 1 is as opposed to Group 2.

Group 1 has access to most things. Dad and Jordan use the computer for just about everything, except the system tools. It is really not necessary for them to be playing around with these, anyway.

Group 2 users consist of a four-year-old, five-year-old, and a six-year-old. Their system settings consist of the bare minimum. They can play their games, practice homework, and that's it. They have absolutely no access at all to anything that deals with computer settings.

Adding Users

If you're established as an administrator, you can start adding people to your network.

To Do 15.1: Adding Users

1. Open My Computer.
2. Open the Control Panel.
3. Double-click on Users and Passwords.

FIGURE 15.1

This is the User and Password section, which is shown in Figure 15.2. This is the place you come anytime you want to add or delete a user or work with passwords.

FIGURE 15.2
The Users and Passwords control center.

4. Click the Add button.

   Complete the required information.

5. Click Next.

   Type in the new user's password. You can either ask the user what he wants his password to be or just assign a password. You're the administrator, so do what feels good, what feels right, what feels better. Whatever.

6. Type the password again to confirm.

   This is done to make sure you didn't make a typing error and that you are certain you know what the password is.

> You'll see asterisks (*) when you type, not real letters. I suppose this is so that all those government spies peering over your shoulder can't see the password.

7. Choose the level of user.

   This takes some thought. You have several levels of users, each level with its own amount of power and privileges. Read the list as shown in Figure 15.3 and decide whether you want users to be able to adjust their computers or just read and save documents. Click on Other and you have additional options. The box under each option gives a brief description of each user. Table 15.1 gives the complete list for you.

FIGURE 15.3
The user status in the Add New User box.

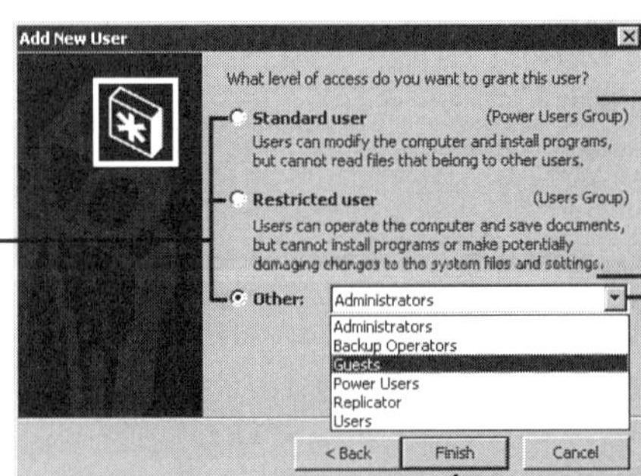

TABLE 15.1 User Definition Guide

User Type	*Definition of Usability*
Standard user	Users can modify the computer and install programs.
Restricted user	Users can operate the computer and save documents, but cannot install programs.
Administrator	Administrators can do anything they please(full access to everything).
Backup operator	This operator can only use a backup program to backup files and folders. Bummer.
Guest	Guests can operate the computer and save documents.
Power user	Power users can modify the computer and install programs.
Replicator	Replicators support file replication in a domain.
User	Users can operate the computer and save documents, but they cannot install programs or make changes to the system files and settings.

8. Click Finish.

Now your new user is listed with all your other users.

If you are following the advice I gave earlier about not staying in administrator status while doing non-administrator–related work, you need to work through the previous steps for adding yourself in a capacity other than administrator. A standard user is a good choice.

After adding yourself as a standard user, according to the computer, you are actually *two* users. Try to parlay this into two lunch hours.

So, how do you go about switching from a standard user (or any type of user group) to an administrator? Cross your arms, wish real hard, and then blink your eyes. No, that's not it. It's all in the logon process that happens when you first start your computer. Of course, you can log on and log off at any point in time. You don't have to always turn your computer on and off.

Logging On

Many company computers have a logon system to keep unwanted individuals out of the system. You know, government spies, corporate raiders undercover, the cleaning lady, that sort of thing. If you are a private home user, you may also have a logon system so that each person in the family can log on and modify the programs and desktop that fits his or her needs. Windows 2000 also establishes what kind of user privileges you have when you log on; these are determined by the administrator.

Do you need to log on to the computer? No. You don't have to use the logon system at all if you are using Windows 2000 at home, and it's just you who are using it. If that's the case, feel free to skip this logging on section. Follow the steps in the To Do which follows if you want to *fix* your computer so there isn't any logon process.

To Do 15.2: Removing the Logging on Process

1. Double-click My Computer.
2. Double-click the Control Panel.
3. Double-click the Users and Passwords icon.
4. Click on the Users tab.
5. Click in the top box to remove the check mark.

   The box says: Users Must Enter a User Name and Password to Use This Computer. Click the box to remove the check mark. This is for those that don't want to bother with the logging in process.
6. Complete the Automatic Logon information.

   You still have to give everyone a password. This just gives you choices. You can arrange it so that no one has to log on or that only certain people have to log on. Perhaps you don't like Rod down the hall because he smokes smelly cigars; so you make him log on all the time. But you like Molly, so you set up her computer so she doesn't have to log on. Figure 15.4 illustrates the Logon box.

FIGURE 15.4
The Automatically Log On box.

7. Type the password again to confirm you typed it correctly.
8. Click OK.

If you are hooked up to a network, or you are the network administrator and are going to require all the users on your network log in and out of the computer, you might want to require a logging in process. More information about networks can be found in Hour 14, "Using the Local Network."

First of all, you have to set up the user and password information before your computer knows that it must require a user to log on.

To Do 15.3: Setting up the Logon System

▼ To Do

1. Double-click My Computer.
2. Double-click the Control Panel.
3. Double-click the Users and Passwords icon.

   This Users and Passwords box is where you'll set things up.
4. Click on the Users tab.

   This brings the Users tab forward.
5. Click in the top box to add a check mark.

   The box says: Users Must Enter a User Name and Password to Use This Computer. Click the box to add a check mark.
6. Click the Advanced tab.
7. Look for the Secure Boot Settings area.

   Click on the box next to Require Users to Press CTRL+ALT+DELETE Before Logging on. Pressing CTRL+ALT+DELETE before logging on guarantees that the Windows 2000 logon prompt appears. Requiring the use of CTRL+ALT+DELETE increases security and helps protect your computer from programs that can potentially be dangerous to your system.
8. Click OK. ▲

This gets you out of the Users and Passwords box. Now you're ready to try this sucker out.

To Do 15.4: Logging on to the Computer

▼ To Do

1. Start Your Computer.

   You'll probably have to shut your computer off before you can start it again. So go ahead and shut down Windows (or better yet, just choose Restart).
2. Press CTRL+ALT+DELETE.

   This takes you to the Log on to Windows dialog box.
3. Enter your name and password.

   Two boxes are available, one for your name and one for your password. This is the password you made up when you first started your computer and were asked for your name and a password. Hope you didn't forget it!
4. Click OK. ▼

A couple of cautions here: First, the password is case sensitive and can be up to 14 characters long. If your password is typed SanTa, you have to type it that way every time, or the computer won't recognize it. Second, if you continually type in the wrong password, Windows will lock up and stop offering you a chance to type in the right word. The only way to get out of this is to turn your computer off, and then go and beg your administrator for your password.

Your desktop will spring forward, just as you will have set it up.

I need a change in my life, but changing my hair color seems a little drastic. Hey, why not change my password? Yes, it's acceptable to do so. Press CTRL+ALT+DELETE and then click Change Password. Type your old password (just to make sure it's really you who is doing the changing). Type your new password, and then type it again to verify you typed it the way you wanted it to be. And folks, get creative. Don't use your name as the password. But don't make it so hard that you can't remember it. Oh, and don't put a yellow sticky on your desk with your password name on it either. That's really dorky. And stop being so stodgy about the hair color thing. It will always grow back.

Logging Off

The purpose of logging off the computer is to close all your programs and to disconnect from the computer and the network. It's also used when another person (user) is going to use your computer.

To Do 15.5: Logging Off Your Computer

1. Click the Start Button.

   Clicking the Start Button—located at the bottom left of your screen—brings up the Start Menu.

2. Click Shut Down.

   The Shut Down menu comes forward. The question, What Do You Want the Computer to Do? is listed. Too bad Make Dinner isn't one of the options.

3. Click the Down arrow.

   Clicking the down arrow brings out your list of choices. Selecting Log off puts that option on the box. Just as a reminder: Windows passes you a little note that says this choice "ends your session, leaving the computer running on full power." Oh, okay. See Figure 15.5

FIGURE 15.5
Shutting down Windows.

4. Click OK.

You are now logged off, and the computer is ready for a new person (known as a user) to use it.

> You can also log off your computer by pressing CTRL+ALT+DELETE and then clicking Log off.

Creating a Password

I'll be honest; if your password is easy to figure out, you don't need a password. A password is meant to keep people out of your computer; so be smart about what you use.

Here are a few tips:

- Don't use your name or any version of your name as a password. Bad passwords: Sandy, SandyG, Sandra, Sandi. Get the idea?
- Don't use kids, family, or pet names.
- Don't use a common word or name. For example, if you work at a bank, you don't want the password to be *money*. That would be too simple.
- Use both upper- and lowercase letters in addition to any symbol found on your keyboard.
- Have your password at least seven characters long. This isn't a Windows rule; it's just harder to break a password that is longer than a few characters.
- Don't write down your password. Memorize it.
- Don't tell anyone your password. If you're going to tell, you defeat the security measure of having a password.

- Have a different password for different purposes. Don't share. For example, don't have your computer password the same as your ATM, which is the same as your keyless lock password. They should all be different.
- Change your password every few months.
- No birthdays or anniversary dates.

Summary

This hour should have made clear the differences between being an administrator and a user. You also should have learned some of the tips for creating and using a password, as well as how to share information with your user compatriots.

Q&A

Q Can I add myself as more than one user?

A Sure! But why? I suppose you might want, for example, to have one personality as administrator, another for working, and a third for playing games. But why bother when you could just remove the passwords altogether and use the computer as a single user?

Q Can I change a user's access level?

A Yes. Go into the Users and Passwords section (from the Control Panel). Click on a user name, then choose Properties. Click the Group membership tab and then change the type of user.

Workshop

The workshop includes quiz questions to help gauge your grasp of the material and exercises to help reinforce your learning. You'll find the answers to the quiz and exercises in Appendix A, "Answers."

Quiz

1. Why and when would you need to log on as other than administrator, if you are indeed the network administrator?
2. What is the Multiple User concept?
3. Why should you log off of a computer when another user is waiting to use the very same program on which you are currently working?
4. *Bonus question*: What is the lowest point on the earth's surface?

Exercises

1. If you are logged on as an administrator, add yourself now as a user. Determine your basic user access, rights, and password—then change them around again.
2. Think of your favorite character from literature: Change your password to that. Consider your favorite date of the last millennium; change your password once again. Now change it back to that one perfect password, suited just for you.
3. Log on to a computer on your network. Or, if you are already logged on, log off now. Now log back on. Now finish that pile of work your boss has been waiting for. Then go crack open a bottle of water and enjoy the rest of your day.

Vocabulary

administrator—A person responsible for setting up and managing networked computers and their users. They assign passwords, allocate the amount of access each user has, and basically have the responsibility to help others with their networking issues.

password—This is a secret word (or acronym or number series) that you must give the computer in order to allow the network to recognize you as a member.

user—A person with the OK to use a networked computer, along with selected programs and information contained therein. A user must rely upon his administrator to define the extent of his access to information and capabilities.

TIME OUT 3

Minesweeper: The Blowup Game

Minesweeper is one of those old computer logic puzzles. It goes like this: Suppose that you have a grid, under which are several mines. You can look under any tile in the grid for a mine. If you find a mine, *BOOM!*, you blow up. (Actually, Bob blows up. Bob is the smiley face above the grid.)

If you don't find a mine, you see a number. The number tells how many tiles around you have mines under them. See? It's amazing that some people really like this game. There are those who would say that this game is enjoyable because of the thrill of defying death. Yeah, whatever.

Learning to Play

The Object

The object of Minesweeper is to find all the mines without getting blown up in the process.

Playing the Game

When you first open Minesweeper, a new game is ready for you. When you're ready to start another game (because you will quickly and consistently be blown into mincemeat until you get the hang of this), click the Game menu and then click New—or you can also just click on Bob's face. The timer starts when you click any square on the playing field.

Just start clicking blank tiles. There's no trick or skill that tells you which one to start with. Just click. Although Bob does give you a fighting chance, the first tile you click is always safe. You can never be blown up on the first turn. After that first click, you must determine where a mine lies, based on the numbers you see. Use cunning, guile, and your computer mouse.

When you think you've found a mine, right-click that tile. This marks the tile with a little flag, meaning "Mine here!" These flags will later help you determine (or guess) which other tiles are safe and which ones come with fireworks.

For example, the grid nearby shows several uncovered tiles, but two of them have been flagged as mines. (That's because the 1 by each tile is touching only that one tile, meaning that a mine is there.) The 2 between the two flagged mines is already touching two mines, so the other blank tiles it's sitting next to are probably not mines. You can click them with the mouse to uncover their secret numbers, which tell you more about the rest of the tiles, and so on, until you solve the puzzle. Figure TO3.1 is peeking in on a game already in process. Bob seems happy; he's smiling!

FIGURE TO3.1
Watch out, Bob!

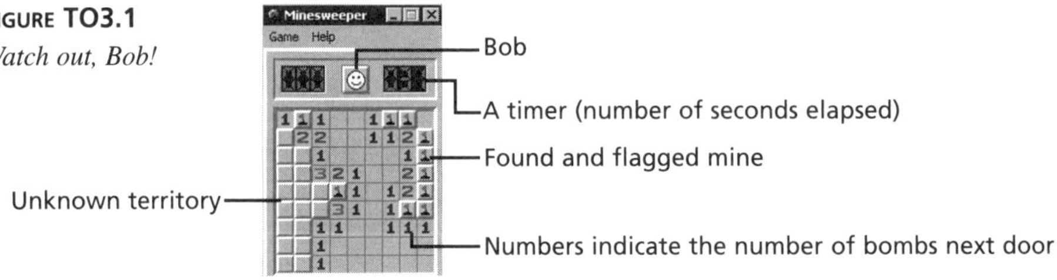

As you click each tile to see what's underneath, Bob gets nervous.

If you click a mine instead of marking it as a mine, regrettably, Bob dies.

If you win, Bob gets cool, and you get to enter your name into the high score sheet.

I think that Bob needs a flack jacket.

Tips and Tricks

You can set the size of the minefield by choosing various options in the Game menu: Beginner, Intermediate, Expert, and Custom (to create your own minefield). Each size is larger, with more mines to uncover, or more literally, to avoid uncovering.

Sometimes you might be uncertain about a square but want to remind yourself to come back to it later. Simply right-click the square twice, and this marks the square with a questions mark (`?`), alerting you that you have to make a decision about the square.

Hunting Down Other Games

There are also the Microsoft Game Pack and the Arcade Pack, which contain games designed to keep you from doing any real work on the computer. `Filemine.com` is one of those places to find other games that will keep you busy for hours and hours.

`http://www.filemine.com`

PART IV
Managing Your PC

Hour

HOUR 16

Organizing the Desktop

The first thing you see when Windows starts is your desktop. When you're finished with a document or task, you close it and there's your desktop again. Because you're always looking at this thing, it might as well be something nice, perhaps pretty or clever. And while you're at it, you can also doctor it up enough so that this desktop is as helpful as it possibly can be.

The highlights in this hour include the following:

- Sticking files on your desktop
- What should go on your desktop; what shouldn't
- Having an Active desktop
- Adding Web content to your desktop

What Should Go on Your Desktop

Your desktop can be customized to look and work just as you want it to, within the boundaries of the Windows 2000 world, of course. Although it would be nice to put curtains on the desktop or drill a hole and hide your safe there, it's just not possible. But, to a point, you do have options as to what is on your desktop.

Certain things are stuck on the desktop. You cannot remove these things:

- Recycle Bin
- My Computer
- My Network Places

Everything else you might see on your screen can be moved.

These are the items that I would suggest you have on your desktop:

- The My Documents folder, plus shortcuts to any other folders you frequently access.
- Shortcuts to programs you frequently open. (But, put your most popular programs on the Quick Launch bar.)
- Shortcuts to documents you frequently use.

Of course, you're not limited to these items. You can have a skinny desktop with only a few icons, or you can litter the desktop with one icon for every ding-dang-dong file on your PC! It's all up to you.

My Documents Folder

Your My Documents folder is where all the documents you create are stored. Having this icon on your desktop makes getting into that folder quick and easy.

However, if you don't want the My Documents folder on your desktop (it is your choice), you can remove it. Unlike other icons that you can just drag to the Recycle Bin, removing the My Documents folder requires special steps.

To Do 16.1: Removing My Documents from Your Desktop

To Do

1. Open the Control Panel.

   Remember that the Control Panel is found when you open My Computer.
2. Double-click on Folder Options.
3. Click the View tab.

   This brings that tab forward.
4. Click in the box next to Show My Documents on the Desktop to remove the My Documents folder from the desktop.

> Obviously, performing these steps and checking the box next to Show My Documents on the Desktop would put that icon back, should you want it there or somehow find it missing.

Sticking Popular Documents on Your Desktop

Most folks use the same documents over and over: travel reports, to do lists, incessant projects you'll probably never finish, and so on. To make getting at these documents a lot easier, you can slap them right down on your desktop. Or, if you like, you can put them all in a folder and put that on your desktop. Either way, you get easy access to your most commonly used documents.

To Do 16.2: Sticking Documents on Your Desktop

1. Right-click My Computer.
2. Choose Explore.
3. Choose the program you want to put on your desktop.

   Hour 18, "Maintaining and Cleaning Files," delves into greater detail on how to use Explorer.
4. Click once on the program or file to highlight it.
5. Click File from the menu bar.
6. Choose Create Shortcut.

   This creates a shortcut icon as shown in Figure 16.1

FIGURE 16.1

7. Click and drag the shortcut icon to the desktop.

Popular Desktop Programs

Not everyone works the same way, so feel free to disagree with the following recommendations. I have listed a few things that I know tend to be popular icons resting on many desktops.

Internet Explorer

Internet Explorer (or whatever Internet software you use) is a good choice to have on your desktop. It's one of those things that you'll find you use all the time after you get comfortable using the Internet.

Word Processing Programs

A word processing program, such as Word, is commonly put on the desktop. You need something like Word to type documents, such as letters or memos.

Current Projects

Projects that you have to visit everyday are good items to have on your desktop. Because adding a program to the desktop is really just adding a copy, you can put a folder there until your project is finished. Then just delete the folder to clean up your desktop.

General Work Items

The Windows calculator, a game, or a graphics program can all be put on the desktop. But only put these items there if you find that you use them often.

> You can also put popular items on the Quick Launch Bar, which is covered in Hour 7, "The Taskbar Is Your Friend."

What Should Not Go on Your Desktop

There is no rule about what not to put on the desktop; you can really stick anything there you want. Traditionally, however, only *shortcuts* are placed on the desktop, not real files, icons, or programs.

If you stick to using only shortcuts on the desktop, you'll never run the risk of accidentally deleting a real file or program.

Also, it's a good idea not to put too much junk on the desktop. My philosophy is this: The most popular programs I use go on the Quick Launch bar (Word, Explorer, Excel, and so on); the next most-popular programs go on the desktop; and then everything else goes on the Start/Programs menu.

Creating Your Own Desktop Folder

I work on a variety of documents on a daily basis: random to do lists, notes to myself, graphics I play with, the list goes on. You might find yourself in the same situation. So for these random tasks you find yourself doing, you can create your own folder of just *stuff* (or any creative name you come up with).

To Do 16.3: Creating a Desktop Folder

To Do

1. Right-click on the desktop.
2. Choose New.
3. Choose Folder.

   There is a new folder on your desktop, just waiting for you to give it a new name.
4. Type a folder name.

   Be creative! Be descriptive!
5. Press Enter after you type the name.
6. Click on a blank area of the desktop.

   This seals in the name, kind of like sealing the envelope.

If you decide you don't like the name of the folder, right click on the folder, choose *Rename*, then type a new name for your folder. You can do this with any folder you use.

Information about folder naming and organization can be found in Hour 9, "What's in Them Folders and Files."

Arranging Icons

After you've added all these nifty new icons to your desktop, you'll want to keep them organized. You can arrange your icons by their names, by their types, by size or by the date you put them there. Or you can ask Windows to please help you with this decision and have the computer auto arrange them.

To Do 16.4: Arranging Your Desktop Icons

To Do

1. Right-click on a blank part of your desktop.
2. Choose Arrange Icons.

   A list of options rolls out, as shown in Figure 16.2.

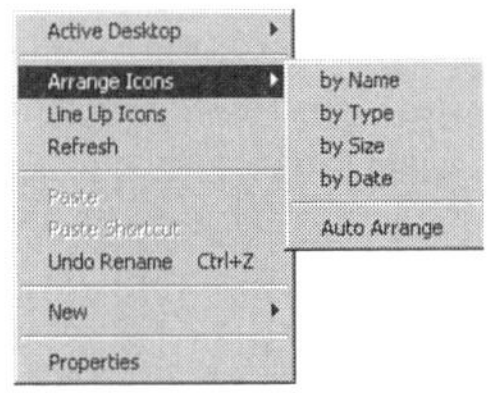

FIGURE 16.2
Arranging icons.

3. Choose which way you want to arrange the icons.

   You can work through these steps several times—making different choices, just to see how things look.

> You can even click and drag your desktop icons anywhere on the screen for that specialized, throw-organization-to-the-wind, custom look.

The Active Desktop

The purpose of the Active Desktop feature is to make Window's 2000 desktop look and work like a Web page. You can display Web content directly on your desktop and have the content updated automatically which, I suppose, makes the desktop "active."

Does this imply inactivity if you don't use this feature? I don't know.

The Active Desktop has many capabilities, such as putting Web channels or updated information right on the screen. For example, you can have a channel to a news page that will update the news as it happens, or you can see a list of stock prices or sports scores. All that happens with Active Desktop activated, synchronized, and dialed into the Internet. But first things first: Turn on Active Desktop.

To Do 16.5: Turning on Active Desktop

1. Double-click the My Computer icon.

   This icon is sitting on your Desktop.
2. Open the Control Panel.
3. Click on the Folder Options icon.
4. Click the General tab to bring it forward.

Figure 16.3 shows an example of your Folder Options screen.

FIGURE 16.3
The Folder Options window.

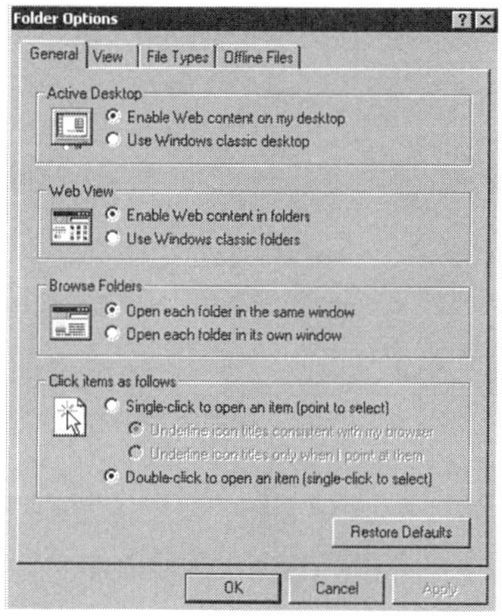

5. Choose Enable Web content on my desktop.
6. Click OK.
7. Close the Control Panel.

   Either Choose File, then Close, or click the X in the upper-right corner.

Windows automatically selects your Home Page to display as your Active Desktop.

If this Home Page is a little too busy for your liking, you can do one of two things:

1. Change your Home Page (covered in Hour 11, "It's a Wild World Wide Web We Weave").
2. Remove the option to show your Home Page. Do this by right-clicking on an area of your desktop (not on the Home Page area). Choose Active Desktop. This shows another menu. Click on the bottom option, My Current Home Page. This will remove the checkmark, and also remove your Home Page from the screen. Ahhh, that's better. Back to your desktop. See Figure 16.4.

FIGURE 16.4
The path to My Current Home Page option.

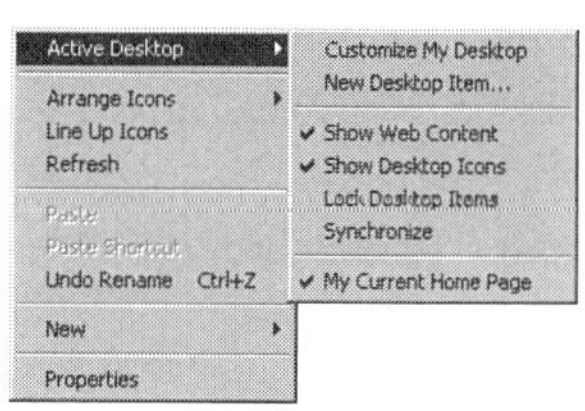

> You can also turn on Active Desktop by right-clicking on a blank area on your desktop, choosing Active Desktop, and then choosing Show Web Content. See Figure 16.5.

FIGURE 16.5
The Active Desktop options.

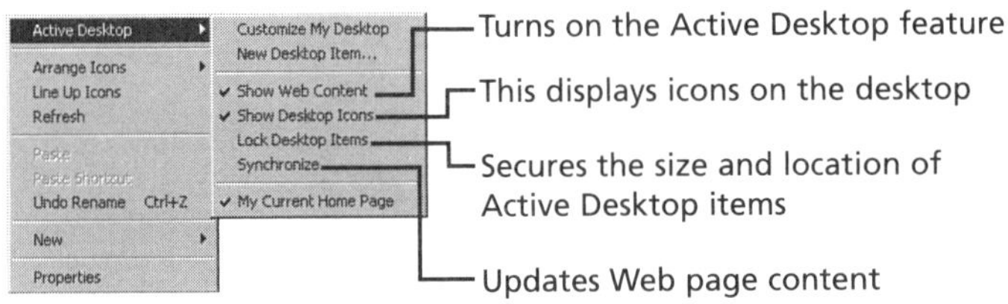

Adding Web Content to Your Desktop

Before you start adding Web content to the Active Desktop, make sure Active Desktop is turned on. Do this by selecting Enable Web Content on My Desktop option in the Folder Options dialog box (this was discussed earlier).

To Do 16.6: Adding Web Content

1. Right-click a blank area on the desktop.
2. Point to Active Desktop.
3. Click New Desktop Item.

   This is the first step in deciding what item or items you want on your desktop. See Figure 16.6.

FIGURE 16.6
The Active Desktop Item Dialog Box.

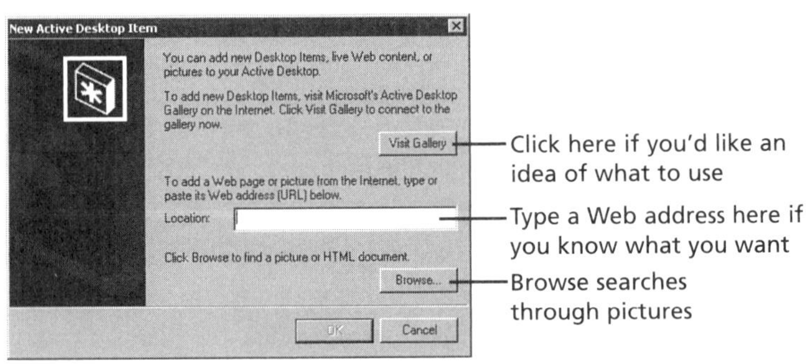

If you know exactly what you want to put on your desktop, type in the Web address next to the Location box and click OK.

If you need some ideas for your desktop, click the Visit Gallery button, and you are immediately connected to the Internet. Figure 16.7 shows the Active Desktop Gallery.

16

FIGURE 16.7
The Active Desktop Gallery.

The Gallery Index has six options: news, sports, entertainment, travel, weather, and cool utilities. (Ever wonder why they don't have "Waste of Time utility"?) Click each one of these to get a description. Figure 16.8 shows an overview of the entertainment options with the Audio Net item selected.

FIGURE 16.8
The entertainment options.

Tour around the site. Pick what you want, then click the orange Add to Active Desktop button. You'll get asked if you want to add an Active Desktop item to your desktop. They're just making sure you know what you're doing. Well, you probably don't know what you're doing, but that's okay. Click Yes. (You can always click No if it seems too weird, and you don't want to go through with it.)

Figure 16.9 shows another item you must agree with to get this Active Desktop thing working. It's just an acknowledgement of what you're doing. Click OK.

FIGURE 16.9
Adding an item acknowledgement.

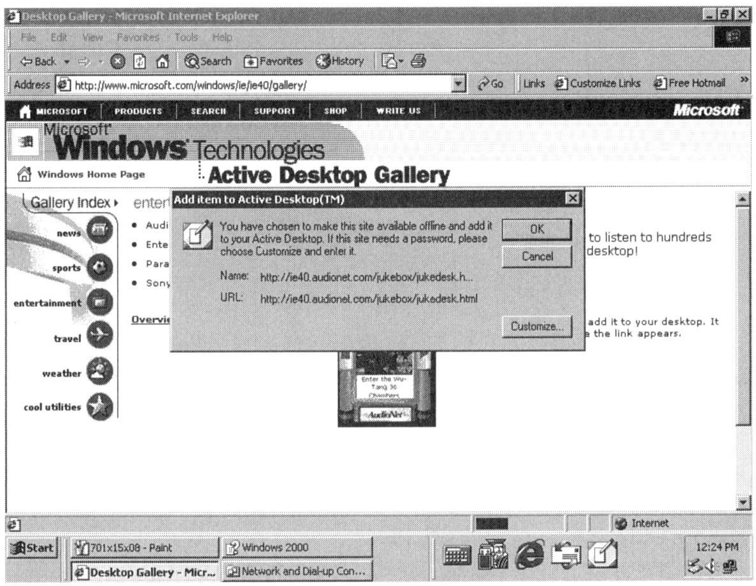

Viewing Active Desktop Programs

Figure 16.10 shows you what adding one of the Active Desktop Options does to your screen—it makes things rather busy. Of course, you can click and grab one of the corners of the window of the item you just added to your desktop to make it bigger or smaller.

FIGURE 16.10
Your screen after Active Desktop.

You can also click and grab the Active Desktop item and arrange things where you want them.

Hover your mouse pointer near the top of the Active Desktop Window. A mysterious toolbar appears. Click the down arrow to see the options that are shown in Figure 16.11.

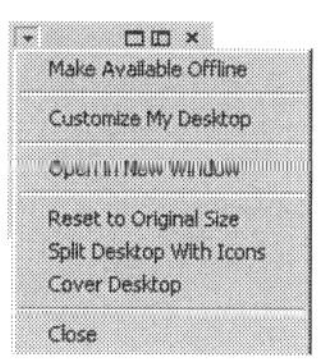

FIGURE 16.11
The mysterious Active Desktop toolbar.

The menu items shown in Figure 16.11 enable you to control your Active Desktop program. The descriptions of each option are as follows:

- Make Available Offline—This enables you to read your Active Desktop program without requiring that the program be connected to the Internet.
- Customize My Desktop—Choose this to add a new Active Desktop Program. This opens the Display Properties box. Click the New button to reach the New Active Desktop Item box (the box where you decide what program you want to add to your desktop).
- Open in New Window—This opens your Active Desktop item in Internet mode.

- Reset to Original Size—Opens the Active Desktop item to the original size.
- Split Desktop With Icons—This splits your screen so you can see your desktop icons on one half the screen and your Active Desktop program(s) on the other side of the screen.
- Cover Desktop—This option hides all your icons and covers the complete screen with the Active Desktop item.
- Close—This option completely closes the Active Desktop item.

Turning off Active Desktop

I've yet to find anyone who enthuses about the Active Desktop. More commonly, I find people who are annoyed by it. Sure, at first it seems fun. But then the fun is gone. And so am I. Ciao!

There's also the fact that your computer can randomly call the Internet without your knowing or asking it to. I personally find that disturbing.

So, if you turn on the Active Desktop to try it out for awhile, then find it just isn't for you, you can turn it off.

To Do

To Do 16.6: Turning off Active Desktop

1. Right-click a blank area on your desktop.
2. Choose Active Desktop.
3. Choose Show Web Content.

This removes the check mark next to this option and, thus, removes the Active Desktop feature. Safe, safe, safe are you from the constant phoning of the Internet.

"Honey, is someone using the computer? It's 3:30 in the morning!"

"It's just Active Desktop checking the stock prices for the Asian markets . . ."

"Can't *anything* wait any more?"

Summary

In this hour, you should have learned to customize your desktop with goodies such as your favorite tools, most-used projects and folders, and, of course, all kinds of cutting edge information via the Internet. You should also now be able to get rid of any extraneous stuff cluttering up your desktop.

Q&A

Q I accidentally moved an icon to the desktop. What should I do?

A Immediately press Ctrl+Z, the Undo keys. That should move the file back to its original location. (Click Yes if you're asked.) Then try again. As a tip, I usually drag files to the desktop using the *right* mouse button, which always pops up a menu where I can choose Create Shortcut(s) Here.

Q Do I have to keep the Active Desktop on all the time?

A No, as a matter of fact. Some people find it distracting if they don't really need this option for their daily work. You can turn Active Desktop on and off any time you want. In fact, you don't have to use this feature at all.

Workshop

The workshop includes quiz questions to help gauge your grasp of the material and exercises to help reinforce your learning. You'll find the answers to the quiz and exercises in Appendix A, "Answers."

Quiz

1. Name three items that you are *not* able to remove from your desktop.
2. Why shouldn't you put every application you use in a convenient spot right on your desktop?
3. Under what circumstances might it be more productive to ignore all this Active Desktop stuff?
4. *Bonus question*: Dolphins live in the Amazon River. What color are they?

Exercises

1. Create a folder called "Notes to Self," then stick it right up there on your desktop. Now rename it, preferably something more applicable to your daily musings, such as "Reasons I Should Rule the World."
2. Choose a game or tool (like FreeCell, Solitaire, or a calculator) to put right up on your desktop. Put it there.
3. Search around the Active Desktop Gallery. Choose a couple types of information you would like to see updated on your desktop. Now activate your Active Desktop and then add at least one of these. You can remove it later, if you wish.

Vocabulary

Active Desktop—In this state, your desktop will work similar to a Web page, periodically interfacing with particular Internet sites in order to update certain information on your desktop.

Active Desktop Gallery—A showcase of Internet info you might wish to add to your Active Desktop. The Gallery will help you find the info and show you how to get the latest info. It offers six separate wings: news, sports, entertainment, travel, weather, and cool utilities.

copy command—This command is used when you want to make a copy of something, such as a file, folder, words, pictures. Whatever.

shortcut icon—A means to gain quick access to a folder.

synchronizing—The process by which your computer intermittently keeps in touch with the appropriate Internet site(s) necessary to keep your desktop "active."

HOUR 17

Fussing with the Printer

Printing is the end-all of using a computer. It's the hard copy, the living proof, and the end to the rumors that you do nothing all day other than sit and play games.

Having a computer and having a printer doesn't necessarily mean you can just automatically print something. Your computer has to know that you have a printer and what kind of printer it is. It might also want to know how you met the printer and just what it means to you, but I will leave that for you to deal with in your own way.

This hour is dedicated to the process of getting your printer to work. I'm going to assume you've already connected the printer with the appropriate cables and such, so I don't have to tell you how to do that.

The highlights in this hour include the following:

- Adding a new printer
- Selecting and configuring a main printer
- Using the print queue
- Understanding faxing

Finding the Printer

Your computer's printer control station is the Printers folder. That's where you control any printers attached to your PC or add new ones.

To Do 17.1: Finding the Printer Icon

1. Pop-up the Start menu.
2. Choose Settings, then Printers.

   You can also access the Printers folder from the Control Panel (and there are a million ways to get to the Control Panel).

FIGURE 17.1
The Printer Icon.

The Printers folder contains an icon for adding new printers, plus icons representing any printers or faxes already installed on your PC (see Figure 17.2).

FIGURE 17.2
The Printers folder window.

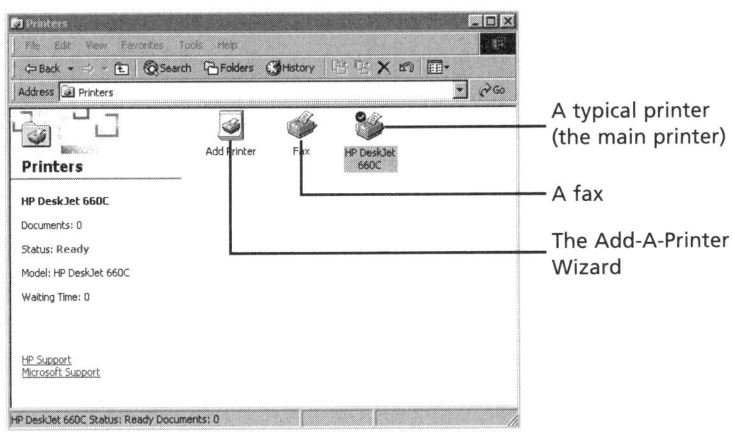

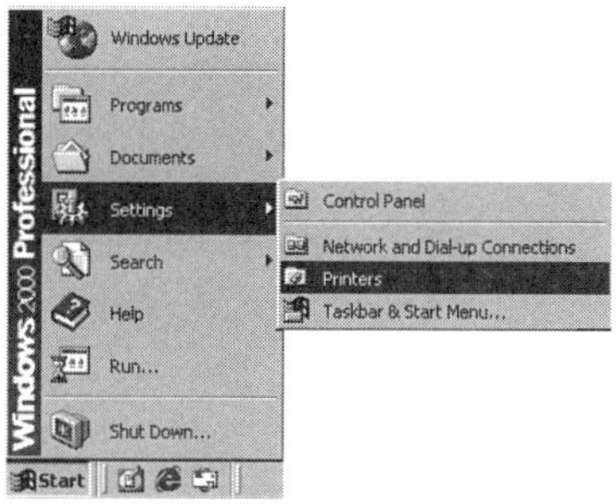

FIGURE 17.3
An alternate path to the Printers folder.

Adding a Printer

Most PCs have only one printer port, so they sport only one printer. You can add a second printer by plugging in a second printer adapter to your PC or, more commonly, more printers are added through the network. You can also use a printer switch box to connect multiple printers to a single PC. Whatever. All those printers will show up in the Printers folder.

Adding a new printer is done by using the Add Printer icon, which runs the Add Printer Wizard. You'll need to know the printer's manufacturer and the model number. If the printer came with any special disks, you should have them handy.

To Do 17.2: Installing a Printer

1. Double-click the Printer icon.

   This is located in the Control Panel.

2. Double-click the Add Printer icon.

   You see the formal Welcome. Yeah, yeah, yeah.

3. Click Next.
4. Choose either Local printer or Network printer.

   A local printer is physically attached to your computer. It should be close by, connected by the printer cable right into the computer box. Follow the cable with your fingers should you doubt me.

   A network printer is some other printer connected to some other computer on a network. It's probably that nice new color laser printer in the boss's office (even though the boss is always out of town).

5. Click Next.

   There is a notice that says Windows will automatically look for your printer. Click no. Not that I'm untrusting here, but if you already know the printer's make and model you'll save yourself some time here.

6. Click Next.
7. Click either Local printer or Network printer.

   Good questions here. Is the printer a local printer (meaning it is physically attached to your computer—the clue is that you can see it sitting close by) or a network printer (meaning it's attached to another computer, maybe even down the hall somewhere).
8. Click Next.

   There is a notice that says Windows will automatically look for your printer. Click yes, that you want it to do the work for you. From this point, you might be sent on your way, or you might have to click the Add Printer icon and start the Wizard again.

   If you're sent back (and we'll pretend here that you are), click the Add Printers icon, click Next, and this brings you to the Select the Printer Port box. Continue.
9. Pick a port.

   Most computers use the LPT1: port to communicate with a local printer.

> Printers typically connect to a parallel port (known as an LPT port), and modems use a serial port (known as a COM port). This should help with your selection.

10. Click Next.
11. Find your printer.

    Select the manufacturer and printer type. If you have an installation disk that comes with your printer, click Have Disk. (You don't have to find your manufacturer and printer type if you have the disk.)

> Make sure the right drive is listed for your disk. Remember that the drive for a floppy disk is different than a drive for a CD-ROM.

12. Name your printer.

    Type in the name of your printer. Be clever. You don't have to use HP OfficeJet. You can use real, fun names like Bert or Melvin.

13. Make it your default printer.

    In computer lingo, *default* means the one to use when you can't make up your mind. So choosing a default printer means you're picking the printer the computer uses all the time. You can choose another printer (if you have a choice). Otherwise, your only printer is the default by default.

14. Click Next.

    Do you want to share this printer? If you choose Share, then other computer users will have access to your printer on the network. Of course, you're not required to share (unless the boss-lady says you have to).

15. Click Next.

    Name a location for the printer. This is for those that might not know where Bert the printer is located. You could be nasty and write `somewhere in the state of Idaho`. Or, you could be more specific, `Office 210`. Make a comment if you want: `Don't disturb during naptime: 1-2 PM every day`.

17. Click Next.

    Check Yes. You do want a test page. Really, you do.

18. Click Next.

    Hurray! This is the "you've done good" page. All the information the Printer Wizard gathered is collected and displayed here. If any of it doesn't look right, click the Back button until you get to the point where you'd like to fix the information. Maybe you're starting to think that Bert is a rather silly name for a printer. So go back, and change it to Ernie. Much better.

19. Click Finish.

    You are done.

Choosing a Main Printer

Odds are that you have only one printer. If so, it's automatically your main printer (because there are no other choices). But if you have more than one printer or you have printers available on a network, you have to choose one of them as your main printer. This is also known as the default printer (the printer Windows always chooses to print from).

To Do 17.3: Picking a Main Printer

1. Double-click My Computer.
2. Double-click the Control Panel.
3. Open the Printers folder.
4. Right-click on your printer.

   Choose the printer you want to select as your main printer. Make sure it's a printer and not a fax machine. Right-click the mouse. The shortcut menu appears (see Figure 17.3).
5. Choose Set As Default.

   If there is already a ✓ check mark by this item, that printer is your main printer. If not, choosing Set As Default makes it your main printer (see Figure 17.4). That will now be the printer Windows uses whenever you print anything.

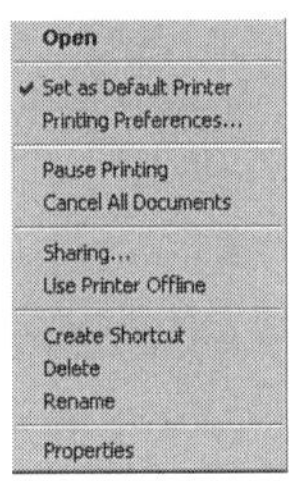

FIGURE 17.4
Setting the default printer.

FIGURE 17.5
The check mark represents that this printer is your default printer.

Changing Printers

You can also, at a moment's notice, change printers for just one document. Do this by choosing an alternative printer in the standard Print dialog box (see Figure 17.6). That way you can use the other printer (or fax), providing you have one. For example, choosing a color printer instead of the dull gray laser printer.

Say, for example, you need to send a copy of the staff meeting minutes to Don. He wasn't invited to the meeting because he's really more of a distraction than anything else. You can print the minutes directly to the printer in Don's office (provided, of course, that you are networked to Don's printer and he has set his printer up to be shared, which was the topic of Hour 14, "Using the Local Network").

Use the drop-down list in the Print dialog box to pluck out another printer. All the printers that have been introduced to and installed on your computer are listed. Choose the one you want.

Windows continues to use the nondefault printer as long as you use that program. If you quit the program, or print from another program, the original default printer is used again.

The Print dialog box, as shown in Figure 17.6, can be a fun place. You have all kinds of printing decisions that range from the number of copies you print to the pages or sections of text you print. It's exciting, really.

FIGURE 17.6
The Print dialog box.

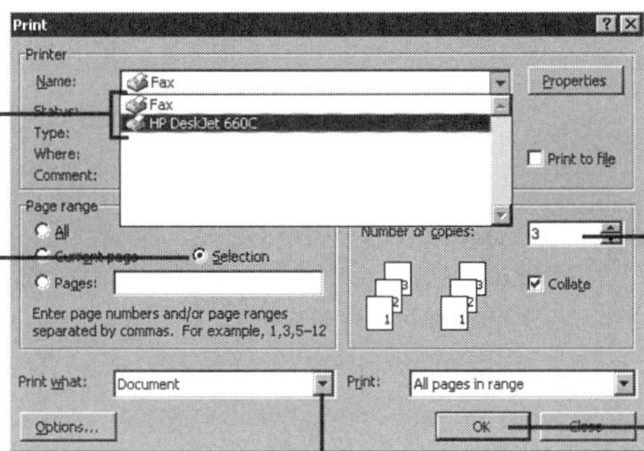

Printer Properties

Like almost everything else in Windows, your printer has its own Properties dialog box, chock full of options and gizmos. Check out Figure 17.7.

To Do 17.4: Finding the Printer Properties

1. Double-click My Computer.
2. Double-click the Control Panel.
3. Open the Printers folder.
4. Right-click on your printer.
5. Choose Properties.

This option is located at the bottom of the list.

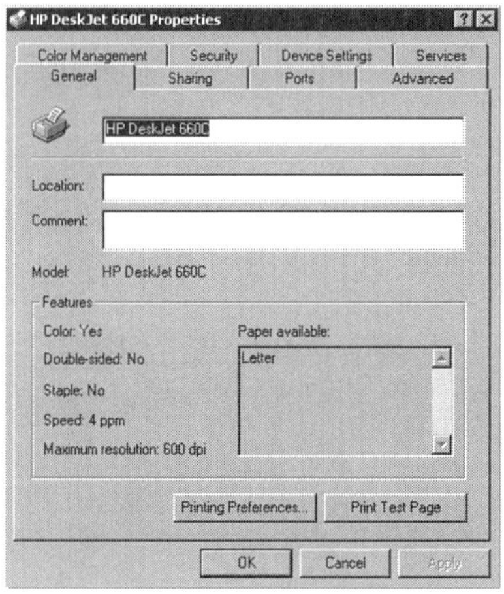

FIGURE 17.7
A typical Properties dialog box.

> Network printers might lack certain control features in their Properties dialog box. In some cases, you can only set specific printer options at the computer directly connected to that printer.

Playing with the Queue

The word *queue* (pronounced Q) means a waiting line. It's kind of a British word. I like to try to work it into loud conversations while in the ticket line at the movies, so people will think I'm more interesting and international. Anyway, when you print something in Windows, the document sits and waits in line, er, the queue until its turn to print comes up.

When it's time to print, Windows prints a little bit of your document at a time, sending small bits of it out to the printer so as not to disturb anything else you're doing in Windows. This is known as *spooling* and it's what allows you to keep working while Windows prints. So you could print several documents and continue to work while they're printing.

Finding the Printing Queue

To see the printing queue, you open your printer's icon. If you have a really quick printer, you might never see anything like what you see in Figure 17.8.

▼ To Do

To Do 17.5: Opening the Printing Queue

1. Click the Start button.
2. Hover the mouse over Settings.
3. Double-click the Printers folder.
4. Double-click on the printer icon.

▲ This opens the printing queue.

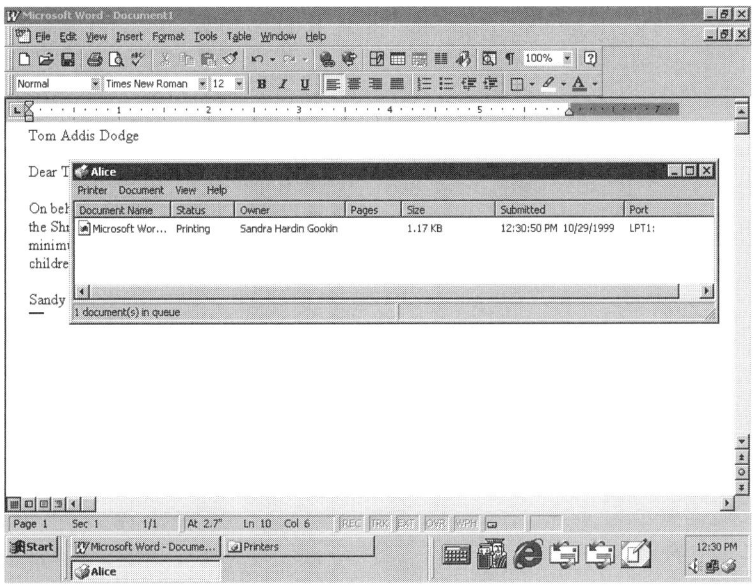

FIGURE 17.8
The printing queue.

Moving Documents Around in the Queue

Things print in the order you requested that they be printed. But if you decide that the item on the bottom of the list needs to be printed immediately if not sooner (for that meeting you're already late for), simply click on the document's icon and drag it up. However, this only works on local printers. You can't, for example, cut in line in front of your colleagues on the network printer.

Deleting Documents in the Queue

Sometimes you might not want something to print. For example, you just typed a great letter to your new mother-in-law and found that you misspelled her name. Well, forget what your analyst might say about Freudian slips and all; Norma and Moron use very similar keystrokes!

Open your printer's window to see the queue. Locate the offending document and click on it once with the mouse to highlight it. Now choose Document, and then Cancel Printing. ZAP! The document will not be printed. All action has stopped, ceased, halted; you get the idea.

If you choose Printer and then Purge Print Jobs from the menu, every print job is purged.

Faxing: Another Print Job

Faxing is nothing more than printing using a fax machine and a phone line. It should be that simple, but there are a few hoops to jump through.

Before sending any fax, work through the steps below. This is to set up your User Information sheet (see Figure 17.9). This information is what appears on the cover pages of your fax, which heralds the arrival of your document to the recipient.

To Do 17.6: Preparing the User Information Sheet

▼ To Do

1. Right-click the Fax Icon.

   This icon is found in your printer's folder.

2. Choose Properties.
3. Click on the User Information tab.
4. Complete the information.

▲

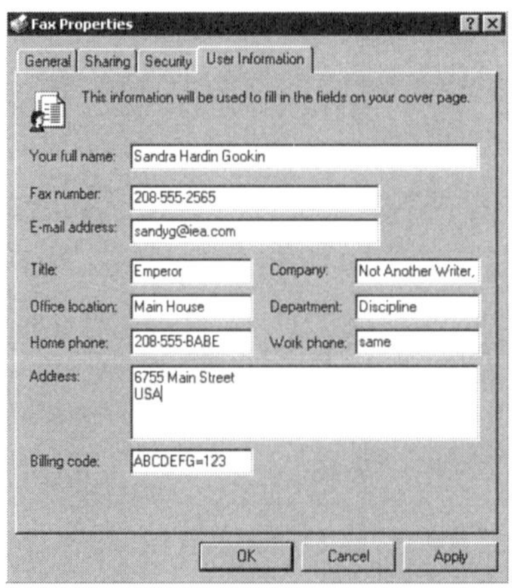

FIGURE 17.9
The User Information sheet.

Now you're ready to fax. Jump right in, get your document ready, and fax away!

To Do 17.7: Sending a Fax

▼ To Do

1. Create the document to be faxed.

   Faxing is like printing, so go ahead and use any application that prints something to create your fax. For example, use Microsoft Word to create your fax. You don't have to quit your program to send the fax; just save it to disk before you fax it.

2. Select File.

   File is an option on the menu bar at the top of the screen.

3. Select Print.

   This brings up the Print dialog box. Figures 17.10 and 17.11 show two different Print dialog boxes. Both are possible options, depending on the program that you use. Both work about the same. Just make sure you review all the printing options before you move to the next step.

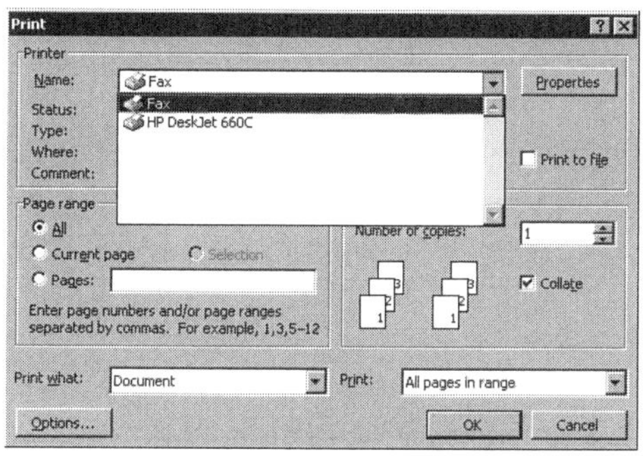

FIGURE 17.10
The Print dialog box option #1.

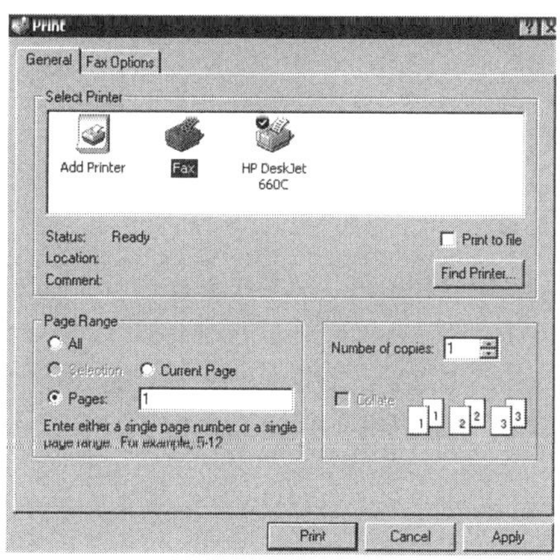

FIGURE 17.11
The Print dialog box option #2.

▼ 4. Choose the Fax as the printer.

Depending on the Print dialog box, you need to choose Fax as your printer. This is done either by clicking on a drop-down list of printers or by just clicking the Fax icon in the Print dialog box.

5. Review your options.

   Now is the time to decide how many copies you want to fax, what pages you will fax (you can choose to fax only page two of a six page document, for example), and if you want the pages to be collated as they fax.

   Figure 17.11 shows a Fax Options tab in that particular print dialog box. You can click on this tab and choose when the fax will be sent, the paper size, and the orientation of your paper. The Paint Program in Windows has this print option, so check it out if you have a few moments.

6. Click OK (or Print).

   The Welcome to the Send Fax Wizard practically blinds you. Thanks. This Wizard is going to hold your hand as it walks you through the steps of sending a fax.

7. Click Next.

   The picture in Figure 17.12 will only be seen the first time you run the Fax Wizard. The purpose of this box is to ask you to complete the User Information. This was the stuff you did in Task 17.7, so if you were good and did what you were told, you can click on the Take No Action button. If you ignored my instructions and didn't work through To Do 17.7, then click the Open Fax Control Panel and complete the information. Maybe next time you'll listen to me. When you're finished, click OK.

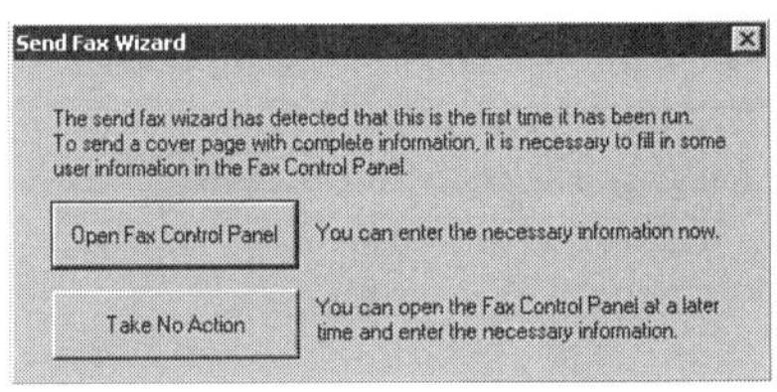

FIGURE 17.12
The Send Fax Wizard Opening Dialog Box.

8. Complete the Information.

   This is the dialing information; where the fax is going. You can't ignore this box or your fax won't work. If you have several people to fax a document to, type their information, click the Add button, and type in another fax number. You can keep adding recipients until you have your list complete.

9. Click Next.

   You can add a cover page if you want. Click in the box next to Select a Cover Page Template with the Following Information. This highlights the rest of the box where you can choose the cover page, and then type in the subject and a note.

10. Click Next.

    When do you want to send the fax? Make your choice and click Next. If you want to send your fax during a specific time (when rates are lower to dial long distance, for instance) you can type in the time—or use the up and down arrows to adjust the time. If you are using a dialog box as shown in Figure 17.11, then the time information you completed in the Fax Options will be reflected here.

11. Click Finish.

    You'll hear the beeping and buzzing of the modem working if you chose to have your fax sent now.

> Rather than endlessly typing the same fax numbers in over and over and over again, use the Windows Address book. More information can be found in Hour 24, "Time and Sound in Windows 2000."

Summary

This hour, you have gotten acquainted with your printer and all the ways to fiddle with it to make it work better for you. You should have discovered how to install a new printer and how to make your computer favor one printer over the others. You should have also learned how to prioritize or delete a print job after you have asked your computer to print it. And finally, I hope, you got a little more comfortable with faxing from your desktop.

Q&A

Q Is it possible to print on both sides of the paper, or do you have to use a copier for this?

A Windows 2000 does support the feature to print on both sides of the paper. Open the Printers folder, right click on the printer you will use, click Printing Preferences, click the Layout tab, and then choose the Print on Both Sides options. The wrench in this clever scheme is that you have to have a printer that supports printing on both sides (which is called duplexing), or the option isn't even available.

Q How can I schedule a fax to send at 9:00 in the morning when I'm not yet up to use the computer?

A You can either click on the Fax Options (shown in Figure 17.11), or wait for the Scheduling Transmission box to appear. Click on the option, Specific Time in the Next 24 Hours, and then use the up and down arrow keys to find the time you want your fax to be sent. You do need to leave your computer on for this to work. If you shut your computer off, this faxing won't happen.

Q Where are the good scissors?

A I told you, they are in the top right drawer in the kitchen where the candles and napkins are kept. Don't make me look for them myself.

Q I have a local and a network printer, but want to make the network printer my default. Is that okay?

A Sure. You can choose any printer you want as your default printer.

Workshop

The workshop includes quiz questions to help gauge your grasp of the material and exercises to help reinforce your learning. You'll find the answers to the quiz and exercises in Appendix A, "Answers."

Quiz

1. What is the purpose of designating a printer as your default printer?
2. What is the purpose of the stuff you put in the User Information Sheet?
3. Which port do most computers use to communicate with printers?
4. *Bonus Question*: How big is the actual *Mona Lisa*?

Exercises

1. Look to see how many printers are installed on your computer and note which is designated as the default printer.
2. Use the Printer's Properties dialog box to change the paper orientation from portrait to landscape and back.
3. Change the paper size to legal.

Vocabulary

local printer—A printer that is connected directly to your printer.

modem—Hardware that enables your computer to communicate over a phone line. Modems are necessary for faxing documents and for connecting to the Internet.

network printer—A printer shared with other computers in your network. It may be located in another room or even on another floor.

queue—Basically just a pretty word for your run-of-the-mill waiting line. Derived from the Old French, it can also be used to describe a pigtail, ponytail, or anything in a line.

HOUR 18

Maintaining and Cleaning Files

Don't you find it strange when you visit someone's office and there is *nothing* on the desk? Sometimes they wink and show you the other room, where the real work gets done. That room usually has a messy desk. But clean desks? No way! There's a theory that states that no matter how big your desk is, you'll always fill it. And if there isn't such a theory, there should be!

Computer hard drives work a lot like desktops. Eventually, your hard drive will accumulate files that, like a desk in an office, will fill with clutter and eventually become less than useful. This hour is dedicated to maintaining and cleaning up files. Keeping things tidy in your computer so that programs continue to run smoothly and as quickly as possible is just as important as anything you do with your computer.

The highlights in this hour include the following:

- The Disk Cleanup Program
- Emptying the Recycle Bin
- Removing unnecessary files

- Backup
- Using Explorer

Cleaning Your Hard Drive

To clean your car, you need a vacuum and a bag in which to put all the trash, French fries, and scraps of paper that accumulate. To clean your computer's hard drive, you need the Disk Cleanup program.

Like cleaning the car, Disk Cleanup's job is to scour the hard drive and remove (or inquire about) files that you may or may not need. It then sweeps the useless matter quietly off into bit eternity, giving you more room on the hard drive and fewer files to fuss over.

To Do 18.1: Using the Disk Cleanup Program

To Do

1. Double-click My Computer, located on the desktop.
2. Right-click drive C.

   You can also work this process if you have a drive D, too (or any additional hard drives you have).
3. Choose Properties from the list.

   In the drive C Properties window, you'll see various information about the hard drive. This is stuff you'll never remember, so don't try to make sense of these numbers. Figure 18.1 describes a little of what's going on with this box.

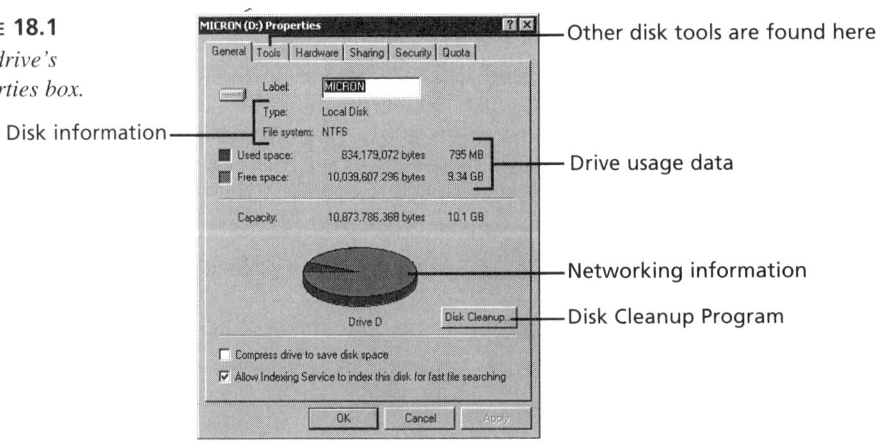

FIGURE 18.1
Your drive's properties box.

4. Click Disk Cleanup.

   Windows examines your disk drives and starts calculating how much wasted space you've accumulated. (Yes, it's possible to accumulate wasted space; ask a physicist.)

Just like your mom looking under your bed for dirty socks, Disk Cleanup finds accumulated waste on your hard drive. The Disk Cleanup for Drive C (or whichever drive you're working on) dialog box appears, as shown in Figure 18.2.

FIGURE 18.2
The Disk Cleanup dialog box.

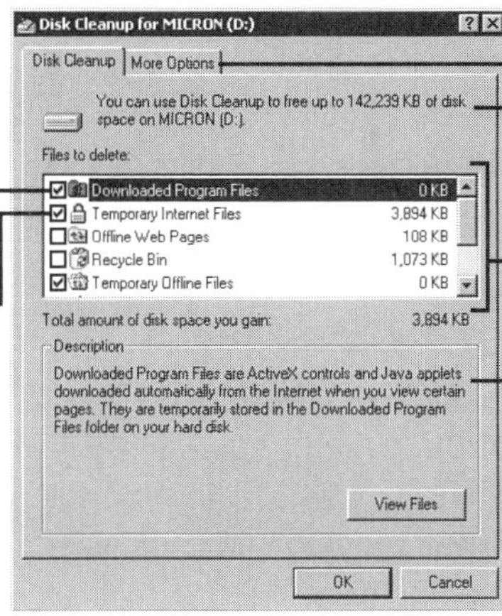

5. Read through the list of options.

   You must decide whether to delete a file. Reading the descriptions can help you decide what you want to get rid of and what you want to keep.

6. Choose your files.

   Clicking on an item puts a check mark in the box to select it for deletion. If you're still not sure about a file after reading the description, click the View Pages button at the bottom of the dialog box to get a glimpse of the files. That may help you decide.

7. Click OK.

   Oh dear, a warning! `Are you sure you want to delete files?`

8. Click Yes.

   Disk Cleanup removes the files. You might see a tiny dialog box indicating Window's progress. Then, it disappears.

9. Click Cancel to close the Drive C Properties dialog box.

18

> If you want to clean up another hard drive, right-click the drive, and choose Properties from the menu. Click the Disk Cleanup button, and you're on your way.

You should run the Disk Cleanup program at least once a month to keep your computer running smoothly. You can also clean any hard drive or a removable disk such as a Zip or Jaz drive using Disk Cleanup. You cannot clean CD-ROM drives; they're read-only. And you cannot clean drives on other people's computers on the network—no matter how upset you get over them!

Taking Out the Trash: The Recycle Bin

All things that die must go somewhere. This includes deleted files, folders, old documents, and graphics that turn out ugly. You name it. On your computer, the deleted stuff goes to Windows purgatory, officially called the *Recycle Bin*.

The Recycle Bin is Microsoft's attempt to show its understanding that at times we can all be a little hasty when pressing Delete, meaning that when you delete an item, regardless of what it is, the Recycle Bin holds it for a spell. That way, you can fish it out later, should you change your mind. Or you can destroy the file utterly by "emptying" the Recycle Bin, meaning that the item will be deleted for good.

To Do

To Do 18.2: Emptying the Recycle Bin

1. Double-click the Recycle Bin icon.

   This is the icon sitting on your desktop that looks like a small trash can.

2. Click Empty Recycle Bin.

   Figure 18.3 illustrates the list of deleted items in the Recycle Bin, waiting for you to decide what to do with this so-called trash.

FIGURE 18.3
The "inside" of the Recycle Bin.

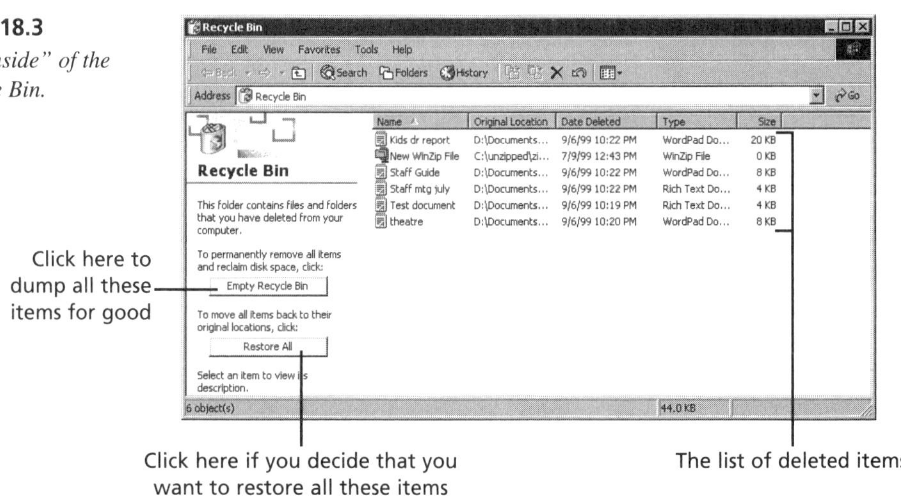

3. Heed the warning!

   Click Yes. Of course, this means that you really, really, really are deleting these items and can't get them back, ever.

   And there you have a nice, clean, empty recycle bin.

Ding, Ding, We're Backing Up

Backing up is hard to do. I'm serious! It's one of the most important things you can do for your hard drive and its data, but few people bother. I suppose that it's like oral hygiene; we know we should floss, but few of us do. And the consequences are painful.

A backup is a copy, a safety copy of all the files and information on your PC's hard drive. It's made and then sits somewhere safe, like a fire safe or vault. The backup copy exists just in case something awful happens and you lose your data. Then you have the backup to restore from. Sounds like a swell idea, but still, few people bother.

> The best way to backup is to get a tape backup drive. This is a special device that quickly copies information from your hard drive to a special backup tape (like a heavy-duty, high-quality cassette tape). The backup drive usually comes with its own software, often better than what Windows 2000 offers. You can even automate the job so that it starts late at night and runs unattended.

If you don't have a tape backup, you can use the backup program that comes with Windows. This allows you to back up to a second hard drive, floppy disks, or some device on the network. It's not the best backup program, but it comes with Windows 2000, so it's "free."

To Do: 18.3: Using the Backup Utility

1. Click the Start button.
2. Choose Programs.
3. Choose Accessories.
4. Choose System Tools.
5. Choose Backup.

   The Backup and Recovery Tools dialog box is displayed, as shown in Figure 18.4. Notice that this is also the dialog box you use for restoring your work or creating the Emergency Repair Disk.

FIGURE 18.4
The Backup and Recovery Tools wizards.

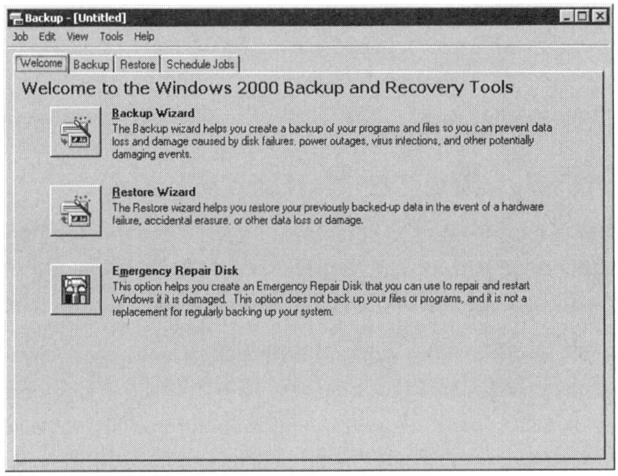

6. Click the box next to Backup Wizard.
7. Follow the directions.

   These steps are rather simple, so rather than walk you through each of these steps, I'm just going to say, "Follow the directions."

> When you get to the dialog box named Completing the Backup Wizard, you can click the Advanced button to set specifics, including scheduling your computer to back up at a later time, such as midnight, for example. That way, you don't have to sit there and wait for all this to happen.

8. When you've worked through the steps, click Finish.

   As the files are backed up, you'll see an animation of your files flying around as your information is being transferred to floppy disk, much like what you see in Figure 18.5.

FIGURE 18.5
The backup progress information.

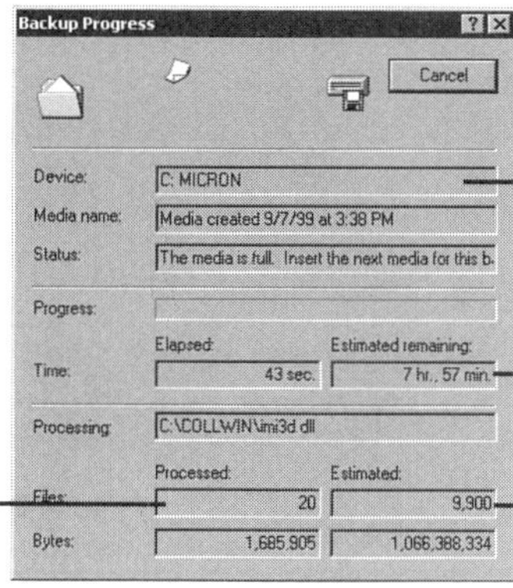

Exploring Your Folders

Windows Explorer is one of your main tools for working with folders. It displays how folders are organized and the files that are in each folder.

To Do 18.4: Finding Windows Explorer

1. Click the Start Button.
2. Choose Programs.
3. Choose Accessories.
4. Choose Windows Explorer

Figure 18.6 illustrates the path to get to Windows Explorer.

FIGURE 18.6
The path to Windows Explorer.

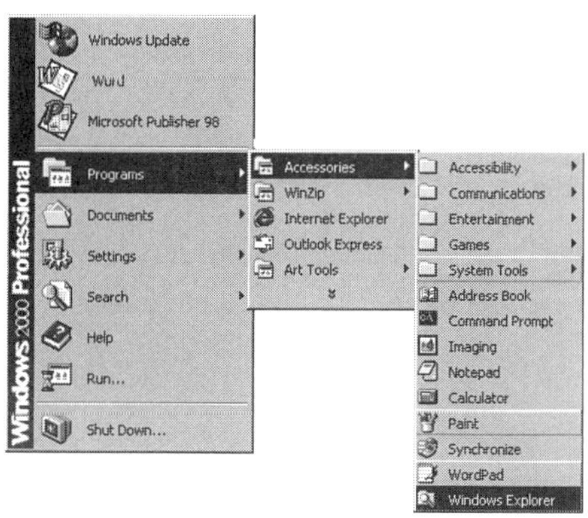

> Now for all of you who like the quick approach to things, you can also find Windows Explorer by right-clicking on My Computer and then choosing Explore. The difference is that this right-click method shows Explorer with My Computer at the top of the list. But, I suppose that this isn't really the "official" way to get there, so maybe you ought not tell anyone you know this. *Shhh*.

Puttering Around the Explorer

The Explorer window appears, as shown in Figure 18.7.

FIGURE 18.7
A peek at Windows Explorer.

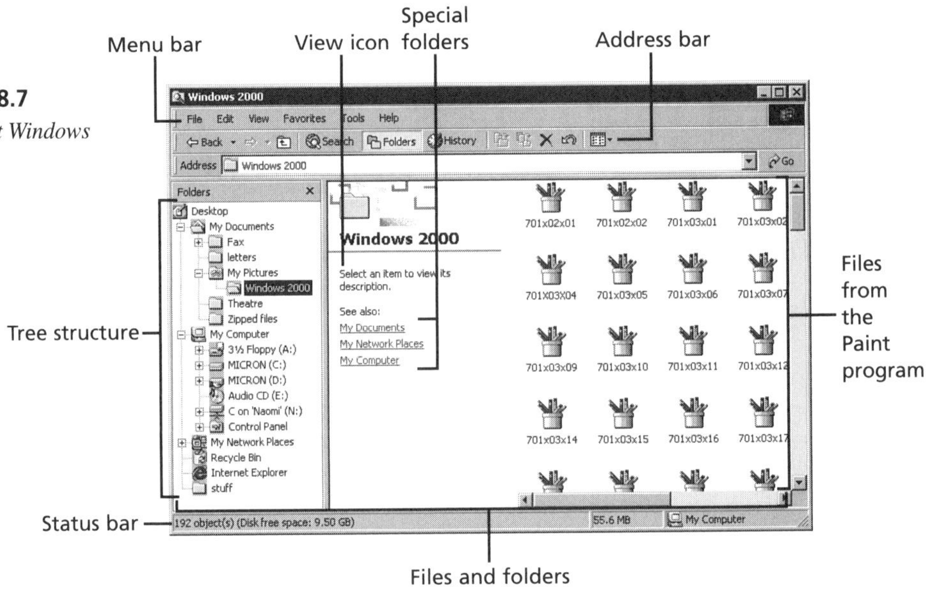

Here are the Explorer features you'll find in Figure 18.7:

- Menu bar—All the adjustments and tinkering in Explorer happen here.
- Address bar—You can see the Address bar by choosing View, Toolbars, and then Address Bar.
- Tree structure—Your computer's tree structure appears here, which is really just a hierarchy of folders and files.
- Plus sign—Click on a plus sign to open a disk or folder, displaying other folders.
- Minus sign—A minus sign means a disk or folder is open.
- Special folders—Folders that live in My Computer.

- Status bar—Choose View and then Status Bar to see this line of information.
- Files and folders—The list of files and folders appear over here, just as in My Computer. Remember, folder side is the left side, and file side is the right side of the Explorer window.
- View icon—Click here to change the way files are displayed.

Working Explorer

The real advantage of Windows Explorer is that it puts you in a position to see which folders various files live in and how things are organized. If you look at Figure 18.7, you'll see a list of files on the right side. But, on the left, you can immediately tell that the folder you're viewing is from My Documents, and you can see other folders nearby.

To Do 18.5: Viewing a Folder

1. Click the plus next to (C:).

   The folders on drive C: are listed (see Figure 18.8). Clicking on the plus opens the "tree," displaying all the folders inside (or beneath) the C: drive. There should be a bunch of them.

   The + opens a folder "branch."

   The – closes a folder "branch."

   Notice how the right side of the window did not change its contents. Only the open folder, shown in Figure 18.8, displays its contents on the right side of the window.

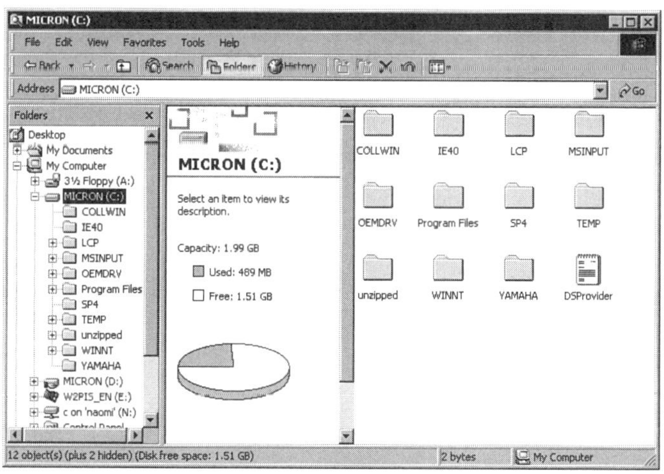

FIGURE 18.8
The exposed C: drive.

2. Click on one of the folders.

   The contents of that folder appear on the right.

> If you've clicked on a folder with a plus next to it, clicking on that folder will simply open it to reveal more folders.

If you are unable to find the file you want, click the Search button. This search button works just like the search described in Hour 9, "What's in Them Folders and Files?"

Working with Groups of Files in Explorer

The Explorer lets you work with files singularly or in groups. (See Hour 9 for information on working with files one at a time.) The commands are the same, although when a group of files is selected, they affect every single file, not just one.

Obviously, the first step to working with a group of files is to select more than one at a time.

To Do 18.6: Selecting a Tag Group of Files

1. Open the My Documents window in the Explorer (if it's not open already).

   You should have a few files in this folder. If not, go to one of your other folders that contains a lot of files—only go to a folder you created. Don't use the folder Windows lives in (C:\WINNT, for example) or any of its subfolders.

2. Press and hold the Ctrl key.

   To select more than one file at a time, press the Ctrl key as you click on each file. This is known as a *Ctrl-click* (control-click). As long as the Ctrl key is down, Windows selects every file you click on.

3. Click on an icon to select it.

4. Click on another icon to select it.

   Both icons are selected—a group is born!

5. Continue Ctrl-clicking icons to select a group.

   For example, you could Ctrl-click on all your graphics icons to select them and then move them to the Graphics folder. Figure 18.9 illustrates this concept.

FIGURE 18.9
Files selected with Ctrl-clicking.

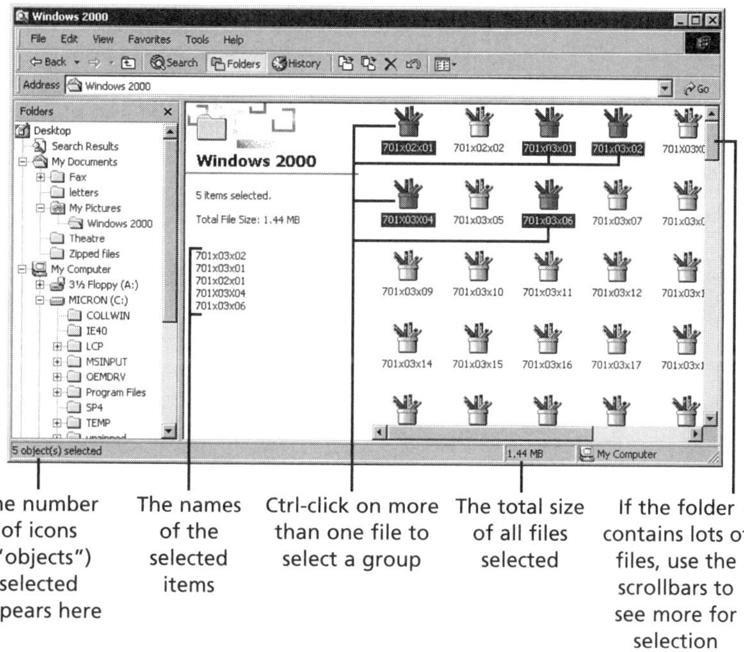

> You can select files in only one folder at a time. If you need to work with files in several folders, you must select each group in each folder, work with the files, and then move on to the next folder.

At this point, you can copy, cut, or delete these files.

> Be careful where you click! If you click anywhere in the Explorer's right window other than on one of the selected files, you deselect the group and will have to start over. Ugh!

When the files are selected, you can work with them as a group: Cut, copy, and delete work on the bunch of them. (You cannot, however, rename a group of files at once.) Pressing the Delete key on the keyboard or clicking the Delete button on the toolbar would destroy them. (Well, deleting would *move* the files to the Recycle Bin, but you get the idea.)

Ropin' Files

Another way to grab a bunch of files is to drag the mouse around them, as Figure 18.10 illustrates. This is good for selecting files when they're grouped near one another.

FIGURE 18.10
Ropin' files.

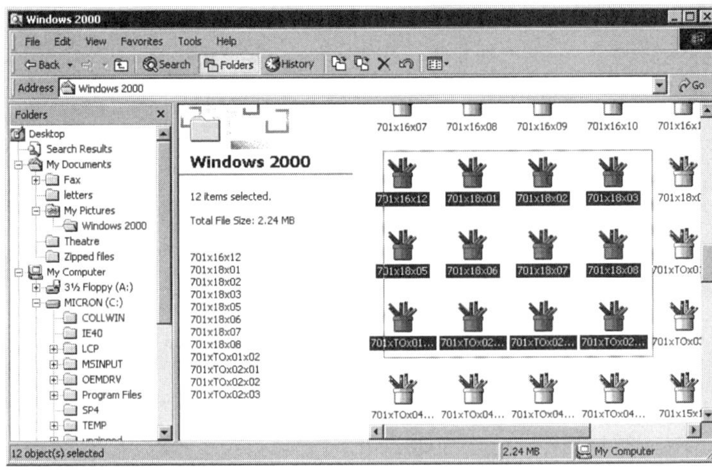

To select a group of files, click and drag the mouse around them. All the files inside the dotted line become selected.

You can even use the Ctrl key when lassoing files. For example, group one selection of files by dragging the mouse around them. Then press and hold the Ctrl key as you drag around a second group, or just Ctrl-click the files you want to add to the group. Windows is versatile when it comes to corralling icons.

Summary

This hour is dedicated to the art of working with your files—cleaning them up, moving them, deleting them from the Recycle bin, and viewing them through Windows Explorer. It's been a busy hour, for sure!

Q&A

Q Are there any other ways to free up disk space, aside from using Disk Cleanup?

A Of course. You can always delete files you no longer need (or copy them to a CD-ROM or backup disk) or uninstall programs you no longer need. I typically do this with games I play. After I'm bored with the game, I uninstall it to free up disk space. It's amazing how much space unused games (or other seldom used programs) occupy on a hard drive.

Q Is there anyway to delete a file without sending it to the Recycle Bin?

A Of course. Use Shift+Delete. Pressing the Shift key when you use the Delete key to remove a file utterly erases the file. After that, the file cannot be recovered from the Recycle Bin.

Q How can I select all but one file in a folder?

A Selecting *all* the files is easy: Choose Edit and then Select All from the menu, or use the handy (and memorable) Ctrl+A key combination. Then you can Ctrl-click the single file you don't want selected to remove it from the group.

Conversely, you can select the single file you don't want selected first; then choose Edit and then Invert Selection from the menu. Try it!

Workshop

The workshop includes quiz questions to help gauge your grasp of the material and exercises to help reinforce your learning. You'll find the answers to the quiz and exercises in Appendix A, "Answers."

Quiz

1. How often should you run the Disk Cleanup program?
2. Why are backups necessary?
3. How can you rename more than one file at a time?
4. *Bonus question*: How many paintings did Vincent van Gogh himself sell?

Exercises

1. Follow the steps in To Do 18.1, and use your Disk Cleanup program.
2. Try the Invert Selection method mentioned in the Q&A section.
3. Practice Ctrl-clicking files to select them.

Vocabulary

backup—A procedure in which files are copied from the hard drive to a backup tape (or disk) for safety reasons. The backup copy can then be used should anything happen to the original files. *Backup* is also, generally, the name of the program that creates the backup copy. (There are various types of backup: A *full backup* means backing up your entire hard drive, which should be done at least once a month. An *incremental backup* means that you back up only those files that have been changed, added, or modified since the last backup. You should perform an incremental backup at least once a week or more often if you modify or change files frequently.

Ctrl-click—Clicking the mouse while holding the Ctrl key at the same time. The Ctrl (control) key modifies the mouse click, performing some special action in Windows, which is usually the selection of more than one object at a time.

disk space—The amount of storage available on a hard drive, either total storage or the specific amount available (which is the total storage minus the storage you've used). Disk space generally decreases over time as you install new software and create new documents and files.

Restore—The opposite of a backup operation. Restoring files from a backup is the process of copying them back to the hard drive. This is done to replace files accidentally deleted or destroyed, or it can be done to recover an entire hard drive, should something very nasty happen to it.

HOUR 19

Installing and Removing Software

Buying a new computer is usually quite an endeavor and a major outflow of cash. Not to burst the bubble of excitement, but you probably aren't finished with the buying part. There is always more to buy. Software, for example, is an ongoing purchase because programs get updated and, even then, there's always yet another program you *must* have.

What is *software?* All the programs you buy for your computer to get work done, to play, or to just help the computer run better. You buy software, you install it, and then eventually you might even uninstall it. It's a vicious cycle.

The highlights in this hour include the following:

- Adding software
- Removing software
- Installing extra Windows components
- Removing Windows components
- Updating Windows

Installing Software

Computer software comes on disks, mostly computer CDs but occasionally floppy disks. To get that software off those disks and onto your computer's hard drive, it must be *installed*. That process involves not only copying the programs but also customizing the new software to work with your computer, letting Windows know that the software has moved in, and setting other options along the way.

To Do 19.1: Installing Software

1. Double-click My Computer.
2. Double-click the Control Panel.

   You can also click Start, and then Settings to find the Control Panel.
3. Double-click the Add/Remove Programs icon.

   The Add/Remove Programs icon is where all software installation and removal must begin. Figure 19.1 shows the Add/Remove Programs Properties dialog box.

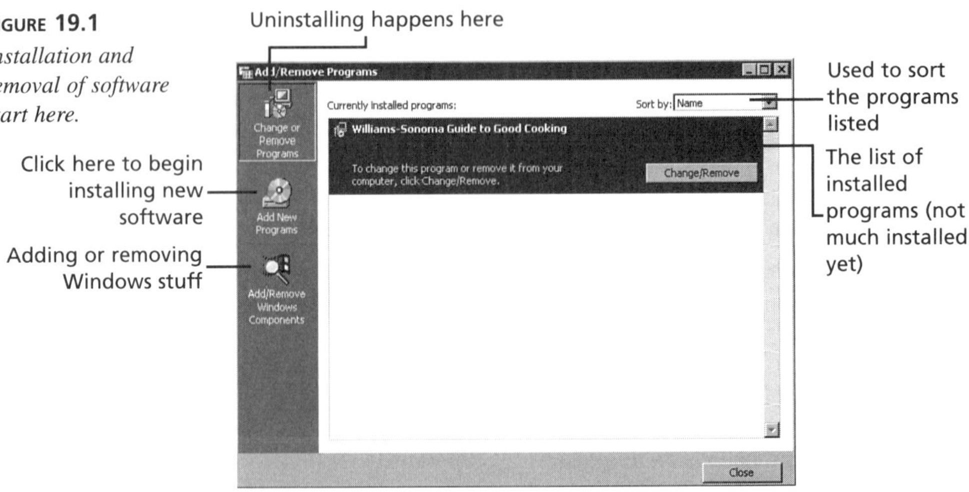

FIGURE 19.1
Installation and removal of software start here.

4. Click on Add New Programs.

   Refer to Figure 19.1 to find this button. It doesn't really look like a button until you point your cursor at the words *Add New Programs*.
5. Choose a location.

You have the option of adding a program from a local disk (the CD-ROM or floppy drive) or from the Internet (the Windows Update button). Most often, it will be the local disk and the CD (see Figure 19.2).

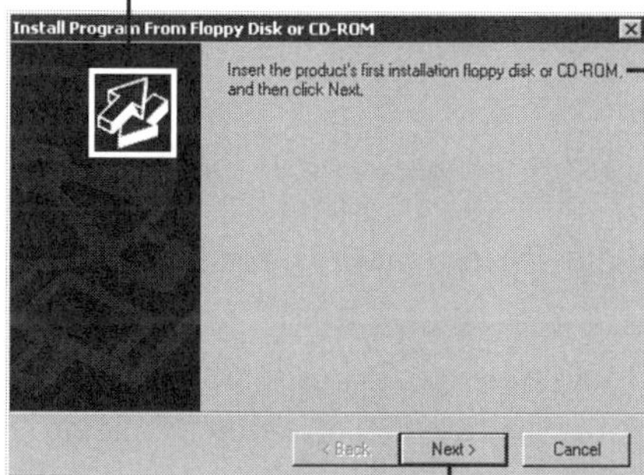

FIGURE 19.2
Installing programs from a disk or CD.

6. Stick the installation disks into the drive.

   If it's a CD, put the CD into your CD-ROM drive, typically drive (E:). If you're installing from floppy disks, put the first floppy disk into your computer's (A:) drive.

7. Click Next.

   You'll see a quick note saying that Windows is looking for your disk or CD. Eventually, it will locate your software's installation or setup program, displaying technical information similar to what you see in Figure 19.3.

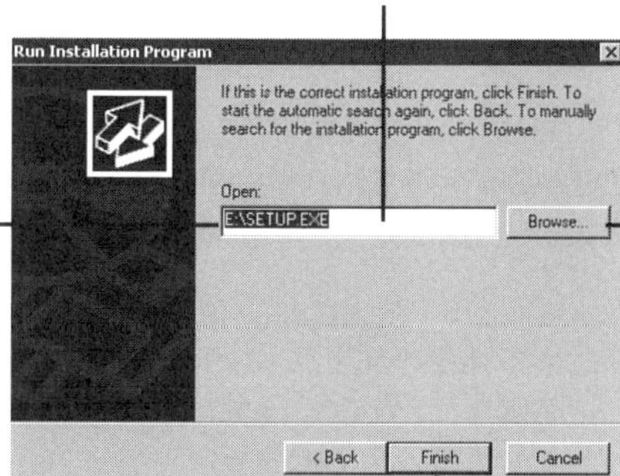

FIGURE 19.3
The Run Installation dialog box.

8. Click Finish.

   Ha! You're not really done. At this point, your job is to read the screen, where you will be asked a variety of questions. Read along and click Yes or Next when necessary.

   You might, at times, see your information being loaded with graphics Windows supplies. It depends on the program you're installing.

   Eventually, a message informs you that installation is complete. One message that I find particularly humorous is

   ```
   All files for (name of program) have been successfully installed!
   ```

   The exclamation point at the end makes it seem as though Microsoft is surprised that it worked.

   You might have to install other programs for your program to work. For example, you might install a game that requires the QuickTime or DirectX programs. Windows walks you through this process, so read carefully and follow the directions. Your computer might have to reboot itself a few times before installation is complete.

> You can also add programs to your system if you're hooked to a network. Follow the preceding steps (open the Control Panel, and click Add/Remove Programs). At the bottom of the screen, you will see a list of programs you are authorized to add. You might have to select Category first if your administrator has organized programs into categories. Select the program you want to add, and then click Add. Simply follow the instructions on your screen from that point on.

Adding More Windows Stuff

Windows comes with tons of stuff—programs, utilities, and lots of support software—most of which isn't installed when you first get Windows. Some stuff isn't installed because your computer lacks the proper hardware. For example, networking programs can't help you if you don't have a network card installed (a network card is considered hardware).

Some programs are not installed when you initially install Windows. Windows itself is fairly bulky, so it saves some things for you to install if you decide you want them. You can look through the list of other stuff that's waiting for you and install the rest of Windows right now, or just a few key programs.

To Do 19.2: Installing More Windows Stuff

▼ To Do

1. Double-click My Computer.
2. Double-click the Control Panel.
3. Double-click the Add/Remove Programs icon.
4. Click on Add/Remove Windows Components.

   The Windows Components Wizard dialog box greets you (provided that the administrator has given you the privilege to get into this wizard). The purpose of this "Wiz" is to walk you through the steps of installing some or all of the rest of Windows. (To help save disk space, you can also remove pieces of Windows that you don't use.)
5. Click Next.

   The Windows Components part of the dialog box is displayed, shown in Figure 19.4. The scrolling list details categories of various Windows components and programs.

   An *empty* box means that none of those components are installed.

   A *shaded* box means that only part of the component will be installed.

   A *check mark* in the box means that all the components are installed.

FIGURE 19.4
The Windows Components Wizard.

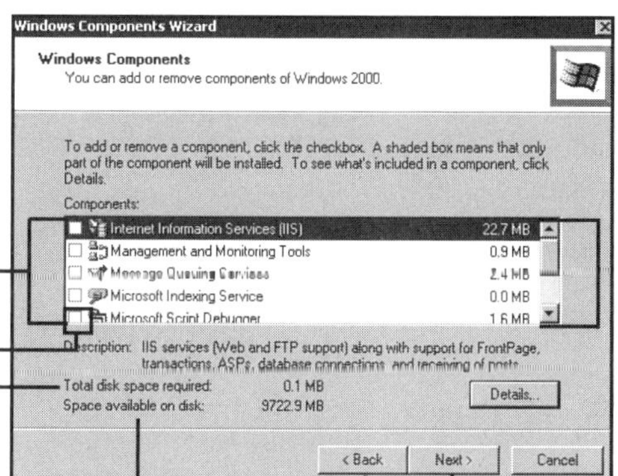

6. Choose a component.

   Click the component once to highlight it.

▼

19

Some components have several programs; others are just one program (such as Microsoft Indexing Service). To tell which components have more programs, look at the Details button. If it's dimmed, there's only one program. If it's available, there are additional choices to make.

7. Click the Details button.

   Another dialog box opens listing subcomponents available (see Figure 19.5). Click in the box next to those items you want to add. Here is yet another Details button, in case even more options are available.

FIGURE 19.5
Adding subcomponents.

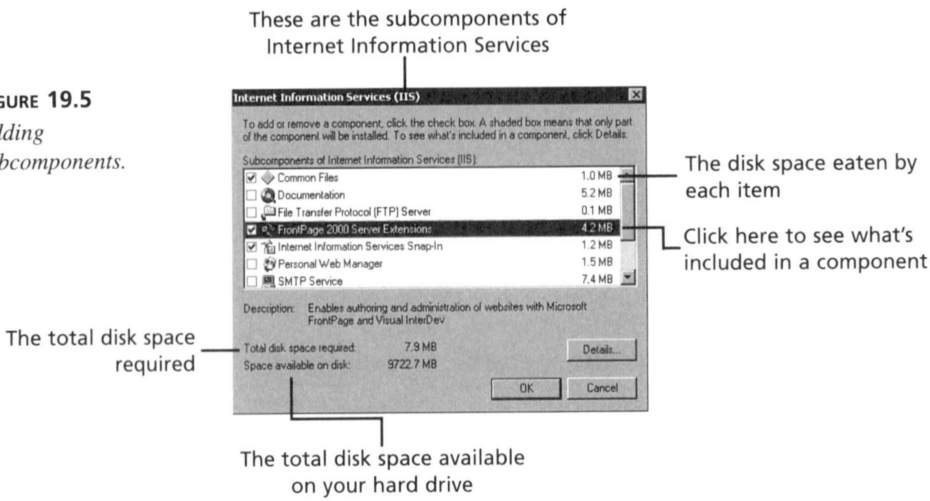

Some items have a gray check mark in their box. This means that only one of several options has been selected. You can click the Details button to select among the options available (covered in step 8).

> You'll notice that most of the selections don't have partially installed items. Either they're installed or they're not.

Remember that check marks both add and remove items. Clicking to add a check mark directs Windows to add a component. Clicking to remove a check mark removes or uninstalls that part of Windows.

8. Click the OK button when you're ready to add your stuff.

Here you might be asked to quit any other programs you're running. This is done mainly to ensure that all your documents are saved to disk should the computer explode or otherwise foul up.

9. Stick the Windows setup disk into your disk drive.

   Stick the Windows setup disk wherever. If you're using floppy disks, don't be surprised if you are asked to remove one disk and insert another.

   Eventually, the changes you asked for will be made. Windows may beg to reset. Let it do so.

Removing Programs

Sometimes you stop liking or using a program. This happens often with kids' games. Or you might have to remove a program to free up some disk space. Whatever the reason, you can easily remove any software you have installed.

> Good items to look for when you want to free up disk space are things like demo software or an old game.

Removing software must be done properly! Never remove programs by dragging them to the Recycle Bin. That works for stuff you create, but *never* for programs. Programs must be uninstalled, not deleted. Only this way can you be sure that you have removed all of the program.

19

To Do 19.3: Removing Programs

To Do

1. Double-click My Computer.
2. Double-click the Control Panel.
3. Double-click the Add/Remove Programs icon.

   Yes, you're back here. This place should look familiar because this is where you came to install programs. Say hello to the wizard guy again. (I like to think that he's a good wizard, not a bad one.)
4. Click Change or Remove Programs.

   A list of installed programs is displayed.

   If the program isn't displayed, check the Add/Remove Windows Components button to see whether what you're trying to kill off is a Windows program.

If the program still isn't listed, you'll most likely need a third-party utility to remove the program. Find something that's Windows 2000 compatible.

5. Select the program to remove.

   Stab it cruelly with the cursor.

6. Click Remove.

   You'll see a Confirm File Deletion dialog box, asking whether you're really sure that you want to utterly remove the program from your hard drive. Be sure that this is what you want to do. If you delete something you actually need, you will have to go back through the whole Install process again.

7. Click Yes.

   After a few spins of the disk, the program is gone!

Removing Windows Components

On the other side of Adding Windows Components is Removing Windows Components. Why would you want to do this? Windows is our friend. We love Windows. We can't get enough of Windows! The answer is that sometimes we have to cut back on the Windows components in order to free up disk space. Or maybe you're just angry at Windows and need a place to vent. Welcome to that place.

To Do 19.4: Removing Windows Components

To Do

1. Double-click My Computer.
2. Double-click the Control Panel.
3. Double-click the Add/Remove Programs icon.
4. Click on Add/Remove Windows Components.
5. Click Next.

   You're back at the Windows Components Wizard.

6. Remove a check mark by an item.

   This is the reverse process of what you accomplished earlier when you added these components. Now you're taking the check marks off, thereby removing them from your hard drive.

7. Click Next.

   You'll see your computer working to comply with your demands. It's still not gonna make dinner, but at this point it will carefully delete whatever it was from your computer, freeing up that much disk space.

8. Click Finish.

Alternative Ways to Remove Programs

Not every application on your computer will be listed in the Currently Installed Programs list in the Add/Remove Programs Properties dialog box. Even so, those programs may sport their own removal program.

The first way to find out whether your program has an Uninstall feature is to browse through its Help file. Use the Index to look up *Setup* or *Install*. Then, check under that heading to see whether there is an uninstall procedure.

Sometimes the removal program is located on the disk you used to install the program. In those cases, it might be necessary to rerun the application's setup program and then choose an uninstall option.

Always remember to try these options first. Never just drag a program from your hard drive directly to the Recycle Bin. Remember that dragging the program off will leave behind bits of refuse that can cause some stinky problems later.

Updating Windows

Microsoft is constantly working to tweak and perfect Windows. And aren't we lucky? This constant tweaking results in some additions and improvements to Windows, which are available on the Internet through something Microsoft calls the *Windows Update*. The Windows Update icon can be seen in Figure 19.6.

You need to do a couple of things for access to these updates:

- Register your copy of Windows 2000 with Microsoft.
- Get connected to the Internet.

FIGURE 19.6
The Windows Update, sitting proudly on top!

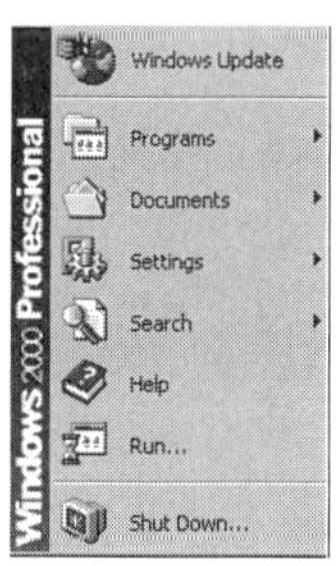

Registering your copy of Windows makes it possible for Microsoft to alert you when these updates are available. To make this really easy, Windows Update is located at the very top of the Start menu. Click the Start menu; then click Windows Update (see Figure 19.7).

FIGURE 19.7
The Windows Update page.

Windows Update was designed with the intention that you use it to constantly update your computer. You can look for outdated system files and automatically replace them with the most recent files.

Finding the New Updates

You can look at a variety of information about Windows, but to get specifics about Windows 2000, look for the heading *Need Help with Windows 2000?* and click on the Windows 2000 Professional link.

You're going to think that this next screen looks mighty familiar. It should. It's the Windows 2000 Help screen. This works just like the Help screen you met in Hour 5, "Getting Help." Double-click on the book to open up more topics. Double-click on the topic to reveal the information.

Updating Your Computer

If you so choose, Windows will go through the steps to update your computer whenever something new and exciting happens. You can participate in this update or just ignore it. It's your choice.

To find this update process, click Product Updates on the Windows Update page. A warning window—take a peek at Figure 19.8.

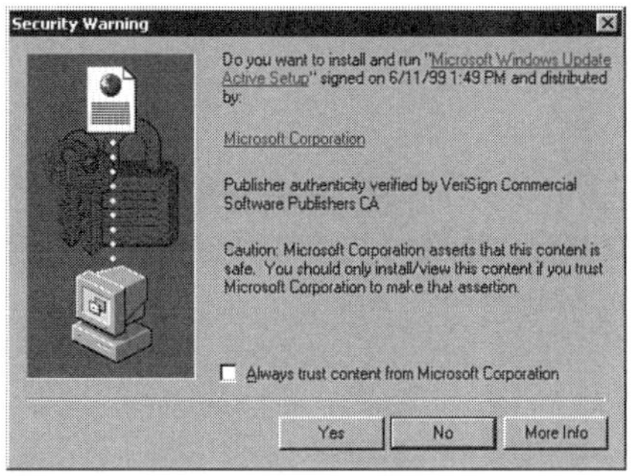

FIGURE 19.8
Hmm, better read this one.

My advice is that you click the More Info button and read about what is about to happen. In a nutshell, clicking the Microsoft Windows Update Active Setup preps your computer to accept new updates when they happen. Read the information carefully and then you can decide. Click yes if you want to do this. Click no if you don't.

Summary

This hour is dedicated to the task of adding to or taking away from what Windows originally gives you. You should be comfortable with installing and removing programs from your computer.

19

Q&A

Q Why doesn't all of Windows install?

A "All of Windows" is a big chunk of hard disk space, most of which you'll never use. Windows sets itself up on your computer with the programs you need the most. Other parts of Windows can be added later, but chances are, those parts aren't really crucial to your PC or to getting your work done.

Q Can I delete programs that Windows installed that I don't think I need?

A No. Don't ever remove a program you didn't install. Windows might have something on your system that you don't think is necessary, but regardless of what you feel, don't remove anything you didn't add.

Q How can I access Windows Update if I don't have the Internet?

A Alas, you cannot. Update CDs or Service Packs might be available through your dealer, but Windows Update is an Internet-only thing.

Workshop

The workshop includes quiz questions to help gauge your grasp of the material and exercises to help reinforce your learning. You'll find the answers to the quiz in Appendix A, "Answers."

Quiz

1. What icon in the Control Panel is used to add more programs to Windows?
2. How do you remove a program that's not in the list of programs Windows can remove?
3. What types of programs can you drag to the Recycle Bin?
4. *Bonus Question*: The properties of matter are solid, liquid, and gas. What do some scientists consider the fourth to be?

Exercises

1. Practice installing new software. Check the pile of stuff that came with your computer for a CD or game you can install.
2. Look through the Windows Components and see whether there's anything there you can't live without; then uninstall it.

Vocabulary

installation disk—The floppy disks or compact disks necessary to install a new program onto your hard drive. Sometimes also necessary to uninstall a program.

partially installed—The status of a program or component when only some of its components or subcomponents have been installed on your hard drive.

Windows Components Wizard—The wizard is your guide through the Windows Components dialog box.

Time Out 4

Something Everyone Can Play: Music

New computers typically come with great sound systems, even if you don't splurge and buy additional speakers or the 350-watt subwoofer. To take advantage of the speakers, I often pop a CD in the computer and listen to some tunes while I work the night away.

Let There Be Music!

To run this exercise, go to your stereo and grab a fun music CD, something funky and upbeat or relaxing and refreshing. No depressing music, please. Oh, and no punk rock.

To Do 4.1: Making Beautiful Music

1. Insert the CD in your CD-ROM.

   The dialog box in Figure TO4.1 appears, asking whether you want Windows to pull up all the Internet links for this particular CD. This could be about the album, the composer, and so on. If you're not connected to the Internet, none of this is going to help you. If you are connected, you might want to click OK in case you get an itch to do a little reading about the music you're listening to.

FIGURE TO4.1
Downloading music.

2. Click either OK or Cancel.

   If you click OK, you will see the Dial-Up Connection box (unless you're configured to have the Internet dial up automatically, explained in Hour 10, "Doing the Internet"). Click Connect to download the information.

3. Ahhhh, music!

   At the same time your computer is buzzing and whistling while it's connecting to the Internet (if you chose to download the information), your music starts to play. Keep reading to find out how to view this downloaded information.

> If your CD player doesn't automatically start for you, you can summon it from the Start menu: Choose Programs, Accessories, Entertainment, CD Player.

Using the CD Player

Your computer CD player looks remarkably like the one you'd find in your car (had you ordered that option instead of listening to your Uncle Walter, who told you it was a gyp). The controls are labeled and work exactly as they do on any stereo or Walkman. An example of your new CD player is shown in Figure TO4.2.

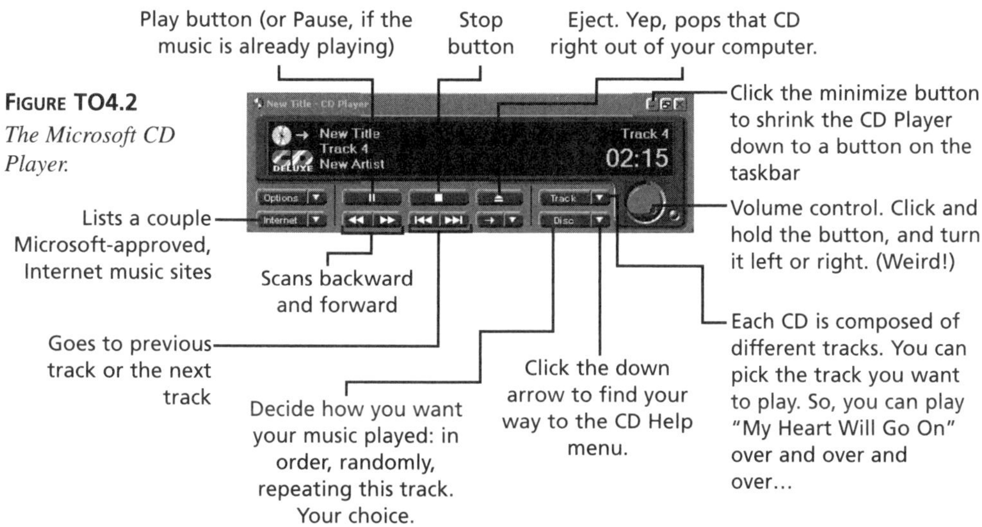

FIGURE TO4.2
The Microsoft CD Player.

Searching for Artists

This CD player is much more than something that plays music for you. It will also help you find information about your favorite artist or album you're listening to. After all, you can't know enough about your favorite Garth Brooks CD, now can you? The trick is that you have to be connected to that darn Internet thing. If you are "hooked to the net," keep going. If you need more information about the Internet, read Hour 10.

To Do 4.2: Finding Album Information

1. Insert your favorite CD into the CD-ROM.
2. Click OK to download information.

   This is in the New Album Found dialog box. Don't be surprised when music starts playing. You've also just started your CD.
3. Click the Internet button. A list of options appear, as shown in Figure TO4.3.
4. Choose what you want to view.

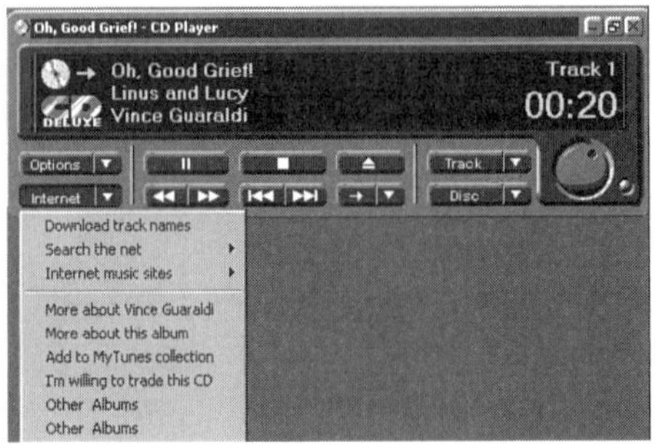

FIGURE TO4.3
Options to view from the Internet.

All the options in Figure TO4.3 are from my Vince Guaraldi CD "Oh, Good Grief"(as in *Oh Good Grief, Charlie Brown*). I can click any one of these options, and Windows will take me to that Internet site, where I can read more about Vince or this CD.

Before you do any of this, you should read Hour 10. The Internet lesson not only gives you direction about the Internet, but it also tells you how to disconnect from the Internet. Better yet, it walks you through the steps so that you will automatically be disconnected from the Internet when you exit. When you click OK to download information about your CD, your modem is on and you're online, hooked to the Internet—and there you will stay unless you disconnect yourself.

Creating Your Own List of Songs

Music can inspire us, give us an emotional lift, make us contemplate our reason for living. It's a powerful thing. I remember having an argument with a college professor who tried to reduce music to nothing but math. Yeah, right! Math? "No!" I said defiantly. Music is soul, spirit. It gives meaning to everything. Music expresses that for which words fail: emotion. This is why there can never be any successful visual equivalent to music; it motivates us at the soul.

Well, that being said (and getting a B– in the class), you might want to arrange the songs on your CD Player. They can be arranged to play in the order that makes you happy, gives you inspiration, brings up visions of math equations dancing in your head, or whatever.

To Do 4.3: Arranging Songs

To Do

1. Click Options.

   It's the button above the Internet button, in the lower-left corner of the CD Player window.

2. Click Playlist.

   On the Playlist tab, click the CD icon.

3. Click Edit Playlist.

   If you don't have a list to edit (some CDs don't have a list), click Create Playlist.

4. Click Clear All.

5. Click the track you want to add.

   This is done in the Available Tracks section.

6. Click Add to Playlist.

Keep repeating these last two steps until you have the list of songs in the order you want them. Your song list is saved in the Documents and Settings folder of your Profile folder. It's a database called deluxecd.mbd.

PART V
Maintaining Your System

Hour

HOUR 20

Fixing Up Your Disk Drives

When you think of the important parts of a computer, disk drives should be right up there with the monitor and keyboard. Surprising? Well, first of all, a disk drive is important to you because it's where you store your applications and all the data and documents you create. Second, much of what Windows does deals with disks (in fact, operating systems used to be called *disk* operating systems). So disks are, more or less, central to your PC's operation. Keeping them happy and healthy, therefore, is important—which is what this hour is all about.

The highlights in this hour include the following:

- The Disk Defragmenter
- Check Disk
- Scheduling maintenance

Time for a Disk Tune-Up

Windows 2000 does some pretty funky things to get information stored on your hard drive. To make room for all your files, Windows 2000 often takes advantage of empty spaces on the hard drive. It takes a file and splits it up—fragmenting the file into smaller pieces so that it fits better on the hard drive.

As the computer operator, you'll never know when a file has been fragmented; Windows re-assembles the file into one piece as it's loaded into memory. Still, that fragmenting and re-assembling takes time, which can result in a sluggish computer after a spell.

When a drive has more than 10 percent of its files fragmented, you should run the Disk Defragmenter tool. This is a special disk utility that puts fragmented files back together. The files are actually rewritten to the hard drive, which makes Windows access them more efficiently. In some cases, defragmenting a badly fragmented drive noticeably improves disk performance.

To Do 20.1: Running Disk Defragmenter

To Do

1. Double-click My Computer.
2. Right-click drive C.
3. Choose Properties from the menu.

> You also can reach the Disk Defragmenter Box by clicking on the Start button, choosing Programs, Accessories, System tools, and then clicking Disk Defragmenter.

4. Click the Tools tab to bring that panel forward.

   You'll see three tools listed as shown in Figure 20.1:

   - Error-checking—This runs Check Disk, the program that finds bad data and missing disk chunks. It's covered later in this hour.
   - Backup—No one uses this, although it's covered in Hour 18, "Maintaining and Cleaning Files."
   - Defragmentation—Aha! This is the one you want. It runs the Disk Defragmenter, which tunes up your disk's performance.

FIGURE 20.1
Drive (C:) Properties box.

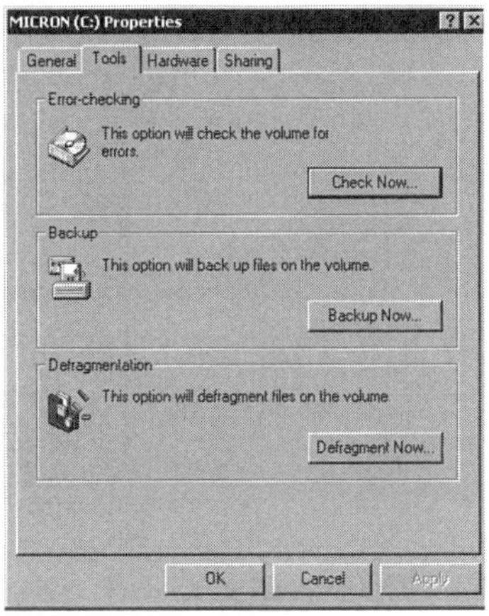

It would only be decent of me to let you know that this operation can take up to an hour or longer to complete, depending on how poorly fragmented your hard drive is. That's another good reason to stay on top of the disk clean up process.

5. Click Defragment Now.

FIGURE 20.2
The Disk Defragmenter busy at work.

Drive (C:). This is the drive being defragmented.

Drive (D:). You may not have two drives. That's OK. Information about your drive.

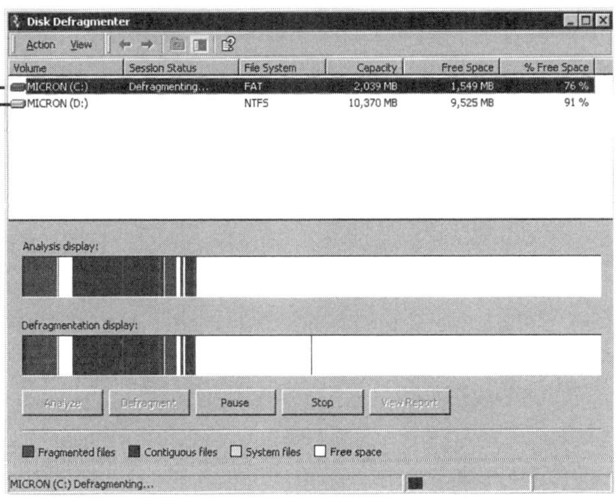

Windows starts working. You can just sit there and watch, but the Defragmenting Drive dialog box is boring. You can do other things while the defragment operation is going on. Doing so, however, slows down the defragmentation process. It's best just to sit and watch, or schedule defragmenting during lunch or after work.

6. The Defragmentation Complete box

   Figure 20.3 shows you this dialog box. But even more interesting is the Defragmentation display in the back. Notice that what was once a squiggle of red, blue, and white lines (oops, this is a black-and-white book—just trust me on this one) is all one color now. The Defragmentation process has put all things back in order. Harmony has been achieved.

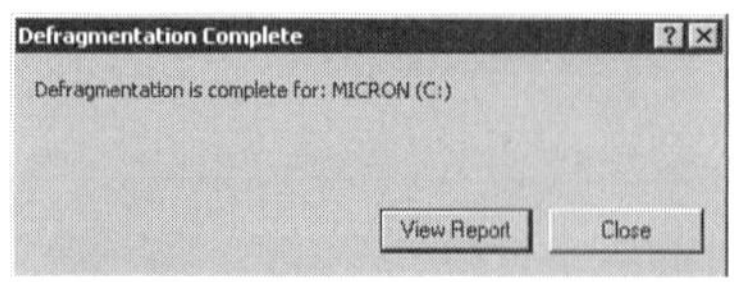

FIGURE 20.3
Defragmentation is complete.

7. Click View Report.

   Figure 20.4 lets you peek in on the report my computer gave me. Use the scroll bar on the right to see more of the report. These numbers may not mean a lot to you, but they are there to view.

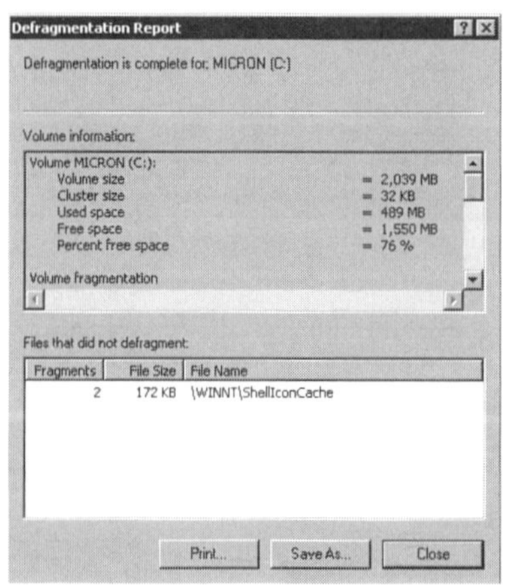

FIGURE 20.4
The final defragmentation report.

8. Click Print, Save As, or Close.

   You don't have to save or print this report. But, if you want to, you can compare all your reports with each other. Maybe, compare to see how messy you can make your hard drive.

9. Click the Close button.

You're done. You can leave the Drive C Properties dialog box open for the next section's tutorial if you like. Otherwise, click Cancel to close the Drive C Properties dialog box and close the My Computer window.

Defragment any hard drive: Right-click that drive, choose Properties from the shortcut menu and continue as described above. You should run the Disk Defragmenter at least once a week or so. Even if there are no files to defragment, or if you have a relatively new computer, you can still run the Defragmenter. It won't take as long as it might for older, more fragmented hard drives, but it still works.

Fine Tuning Your Hard Drive

In addition to other hard drive disorders, there's also the category of file foul-ups. For some reason, files get lost; bits and pieces of them fall off or something. This seems to happen at random and at unpredictable times. Fortunately, Windows has yet another tool for fixing these minor file boo-boos. It's called the Check Disk program, and it has almost spell-casting powers when it comes to fixing weird things that happen to files on your hard drive.

To Do 20.2: Running Check Disk

To Do

1. Open the My Computer icon on the desktop.
2. Right-click drive (C:).
3. Choose Properties from the Shortcut menu.

   This displays the Drive C Properties dialog box.
4. Click the Tools tab to ensure that the panel is forward.
5. Click Check Now.

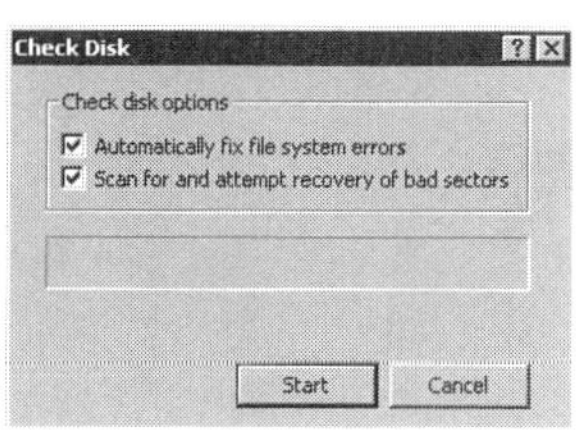

FIGURE 20.5
Pick one or both options.

6. Click each box to make a choice.

20

Your choices are

Automatically fix file system errors, which directs Check Disk to examine and repair any problems with the main (boot) part of the disk. (Windows stores vital information on that area.)

Scan for and attempt recovery of bad sectors, which scans the rest of the disk (beyond the file system) and repairs any problems there.

There's no harm in selecting both options, although it does save time to select one over the other if you know the other isn't the source of your woe.

Check Disk fires itself up. Very little happens at this point. A small box is shown with a thermometer going across to show you how long until the process is complete.

7. Disk Check Complete.

   Click OK.

8. Click Cancel to close the Drive C Properties dialog box.

You should run Check Disk at least once a week, more often if your hard drives are particularly fussy.

Note that Check Disk will not run if the disk is "busy," for example if you're using the disk to download a file or sort a database. Check Disk lets you know this and asks if you'd like to reschedule the disk checking for later.

Cleaning Your Disks

Disk drives don't exactly get dirty, but they do accumulate a lot of junk files. Your programs create temporary files for this or that, then forget to delete them. You accumulate all sorts of temporary files when you browse the Web, and Windows makes temporary files like the ocean makes foam. All that junk takes up space and can easily be removed to give you back that precious hard drive space. The tool that does that is called Disk Cleanup.

To Do 20.3: Running Disk Cleanup

To Do

1. Click the Start button.
2. Choose Programs.
3. Choose Accessories.
4. Choose System Tools.
5. Choose Disk Cleanup.
6. Select the drive you want to clean.

You can click the down arrow to choose from the list of drives available. Figure 20.6 gives an example of the drives to choose from.

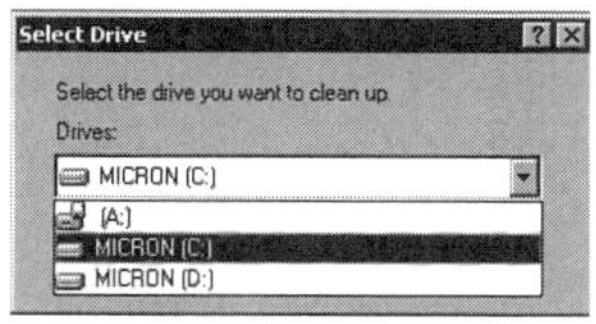

FIGURE 20.6
Cleaning up Drive (C:).

7. Click the drive you want to clean.

   The Disk Cleanup for your disk drive shows you how much disk space you can clean up by running this program.
8. Click the files you want to delete.
9. Click OK.

You should run Disk Cleanup every month or so, more often if you notice that available (free) disk space is decreasing at an alarming rate.

Scheduling Disk Maintenance

Using Windows 2000's disk maintenance tools is necessary, and using them often is always a good thing. It's part of using a computer, but a part most people tend to neglect. After all, you bought your computer to do work, not to be a hard disk maintenance operator. And, hey! Aren't computers supposed to make life easier?

What if the computer reminded you when to run disk maintenance programs? The thing has a clock, doesn't it? It would be simple for it (not you) to look at the clock and say, "Hey! Run Check Disk again!"

Better still, wouldn't it be nice, if instead of just reminding you, the computer suddenly went out and did it? What if, at a pre-appointed time, Windows 2000 suddenly decided to go run Check Disk without your telling it to do so? Nifty, huh?

Say hello to the Scheduled Tasks utility. It's a program that automatically schedules various routine disk operations, plus other chores, so that you don't have to lift a finger.

To Do 20.4: Scheduling Disk Maintenance

1. Click the Start button.
2. Choose Programs.
3. Choose Accessories.
4. Choose System Tools.

5. Choose Scheduled Tasks.

   The Scheduled Tasks box appears.

6. Double-click Add Scheduled Task.

   This starts the Scheduled Task Wizard. The next few steps are going to walk you through how to pick the tasks you want to run and the times you want to run them. Sounds easy enough.

7. Click Next.

8. Look for an appropriate task.

   There are two places to look. One is from the list of applications. The second is to click the Browse button and find the program you're wanting to schedule.

9. Choose Disk Cleanup from the application list.

   Choose this just as a practice run. Click Next.

10. Choose a time when you want to run this task.

    Click on one of the dots beside the date to choose a time.

11. Select the time and day.

    This dialog box looks different depending on which time you chose. Figure 20.7 shows an example of what you see if you choose the Monthly option. Click Next after you've picked your times.

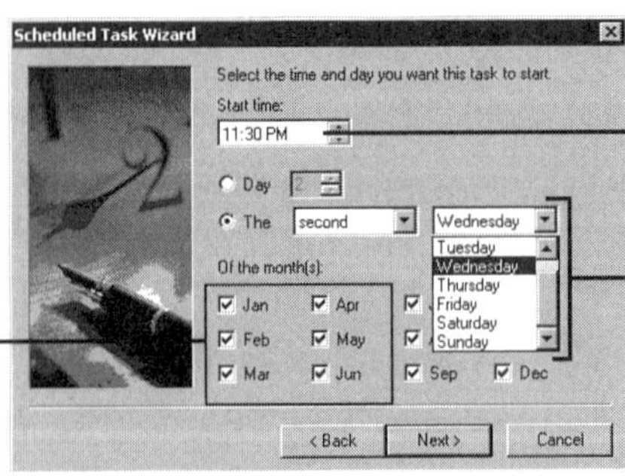

FIGURE 20.7
Picking times to run your program.

12. Enter your password.

    Type the password again to confirm you typed it right. Click Next.

    You'll get a final dialog box stating all the things you've established, such as the task and the time the task is to be completed.

> You'll want to pick a time when you're not doing anything with the computer. That's best.

The computer must be on for this to work. If you're used to turning off the computer when you're done working, the tasks will never be done. (I leave my computer on all the time, so I schedule tasks for early morning, long after I've gone to bed.)

13. Click OK.

The final box you see is the Scheduled Tasks dialog box, which shows the task you've scheduled. You'll also see a memo as to the scheduled date, the next time the program should run, and the last time it ran. Figure 20.8 shows the program just added. Notice the last runtime is Never (because the disk cleanup program was just added).

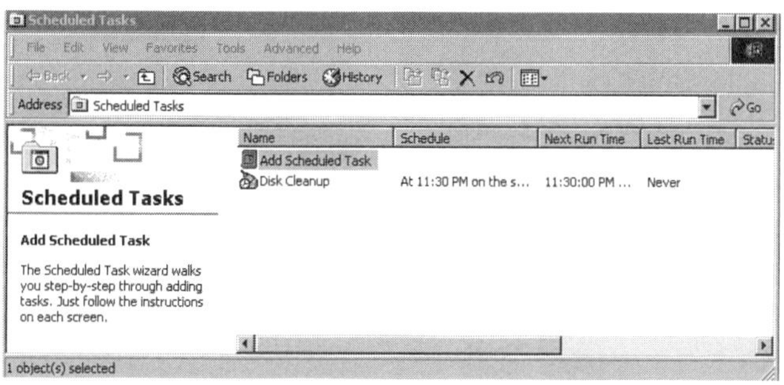

FIGURE 20.8
The Disk Cleanup program is scheduled.

With all the disk cleanup/maintenance programs Windows has, you can be confused about when, where, and how often to do this stuff. Luckily, I know your confusion. Table 20.1 lists the clean up programs and when you should use them.

TABLE 20.1 Cleaning Schedule (aka: Chore Chart)

Program	*Scheduled Time*
Disk Cleanup	Once a week
Disk Defragmentation	Once a month
Check Disk	Every week
Backup	Every week, daily if you change information often

System Information

You know how people like to brag about their computers? You know, what make and mode, how much memory they have, that sort of thing? Okay, maybe you don't need to brag, but often you'll need to know. Tech support might ask questions about your hardware, or you might need to know detailed information when buying an upgrade or to ensure that new software is compatible with your system. Microsoft has a special place for all that stuff. It's called the System Information.

To Do 20.5: Finding System Information

1. Click the Start button.
2. Choose Programs.
3. Choose Accessories.
4. Choose System Tools.
5. Choose System Information.

Figure 20.9 shows you all the secrets of my computer.

FIGURE 20.9
System Information Summary Sheet.

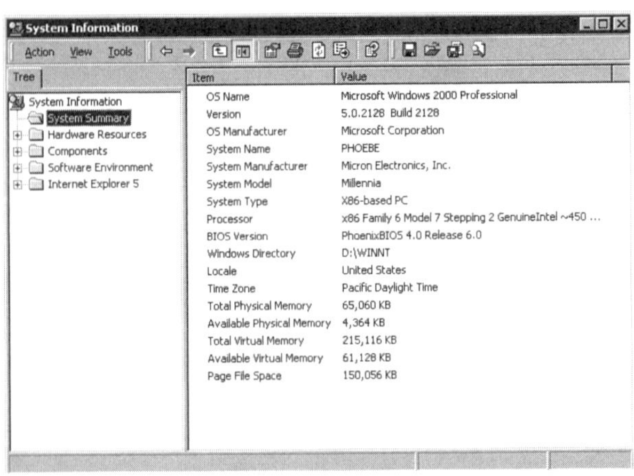

The process of reviewing this information is very similar to working with Windows Explorer. Click on a plus sign to open more folders and watch the information unfold on the right.

As practice, say your modem is acting up and you want to find out some information about your modem. Where do you go?

To Do 20.6: Finding Modem Information

▼ To Do

1. Click the Start button.
2. Choose Programs.
3. Choose Accessories.
4. Choose System Tools.
5. Choose System Information.
6. Click the plus sign next to Components.

   A whole list of options drops down.
7. Click Modem.

   And right before you eyes is a whole list of information about your modem. Device Type tells you whether you have an internal or external modem. Name tells you the make of your modem. All very interesting—most of it understandable, some of it questionable.
8. Click the Close button (X) when you are finished. ▲

Summary

This hour was dedicated to housework. Well, computer cleaning would be more like it. Although computers are supposed to make your life simpler, you still need to do your part in keeping your computer healthy.

Q&A

Q Can Check Disk determine if my PC has a virus?

A Alas, no. Check Disk merely corrects some occasional problems you might have with your hard drive. To fix viruses, you need third-party programs or utilities that scan for and correct virus problems. I can recommend both McAfee and Norton brands of virus protection, but ensure that you get programs that are compatible with your release of Windows 2000.

Q How can I prevent fragmentation?

A The answer is, "Never use your computer." Seriously, you shouldn't worry about it. Windows fragments for good reasons, and the Disk Defragmenter program fixes any sluggishness it causes. No, you'll always be in good shape with Windows 2000 and Defragmentation.

Q Will Disk Cleanup remove the history of Internet sites I've been to? If not, how can I get rid of some of those Web pages that Internet Explorer keeps a list of?

A One sure method to remove those history items is to access the Control Panel's Internet icon. Open it, then locate the Clear History button. Click that button to remove the backlog of Web pages you've been to.

Workshop

The workshop includes quiz questions to help gauge your grasp of the material and exercises to help reinforce your learning. You'll find the answers to the quiz and exercises in Appendix A, "Answers."

Quiz

1. What has happened when your files are fragmented?
2. Which files does Disk Cleanup remove?
3. Can Check Disk be made to operate automatically?
4. *Bonus Question*: What is the name of the monster in Mary Shelley's book *Frankenstein*?

Exercises

1. Work through the steps to run the disk defragmenter.
2. Work through the steps to run Check Disk.
3. Work through the steps to have your computer run Disk Cleanup every Thursday at midnight.
4. Do 10 pushups.

Vocabulary

disk drive—Where you store your applications and all the data and documents you create.

fragment—A piece of a file, one that Windows had to split up to better fit on the disk.

sector—The basic unit of storage on a disk drive. Disks are designated by disk number (or platter—there are several disks spinning in a hard drive), side of the disk, track on the disk, and sector on the track. This is all complex information, although the sector is the final, basic unit of storage on the disk drive.

HOUR 21

Adjusting the Screen

This hour is the tinker's dream. It's for those of you who like to tinker and mess with your computer in every way possible. There is probably very little in this hour that is going to help you be a more productive, smarter person, or more knowledgeable in any way that could ever impress anyone. But heck, it sure is a lot of fun to do this stuff!

The highlights in this hour include the following:

- Using the desktop Properties dialog box
- Altering the screen resolution
- Choosing a new color scheme
- Working with the Screen Saver
- Displaying icons

Starting with the Background

Changing the desktop in your office requires some woodworking skills, a lot of noisy equipment, and time. Changing the desktop in Windows only requires knowing where Windows hides the tools and, of course, time to mess with things.

Within the confines of your computer's monitor, you can do a lot to the desktop, spiffing and spaffing it up to reflect your personal tastes or a spur-of-the-moment whim. You can, for example, choose an exciting pattern for the desktop or an interesting graphical image appropriately called *wallpaper*. Figure 21.1 shows you a few examples of desktop patterns and wallpaper.

FIGURE 21.1
Desktop background examples.

Wallpapering the Desktop

When you want to change the way your desktop looks, you mosey on over to the Display Properties dialog box.

To Do

Task 21.1: Picking out Wallpaper

1. Right-click on a blank part of the desktop.

   This makes the desktop's shortcut menu appear (see Figure 21.2).

FIGURE 21.2
The desktop's shortcut menu.

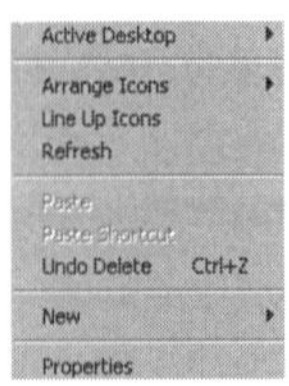

2. Choose Properties from the shortcut menu.

   The Display Properties dialog box appears (see Figure 21.3).
3. Click on the Background tab to bring this panel forward.
4. Browse through your choices.

   There is a long list of options. Click on each one to see a miniversion of what the desktop might look like. This is displayed on the minicomputer in the window.
5. Click on the one you like.
6. Click OK.

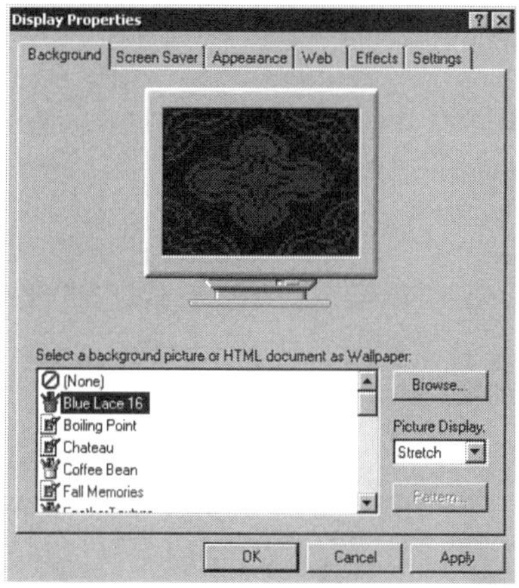

FIGURE 21.3
The Display Properties dialog box.

And your whole desktop is transformed. But whoa! That desktop background you just picked is way too busy for you. That's OK. Just go back to step one and start again, but choose a different background.

You can also play with the Picture Display area. Click on the down arrow and choose from Center, Tile, and Stretch. These change the way each of the wallpaper options looks. For example, if the picture of your cat is too teensy to fill the screen (and the Tile option is too frightening to the computer mouse), consider Stretch to make kitty fill the screen.

> You might select a wallpaper that requires what is known as an Active Desktop. When this happens, you'll see a notice of sorts, such as the one in Figure 21.4. Hour 16, "Organizing the Desktop," discusses the Active Desktop. If you want to review this topic, return there.

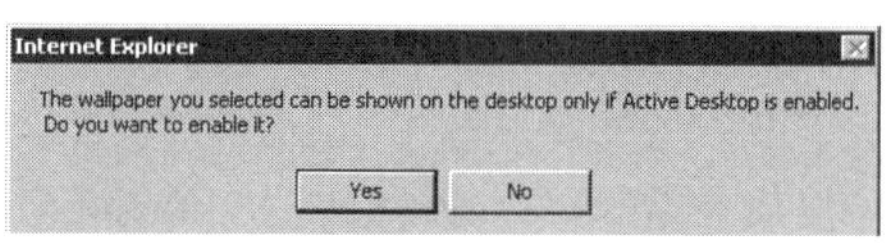

FIGURE 21.4
The Active Desktop notice.

All the Many Screen Options

Here's a tip you'll not often hear: It's possible to increase the size of your desktop without buying a larger monitor. Imagine your cozy 640×480 pixel lot enlarged to an 800×600—or even a 1024×768 pixel ranch—all without buying a new monitor or applying yoga-like stretching techniques to your current monitor! This can be really nice, allowing you to see more windows on the screen, more icons on the desktop, more of everything—without losing a penny.

To Do 21.2: Changing the Screen Area

1. Right-click on the desktop.
2. Choose Properties.
3. Click on the Settings panel to bring it forward. This panel appears in Figure 21.5.

Figure 21.5
The place to change your screen area.

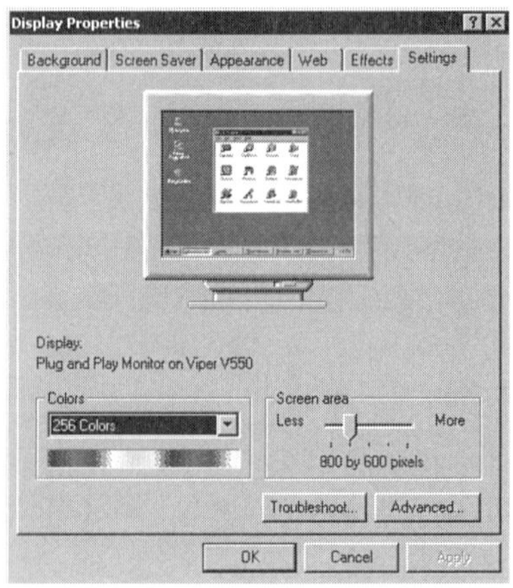

4. Choose a new resolution from the Screen area.

   Don't slam the slider all the way up to the highest value right away. Instead, settle on the next-highest resolution first. For example, drag the slider from 640×480 until you see 800×600 pixels displayed.
5. Click the Advanced button.

   If you choose a higher resolution, you might also want to choose Large Fonts from the Font Size area. Click the down arrow to see the list of options. Click OK when you've made your choices.
6. Choose a new color value from Colors.

   Click on the arrow to drop down the drop-down list. Go ahead and try each of one of the two other choices just to see the differences.
7. Click OK.

   You must click OK to secure any of your changes. Click Cancel if you're just playing around and want to leave things as they are.

As you increase the desktop's resolution, note that the number of colors available might decrease. It's a trade off; higher resolutions can require fewer colors in some computers. Lower resolutions guarantee more colors. So don't get frustrated trying to set both high resolution and colors at the same time. Some video systems just can't hack it.

Windows Color Scheme Can Match You!

Henry Ford once said that his customers could have any color car they wanted, as long as it was black. Bill Gates isn't as limited in his vision of the colors you use in Windows. You're free to change the drab on-screen colors of Windows as much as you like. Just about every element on the screen can be changed to another color, font, and size.

To Do 21.3: Changing the Color of Your Windows Screen

To Do

1. Right-click on your desktop.
2. Choose Properties.
3. Click on the Appearance panel to move it center stage.

   The Display Properties dialog box Appearance panel looks something like Figure 21.6. It shows several on-screen elements of Windows—colors, fonts, and whatnot. Each of these items can be changed, either individually or all at once by using some predefined schemes.

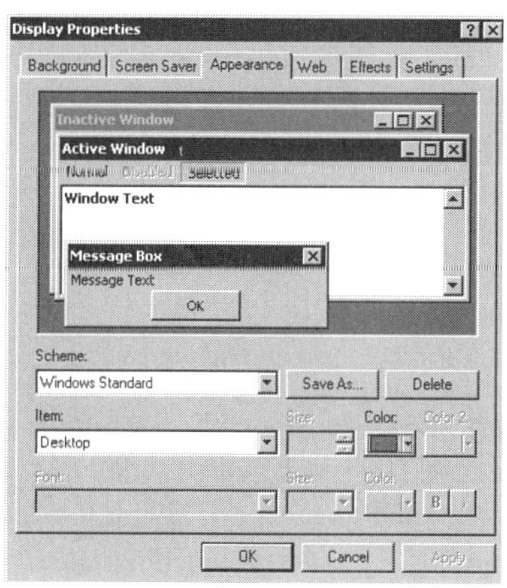

FIGURE 21.6
Windows Standard for the display boxes.

4. Preview new schemes.

   Use the drop-down list box below Scheme to display some of the color patterns dreamed up by the overly creative boys and girls at Microsoft. I suggest previewing Brick, Pumpkin, and Rose to sample the variety.

21

After choosing an option, you'll see how it would affect things in the preview window. If you find a color arrangement you like, move on to step 5. Otherwise, feel free to mess around. Remember: This is also a way to use the computer, so don't feel you're missing out on any serious work or anything.

5. Choose the item to color.

   The Item drop-down list contains all the different elements of Windows that you can tweak. It's easier, however, to change something by clicking with the mouse on that element in the preview window (at the top of the dialog box). For example, click on Active Window to change its colors, fonts, or size.

   You can also change the font in some of these options. However, if Font is dimmed, that means it doesn't apply to the element you've chosen. For example, there is no font associated with a window's background color.

   If you tend to play a lot in this area, click the Save As button to give your new color scheme a name. That way you can retain your choices for later.

6. Click the Apply button.

   If you've made horrible choices, go through these steps and try something new. Or if you're a traditionalist, Windows Standard is the way your computer was originally set up.

Help! Help! Save the Screen!

A Screen Saver is an archaic program designed to prevent something called *phosphor burn-in*. It was a problem that affected early monochrome and color PC monitors; if you left the monitor on for any length of time, eventually the screen image would "burn" into the phosphor.

The Screen Saver saved the screen by blanking-out the monitor, preventing an image from being burned into the phosphor. (Many early PCs often had images of WordPerfect or Lotus 1-2-3 that appeared on the screen even when the monitor was turned off!)

The early Screen Savers merely blanked the screen, erasing the image until you pressed a key, which made the image return. Then along came fancier Screen Savers that offered pictures or animated images—floating toasters and flying toast, for example. Watching a Screen Saver was more like playing a game (or watching laundry tumble in the dryer).

Today's monitors are better made than the earlier monochrome and RGB color monitors. Phosphor burn-in is no longer a problem, but the Screen Saver program survives as a fun pastime.

Setting a Screen Saver

Windows comes with a small selection of Screen Savers, and you can get more from the Internet by searching for *Screen Saver* at any popular search engine or file resource. To set a Screen Saver for your PC, you use the Display Properties box. There are two ways to get there.

To Do 21.4: Finding the Screen Saver Options

1. Double-click My Computer.
2. Double-click the Control Panel.
3. Choose the Display icon.

   The other option is to right-click on the desktop with your mouse, and then choose Properties from the menu.
4. Click on the Screen Saver tab to bring that panel forward.

The Screen Saver panel in the Display Properties dialog box is shown in Figure 21.7.

FIGURE 21.7
The Screen Saver settings area.

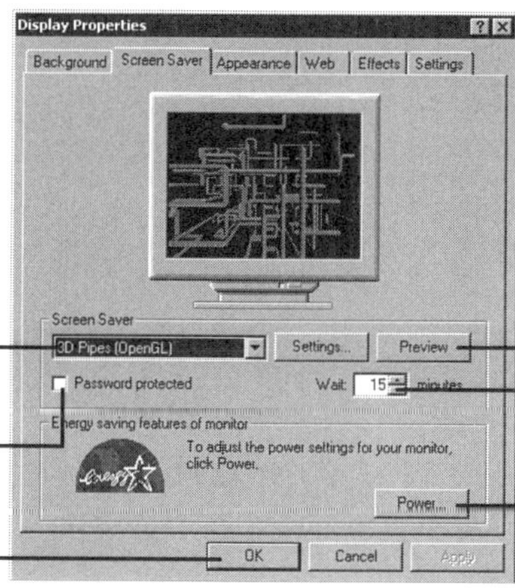

As with other parts of the Display Properties dialog box, the Screen Saver panel encourages play. Pick a Screen Saver, and then follow along below to play with your choice.

To Do 21.5: Choosing a New Screen Saver

1. Click on the arrow next to the name of the Screen Saver.

   A list of options rolls out. Your job is to decide what looks the most interesting or creative. Hmmm. This could be fun!
2. Choose Marquee Display.

This is where the fun starts. Each Screen Saver you choose has its own options for adjusting the graphics that you see. The options for adjustments are different for each Screen Saver, but we'll use the Marquee as an example.

3. Click the settings button.

   Again, refer to Figure 21.7 to find this.

   As you can see from Figure 21.8, you can adjust the position of the text, the speed at which it is flying across your screen (you might want to change that first), the background color, and even what the text says. You can even see that I've already made changes based on my personal preference.

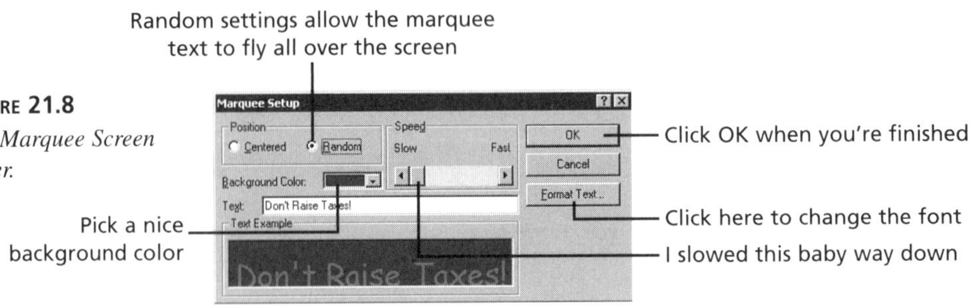

FIGURE 21.8
The Marquee Screen Saver.

4. Click OK.

   The preview window gives you an example of what you'll see.

5. Click the Preview button.

   Ah, the Screen Saver. Is this what you wanted?

6. Roll your mouse around.

   This gets rid of your Screen Saver, and you're back at the Display Properties box. If everything looks good, click OK, and you're finished. If you want to tweak and play more, go back and play.

> The number between the words *Wait* and *minutes* is the place where you can type in how many minutes you want your computer to sit idle before the Screen Saver kicks in.

There are two ways to restore the screen after a Screen Saver kicks in: press any key on the keyboard or jiggle the mouse. If you want to press a key on the keyboard, the Ctrl key is the safest one to press. Pressing Enter, Esc, or even the Alt key can actually trigger some application. The Ctrl key doesn't affect any application, making it the best key to press.

> If you're in a habit of just sitting there and reading Web pages on the Internet, choose a value higher than 15 minutes.

The Sleepy Monitor

Your monitor has a very special capability: It can turn itself off and go into a special low-power mode. The screen goes blank—just as a Screen Saver does—and you save energy at the same time.

To Do 21.6: Putting Your Monitor to Sleep (Shhh!)

1. Open the Control Panel.
2. Open the Display icon.
3. Click on the Screen Saver tab.

   If your monitor is capable of sleeping, you'll see a special Energy Saving Features of Monitor section at the bottom of the Display Properties dialog box (see Figure 21.8).
4. Click Power.

   The Power Options Properties dialog box appears, as shown in Figure 21.9. I have my monitor sleep after 20 minutes of computer inactivity (no typing or mouse movements).

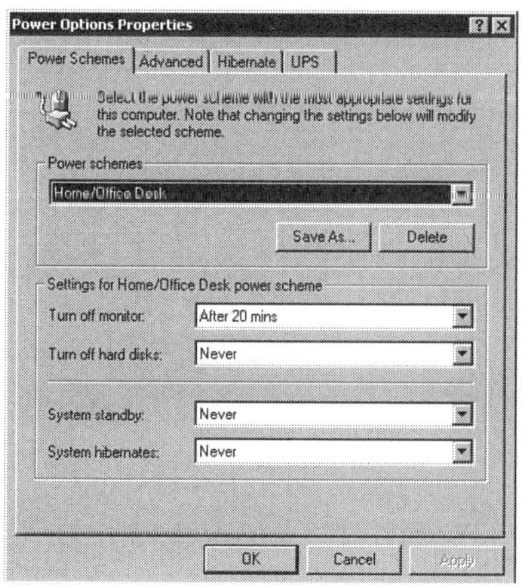

FIGURE 21.9
The Power Options Properties dialog box.

Click the down arrows next to each of these to pick a time.

- Turn off monitor: This turns off your monitor, meaning that the Screen Saver is also turned off. By the way, if you have a Screen Saver that plays sounds, the sounds continue to play even if your monitor sleeps. That's because the monitor is turned off, but not the computer. If you've set the computer to sleep as well, it won't play the sounds.
- Turn off hard disks: This literally stops the hard drives from spinning, which saves power. This option still keeps the computer's electronics on and ready.
- System Standby and System Hibernates: For more information on what Standby and Hibernates mean, refer back to Hour 2, "Let's Get Ready To Rumble…!" These are both different types of options when you want your computer to wait for your return.

> Not every computer can handle sleep mode well. Some of the newer models and laptops do just fine. But if you have any problems with sleep mode, such as the computer becoming comatose and not waking up (forcing you to reset), forget about sleep mode. Instead, just turn off the monitor when you're away for a spell. Shut down the computer instead of sleeping it.

Altering Your Icons

This section is the true computer users' playground. As if you haven't learned enough tinkering, you can also change the way your desktop icons look. Yes, it's true.

To Do 21.7: Changing the Desktop Icons

1. Open the Display properties box.

   The steps are listed earlier in this chapter if you need a quick reminder.
2. Click on the Effects tab.

   Figure 21.10 illustrates the Effects tab. What you see is the current list of desktop icons. Luckily, you don't have to live with this list.
3. Click once on the icon you want to change. For now click My Computer.
4. Click the Change Icon button.

   Figure 21.11 shows you a list of possible icons.

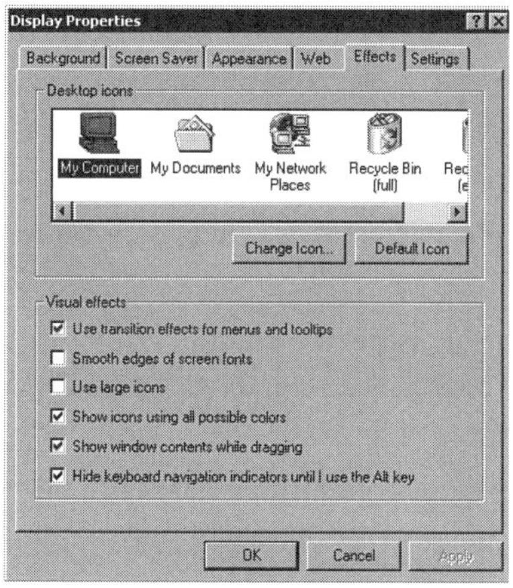

FIGURE 21.10
The Effects tab of the Display Properties box.

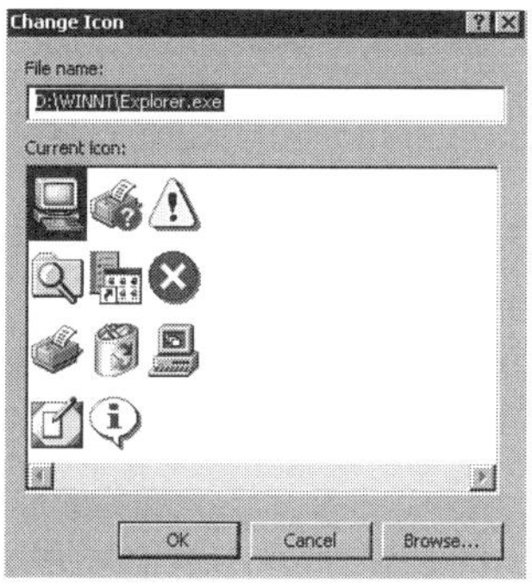

FIGURE 21.11
Change Icon dialog box.

5. Click once on a new icon.
6. Click OK.

   You now have a new My Computer icon. You can see in the list of Desktop icons that the My Computer icon has been changed. Very nice!
7. Click OK when you are finished playing.

Summary

This hour was dedicated to pure play and fun—changing your color scheme, selecting a Screen Saver, and changing your desktop icons. This is serious business!

Q&A

Q How can I get the original Windows color scheme back?

A Return to the Display Properties dialog box, click the down arrow next to Scheme, and choose the Windows Standard item from the list. That restores your desktop to the way it was when Windows first came out of the box.

Q When I am picking a color scheme, are there any colors that don't well work on a computer?

A This is a personal preference, but be careful not to turn everything into one color—for example, making the background and the text all blue. You won't be able to read what you see on your monitor.

Q What if someone else using the computer hates my new color settings?

A This is Windows 2000. Others using the computer should have their own logons and personal information. Your settings will not change their settings. See Hour 15, "Juggling Multiple Users," for information on having more than one person use the computer.

Workshop

The workshop includes quiz questions to help gauge your grasp of the material and exercises to help reinforce your learning. You'll find the answers to the quiz and exercises in Appendix A, "Answers."

Quiz

1. How do you give yourself a larger work area on your screen?
2. How do you change the color scheme of your computer?
3. What was the original purpose of the Screen Saver?
4. *Bonus question*: In Nigeria, all twins have to be given the same names. What are they?

Exercises

1. Click the Settings tab in the Display properties box. Now, click the Settings tab to bring it forward. Play with the colors and screen area to adjust your screen. Remember what settings your screen has now so you can put things back if you don't like the results.
2. Use the color scheme process to change your desktop to a rose color.
3. Activate a Screen Saver.

Vocabulary

pixel—A dot on a computer screen. The dots can be any number of colors, and hundreds of dots on a typical screen clump together to form an image.

scheme—A collection of settings for Windows, which includes colors, fonts, sizes, and other information that describes the screen. You can use predefined schemes for the display or design and save your own.

Screen Saver—A program that runs after a period of inactivity, disguising or blanking out the screen. A practical utility in days gone by, Screen Savers today are mostly diversions that tell you the computer is bored.

sleep mode—The capability of a computer to turn off pieces of hardware after a period of activity to save electricity. Originally created for laptops to save battery life, sleep mode can be used on desktop computers to save power by shutting off the monitor, hard drives, or the entire computer after a period of inactivity or on command.

Hour 22

Those Fabulous, Fantastic Fonts

A font is a type style. It defines the way text looks both on the screen and when your document is printed. Windows comes with a host of fonts, and you can add your own to the mix. By using fonts carefully and creatively, you can add weight or spice to any document you create—even silly things like grocery lists or employee memos. It can be fun.

The highlights in this hour include the following:

- Using fonts
- Installing new fonts
- Previewing your fonts
- Removing cruddy old fonts

Finding the Fonts

Fonts are basically different styles of type you can see on the screen, use in documents, and send off to the printer. With Windows 2000, fonts have collected themselves in one location. Working with and organizing fonts is now a lot easier and a lot saner than it ever was. It's all worthy of a good look.

Using Fonts

Fonts are *applied* to any text you write in Windows. Typically the Font command is found in the Format menu, although some programs use a toolbar drop-down list of fonts. If you change a font, that change will apply to any selected text or, if no text is selected, to any new text you write.

The font's name describes the font's overall appearance.

The Courier font is a basic, easy-to-read typing font.

The Times font is popular for text and easy to read.

Arial is a font used for headings and titles.

The Courier font is an example of a monospaced font. Each character takes up the same space as other characters in the font. So an M is as wide as the lowercase I.

Times is an example of a proportionally spaced font, which is easy to read and professional-looking. Each character takes up only as much space as it needs to.

Times is also an example of a *serif* font. There are small jots and tittles on the ends of the characters, which are called serifs. They make reading easier.

Arial is an example of a *sans serif* font, which lacks the jots and tittles of a serif font. These fonts are best suited for headlines and titles. Because they are harder to read, sans serif fonts aren't well-suited to text.

Beyond the techy descriptions of a font, there are font attributes. These are usually **bold**, *italics,* a ***combination of both,*** or `underline`. Sometimes there are separate fonts for these attributes. For example

- Bookman Old Style
- Bookman Old Style Bold
- Bookman Old Style Italic
- Bookman Old Style Bold Italic

It's usually best to choose the proper font for whichever attribute you want. A specifically chosen font looks better than one you get when you simply tell Windows to make a font bold.

Finally, fonts have size. The size is measured in points, and there are 72 points to an inch. The typical size for most text is either 10 or 12 points, which is a good reading size. Smaller point sizes are harder to read, and larger sizes tend to get obnoxious—although the larger sizes are good for headlines and titles.

All this is rather basic font stuff. What's more interesting is discovering where Windows puts your computer's fonts, how to add more to the lot, or how to remove those you no longer use (which frees up disk space and system resources).

Where the Fonts Are

Windows fonts are kept in their own Font folder, which you can easily get to from the Control Panel. Here's how:

To Do 22.1: Finding the Fonts Folder

1. Open the Control Panel.
2. Double-click on the Fonts folder to open it.

   You'll see its contents displayed, as shown in Figure 22.1. That's the Big Icon view in the figure; as with any other My Computer window, you can change the view to something else.

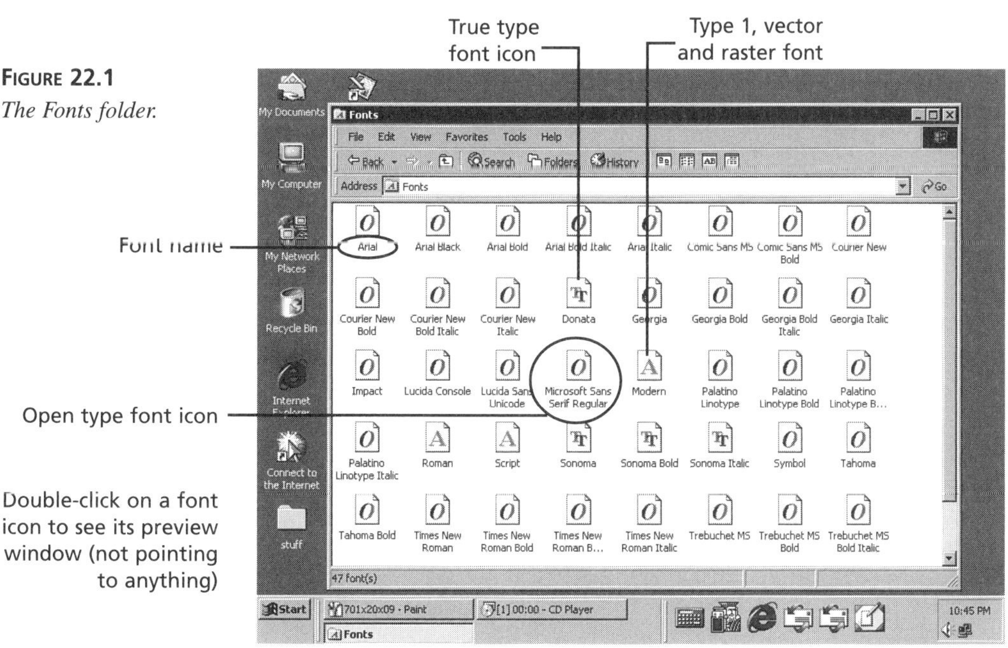

FIGURE 22.1
The Fonts folder.

If the Fonts window is a little busy for your taste, you can choose View and then Hide Variations to cut out the similar fonts All you're left with are the true originals.

Playing with Your Fonts

By having all your fonts in one handy folder, Windows lets you easily peruse the lot, managing and previewing fonts as you need to. This makes it very handy for those times you sit and agonize over fonts (which is a lot more often than you'd think).

Can You Name That Font?

A font, by any other name, would still look the same. But there are different types of fonts for different computer needs. The following list describes some of the font types you might find lurking in the Fonts folder:

- TrueType font. These are the bread and butter fonts, which appear on the screen exactly as printed. They can be stretched or shrunk to any size.

FIGURE 22.2

- Open type font. An improvement upon the basic TrueType font, which looks even better in various sizes.

FIGURE 22.3

- Type 1, vector and raster font. This is also known as the screen font or fixed font. It is an older type of font, primarily used by old Windows applications. It looks good only in a few sizes (as shown by the font's name, such as Courier 10,12,15, which looks good only at 10, 12, and 15 points). The raster type of fonts are designed with a specific size and resolution and cannot be scaled or rotated.

FIGURE 22.4

Other types of

fonts exist as well. For example, your computer might have PostScript fonts, which are designed for use with PostScript printers. These fonts typically live in another folder and have their own utility for font management.

Previewing Your Fonts

To see what a font looks like—the sneak preview—double click on its icon in the Fonts folder. You'll see a special Quick View window displaying all sorts of details, as shown in Figure 22.5.

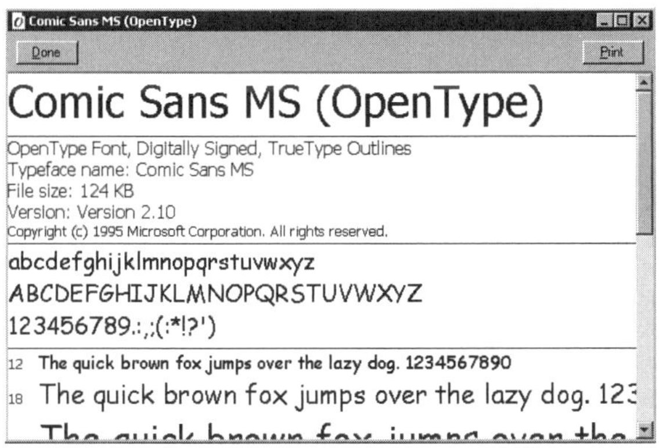

FIGURE 22.5
A sample of Comic Sans—my favorite!

When you examine a font, look for certain special characters such as subtle differences in the appearance of the letters. Pay close attention to the lowercase G for example. Also, look at the big W and the big Q. Even if you think one font is the same as another font, those letters will most likely be different.

Adding Fonts to Your Collection

New Fonts are added to your system using a special command in the Fonts window. You can actually add fonts from one of three places: A Fonts CD-ROM or floppy disk, from the Network, or from the Internet.

To Do 22.2: Adding Fonts from a CD-ROM or Disk

▼ To Do

1. Insert the floppy disk or CD-ROM.
2. Open up the Fonts window.
3. Choose File.
4. Choose Install New Font.

The Add Fonts dialog box appears (see Figure 22.6).

FIGURE 22.6
The Add Fonts dialog box.

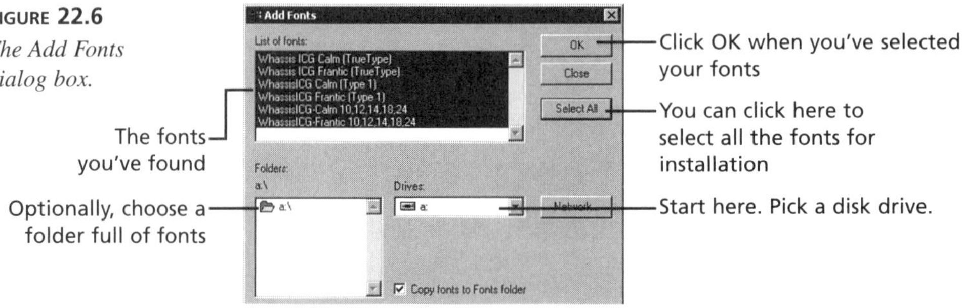

5. Find the fonts.

   Where are you getting these fonts? If you have a disk or CD, click on the drive name. For Figure 22.6, the fonts are coming from a floppy disk, so drive (A;) was chosen. The list of fonts appears in the window. It will take Windows awhile to read in the font names. Be patient.

6. Select the fonts you want.

   You can either Control + click on each font (hold the Control key down and pick each font individually with the mouse) or click the Select All button if you want to select all the fonts that are offered.

7. Click OK.

Windows shows you a brief dialog box that says your fonts are being loaded. Lo and behold, they are now listed in your Fonts window. You might have to scroll around and find them. Figure 22.7 shows the new Whassis fonts just added.

FIGURE 22.7
The new Whassis font.

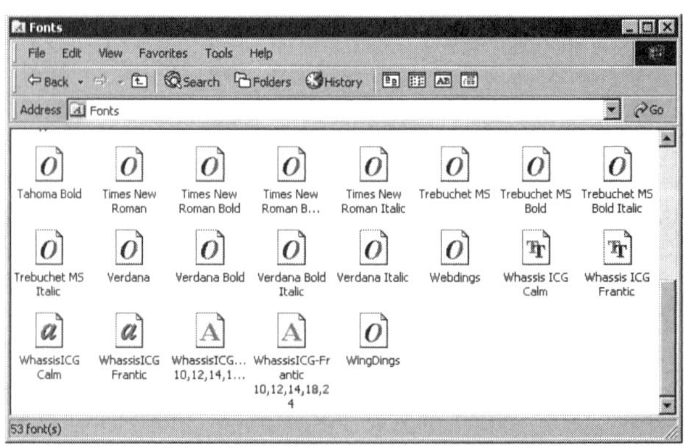

To Do 22.3: Adding New Fonts from the Network

▼ To Do

1. Open up the Fonts window.
2. Choose File.
3. Choose Install New Font.

   The Add Fonts dialog box appears.
4. Click the Network button.

   Lo! The Map Network Drive box we met in Hour 14, "Using the Local Network."
5. Click the Browse button.

   Find the drive and folders where the new fonts live. You might need to refer back to Hour 14 to remember this process. Click the Fonts file to highlight it. Then click Finish.
6. Select the fonts you want to keep.

   Remember, hold the Control key down while clicking on the fonts you want to select.
7. Click OK.

▲

And there they go! All your pretty new fonts.

Printing Hard Copies of Fonts

If you're a big font user, meaning that you like to try lots of different styles of fonts, you might want to print a hard copy of all your fonts. This saves you the repeated process of opening each font to see what it looks likes, closing the font, opening another.

To Do 22.4: Printing a Font Sample

▼ To Do

1. Open the Fonts folder.
2. Double-click one of the fonts to the preview window.
3. Click the Print button.

   A Print dialog box opens.
4. Choose your printer.
5. Click Print.

You'll have to go through each font, one by one, and do this with each one. Put the hard copies in a folder for safekeeping. When you have to decide which font you want to use, just flip through the folder.

▲

Places to Find Other Fonts

Those 10 million fonts-on-a-CD-ROM disk things are neat. And some places charge Big Money for specialty fonts. But there are still fonts to be had for free, and the place to find them is usually the Internet.

You can search for fonts using any Internet search engine. Because the location and reliability of these places is constantly in question, I'm not going to list any specific font locations here. The results from any search engine, however, should be enough to get you some fonts.

Some places even sell fonts on the Internet. You enter a credit card number, and then you download a professional font to your computer.

Removing Boring, Ugly Fonts

Fonts can accumulate on your computer like old socks in a drawer. Although this can give you a nice variety of fonts, you'll also get a lot of duplicates or even fonts you'll never use. These occupy disk space, and loading them all means your applications slow and Windows loses memory.

To Do 22.5: Giving the Boot to Excess Fonts

1. Open up the Fonts window.
2. Select the font(s) you want to kill off by clicking on them.
3. Choose File from the menu bar.
4. Choose Delete.

   A warning box appears, asking if you're sure you want to delete the font.
5. Click Yes.

Argh, Mate, the font be gone!

> As an alternative, you could consider *moving* the font to another location. For example, you could copy excess fonts to a Zip disk or another hard drive. Windows loads only those fonts installed into the Fonts folders. If you put them anywhere else, they won't use system resources (but they still use disk space).

Treasury of the Character Map Program

Opening a Font icon lets you preview the font, but it doesn't let you use any of the amazing characters you can find there. For example, locate the Wingdings icon in the Fonts folder. The preview window shows you many of the delightful characters in this decorative font, but you cannot select the character in the window; and even if you could, there's no Copy command available. Drat!

Thank heavens for the Character Map program. Not only does it preview all the characters in a font, it lets you copy them to be pasted elsewhere.

To Do 22.6: Using the Character Map

1. Click the Start button.
2. Choose Programs.
3. Choose Accessories.
4. Choose System Tools.
5. Choose Character Map.

   Figure 22.8 shows the path to get to the Character Map.

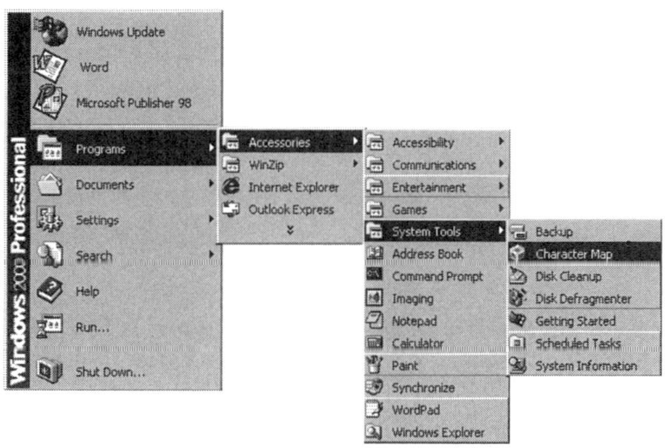

FIGURE 22.8
The path to a good Character (Map).

The Character Map program appears, looking similar to Figure 22.9.

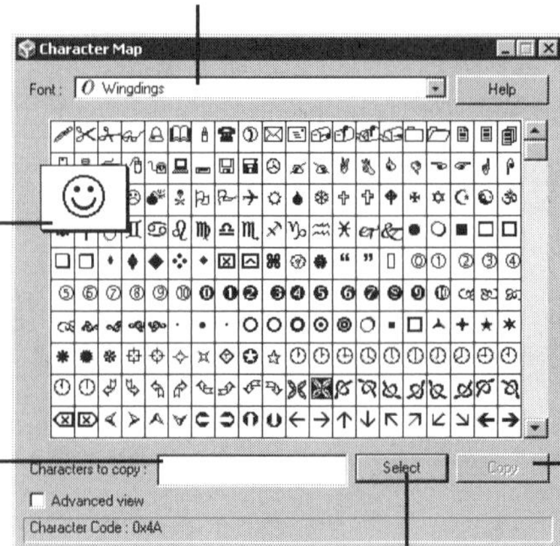

FIGURE 22.9
The Wingdings characters.

6. Choose *Wingdings* from the *Font* drop-down list.

   All the characters in the Wingdings font appear in the Character Map grid.

7. Aim the mouse pointer at a character. Press and hold down the mouse button.

   The character you're pointing at is magnified so you can better see it. In Figure 22.10, I'm highlighting the smiley face guy.

8. Double-click the smiley face guy.

   After double-clicking, that character appears in the Characters to Copy text box. You can continue double-clicking additional characters to insert if you like.

9. Click Copy.

   The smiley character is copied into the Windows clipboard.

10. Click Close.

    The Character Map program goes away.

11. Start WordPad

Before you type, you need to do some formatting. Click the Center tool. Choose a font size of 48 (gotta make it big). Choose Arial from the Font drop-down list. Type `You're Fired!` Press Enter to start a new line of text. Press Ctrl+V to paste the smiley face.

If the smiley shows up too small, select him and choose 48 from the Font Size drop-down list. Your pretty sign should look something like Figure 22.10.

FIGURE 22.10
Great Smile!

In Microsoft Word, you can choose Insert and then Symbol from the Word menu to see a dialog box similar to the Character Map program. You can use that dialog box to insert special characters right into your document.

Summary

This hour was dedicated to the fun and fantastic world of fonts. Fonts add power and expression to your documents, so having and using them properly is important to getting the most from Windows.

Q&A

Q How many fonts can I put into a document?

A The proper answer would be: As many as are necessary. However, as a general rule, try not to use more than three fonts in any document. More than that (unless you are a designer who does such things for a reason) and your document looks amateurish. No, stick to one font for headlines and titles, another for the text, and maybe a third to add some spice.

Q How come I can see some fonts in one program that don't appear in another?

A Some programs have their own, private font stash. Adobe Illustrator, for example, uses its own special fonts that are not available in any other (nonAdobe) program. Also, some applications may filter out the screen fonts and other fancy fonts they don't want you to use.

Q The fonts vanish when I paste text!

A Not every Windows program uses fonts. For example, Notepad doesn't use fonts, so any text you paste into Notepad will appear as raw text only—without fonts or other formatting information. However, pasting the text into a program that understands fonts will yield properly formatted text.

Workshop

The workshop includes quiz questions to help gauge your grasp of the material and exercises to help reinforce your learning. You'll find the answers to the quiz and exercises in Appendix A, "Answers."

Quiz

1. Where is the fonts folder located?
2. How do you preview a font?
3. What is the path to get to the Character Map program?
4. *Bonus Question*: In 1952, who was offered presidency of Israel?

Exercises

1. Make a hard copy of several fonts. As a tip, print the font information out on three-hole paper so you can clamp it in a binder. (You don't have to print all your fonts, because that would be very time consuming. But printing out a few every day will accomplish the task in a few weeks or so.)
2. Install new fonts either through the network or with a font disk.
3. Locate a font you don't use and copy it to the My Documents folder (for safe keeping). Start an application to confirm that the font is no longer available.

Vocabulary

font—A type style. The way text appears on the screen and when printed in Windows.

point—The height of a font. There are 72 points in an inch, so a font 72 points high would be one inch tall. Most users, however, set their fonts to 10 or 12 points.

Sans serif—A font that's useful for headlines or titles, but not as easy to read as a serif font.

Serif—A type of font that's easy to read thanks to various embellishments on the ends of the letters.

typeface—The official typesetter's name for a font. (They're actually called typefaces. A font is a specific typeface, such as Optima Oblique.)

HOUR 23

Installing and Removing Hardware

As you grow to love your computer, you'll find yourself buying it gifts. You may even wrap them and present the gifts to the computer in a surprising manner. "Look what I have for you!" as you flash the PC its new scanner. "Aren't we excited?" you gush.

New hardware happens. You may add a new peripheral, upgrade an external modem, buy a new printer, or take advantage of a new digital camera. Whatever! Windows 2000 needs to know about its new toy. This is the software side of the hardware add-on. Fortunately, Windows uses a special hardware wizard, which makes installing new hardware fairly pain-free.

The highlights in this hour include the following:

- Working with USB devices
- Adding hardware
- Removing hardware
- Troubleshooting hardware problems

Before You Start

Not just anyone can go off on a binge and start installing hardware. I mean, that would just mean mass chaos. You must be logged on as an administrator or a member of the Administrator's group in order to be in the oh-so-important position to install hardware.

If your computer is connected to a network, you may also be prevented from installing hardware. You'll need to ask the person who is in control of your network what your options are. However, if you're a private computer user, hey, go for it (although even as a private user, you need to be logged in as an administrator)!

The USB

The first step in installing hardware is to find out what your computer is capable of when installing hardware. The first thing you need to find out is if you have a USB.

A USB (Universal Serial Bus) is an external piece of hardware that supports what is called *Plug and Play* installation. Using USB, you can connect and disconnect devices without using a screwdriver or shutting down your computer.

Besides the nifty Plug and Play feature, you can connect up to 127 USB gadgets to your computer, including speakers, telephones, CD-ROM drives, joysticks, tape drives, keyboards, scanners, cameras, and even more. Now, that's a lot of gadgets!

> A USB port is a piece of hardware located on the back of your computer. That's for those of you who want to know what is stuck to your computer's backside!

You can easily find out if your computer is equipped with a USB.

To Do 23.1: Finding the USB

1. Open My Computer.
2. Open the Control Panel.
3. Double-click the System icon.
4. Click the Hardware tab.

   This brings the Hardware tab forward.
5. Click the Device Manager button.

   This is located in the center of the page under the Device Manager section.

6. Look for Universal Serial Bus controllers.

   This is your complete list of the devices that are on your computer. If you want to know more about each option, click the plus button next to the icon. This opens that section for more detail (see Figure 23.1).

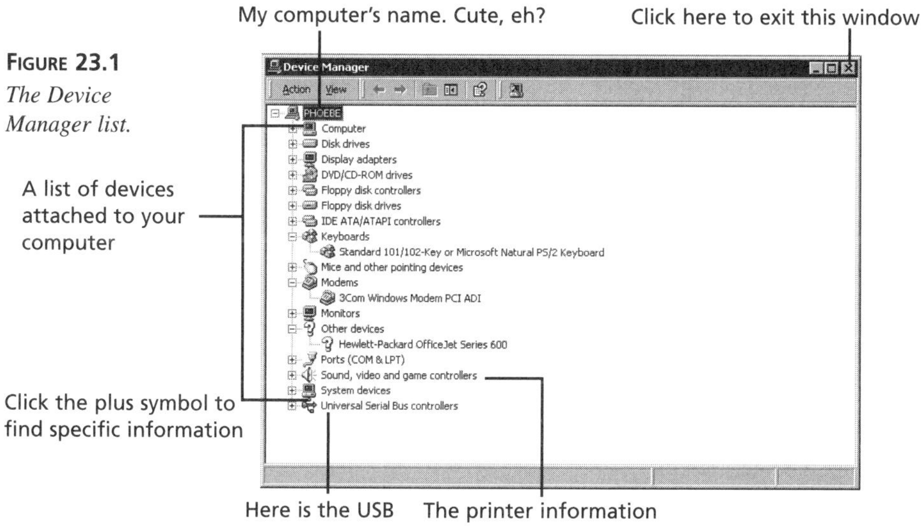

FIGURE 23.1 *The Device Manager list.*

Plug and Play

Plug and Play is just what it sounds like. It enables you to plug in your new computer toy and play with it without painful installation nonsense. The computer automatically detects newly installed Plug-and-Play hardware and configures the appropriate software (called *device drivers*). This saves you from all the techy computer work that is really no fun. So you plug in your new hardware, and then you can play!

Adding a New Peripheral to Your Computer

Pretty much anything you add to your computer these days follows the plug-and-play standard, which means installation will be a snap. If it's a USB something-or-other, it's definitely Plug and Play. Other hardware is harder to tell, although it should say *Plug and Play* on the box. Older hardware may or may not be detected by Windows the same way as Plug-and-Play stuff. But, on the whole, you probably don't want to install older hardware on a PC running something as sophisticated as Windows 2000. This may encourage you to get into the habit of buying a new piece of hardware rather than using an older version that your Uncle Chet gave you because he was bored with it.

To Do 23.2: Installing Hardware

1. Install your hardware.

   If you're installing a USB option, just plug it in. Windows 2000 should recognize it and configure the hardware just fine. If the USB port doesn't see the hardware, check to ensure that the hardware is turned on; some devices—scanners, monitors, and the like—must be turned on before the USB port recognizes them.

   If you're installing any other external items or internal options, turn off the computer. Refer to the hardware instructions for proper installation procedure. (I can't cover everything here.)

2. Turn on the computer.

   Obviously, this step is optional for installing a USB device.

   If you did install a USB device, there is a remote chance you may be asked to restart Windows. Do so.

   At this point, the Hardware Wizard should run, configuring the new hardware you just added. If not, you'll have to manually run the wizard.

3. Close all open programs.

   When you get into the Add/Remove Hardware Wizard, it's going to tell you to close all programs, so you might as well do it now.

4. Double-click My Computer.
5. Double-click the Control Panel.

6. Double-click the Add/Remove Hardware icon.

   This starts the Add/Remove Hardware Wizard. This wizard walks you through the steps of installing the program that goes along with the hardware you just installed.

7. Click Next in the Add/Remove Hardware Wizard box.
8. Choose a hardware task.

   The first option is already chosen for you: Add/Troubleshoot a Device. You are adding a device.

9. Click Next.

   You'll see a brief notice that your computer is looking for the Plug and Play feature, as shown in Figure 23.2.

10. Add a new device.

    This is where you choose the piece of hardware you just installed. Read carefully through this list of hardware. You might even compare this list of technical terms with your hardware manual so that you get the names right.

    If your hardware *is not* listed, click Add a New Device and keep following along.

FIGURE 23.2
Looking for your hardware.

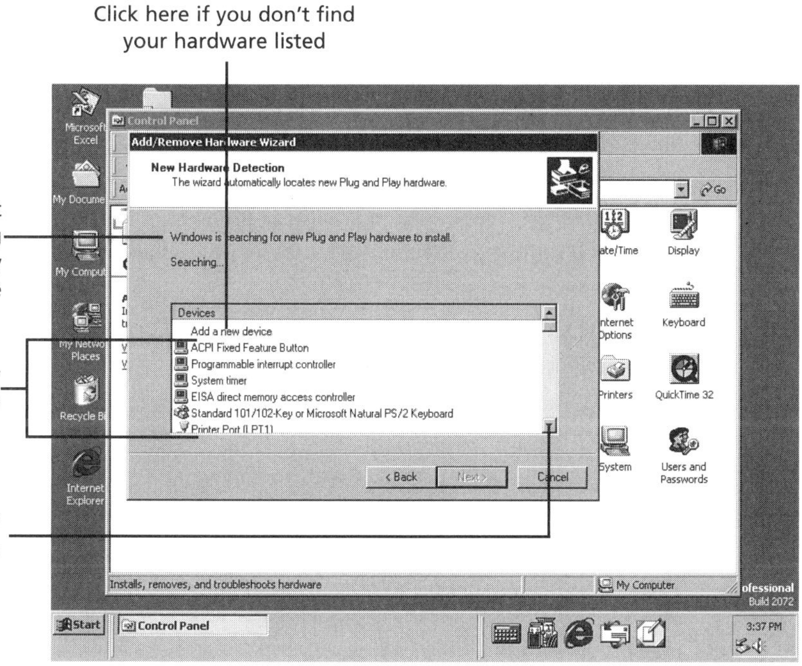

11. Click Next.

    Do you want Windows to search for your new hardware? Absolutely! Make sure that there is a dot next to Yes, Search for New Hardware.

12. Click Next.

    Now the computer goes to work looking for anything new you added. If it doesn't find what you installed, you'll have to continue to work through the following steps. These steps are literally telling the computer what it is you installed.

13. Find your hardware.

    Select a manufacturer and model. If you have an installation disk, choose Have Disk. You'll be asked to insert the disk into the appropriate place; then click OK. This should bring up the right equipment model.

14. Click Next.

    Windows will now install the software that is included for your hardware. Click Next.

15. You're finished!

    Click the Finish button.

You may be asked to reset your computer. If you need to reset, click the Start button, choose Shut Down, and then choose Restart. This works as a reset option.

You may be finished, depending on what was installed. There may be additional verification or configuration. What happens next really depends on what was installed.

Just keep working your way through the end of the wizard. When it disappears from the screen, or in those rare instances when you may need to reset, you'll be ready to start using your new hardware.

If you have any trouble with your new hardware, you can go back through these steps and work through the same method. Click on the hardware you just installed, and this same wizard works as a troubleshooting process.

Removing Hardware

There could be several reasons why you would want to remove a piece of hardware. For example, if you've just changed something like an old SCSI scanner or external drive, you'll have to get rid of the old one.

To Do 23.3: Removing Hardware

To Do

1. Turn off your computer and remove your hardware.
2. Restart Windows.
3. Close all open programs.

   Just a precaution.
4. Double-click My Computer.
5. Double-click the Control Panel.
6. Double-click the Add/Remove Hardware icon.

   Wow, this looks familiar, doesn't it? This is rather like dejà vu, isn't it? You're back at the Add/Remove Hardware Wizard. Only this time, you're going to tell the computer what hardware you want removed.
7. Click Next in the Add/Remove Hardware Wizard box.
8. Choose your task.

   This time you want to check the Uninstall/Unplug a Device option.

9. Click Next.

   You want to choose Uninstall a Device. Even though you've technically gotten rid of the hardware, you must still follow through and tell the computer that the device is no longer a part of the computer family. It has defected!

10. Click Next.

    Choose the device you want to uninstall. Click on it once to choose it.

11. Click Next.

    Are you sure that you want to uninstall this device? Good question by Windows. Think now. Is this what you want to do? Click No or cancel if you change your mind. Click Yes if you want to trudge forward and uninstall.

Your computer may buzz a bit, but then you're finished. That's it. Now you can go get a cup of coffee with the realization you've booted something out of your computer family.

> Removing a USB device is a cinch: Just unplug it You can re-add the device at any time by plugging it back in.

Software Installation

There is also a software side to hardware installation—even for plug-and-play devices. For example, you may add a USB scanner. The hardware installation is a snap: Plug in the scanner and you're ready to go. But you cannot scan anything until you install software to *use* the scanner.

The software is generally some program designed to use your hardware. For example, installing a new joystick can be fun, but until you have a game that uses the joystick, there's little you can do with it.

The process of adding the hardware's software depends on the piece of equipment you're adding. One of two things can happen:

1. You are prompted to insert a CD or floppy disk that came with your hardware during the process of working through Add/Remove Hardware.
2. Adding the software would be the same as adding any software, which is discussed in Hour 19, "Installing and Removing Software." You go to Add/Remove Programs in the Control Panel, click the Add New Programs button, and then follow the instructions. Better yet, read Hour 19.

I had to use option 1 when I installed my Network card. I used option 2 for installing my printer. Weird.

Troubleshooting Your Problems

Troubleshooting is a term that means you're going to work through some problem to see whether you can figure out why you have a problem. Well, sort of. In Windows 2000, *troubleshooting* means that you're going to work through a series of steps in a Windows 2000 Troubleshooter, which is a special program designed to see whether Windows can figure out the problem.

Windows is equipped with several kinds of troubleshooters for different kinds of hardware and problems.

To Do 23.4: Finding the Troubleshooter

1. Click the Start button.
2. Choose Help.
3. Click the Index tab.
4. Type **`Hardware troubleshooter`**.
5. Click Display.

   The Windows 2000 troubleshooter window is brought forward for you to review. Read through the list of problems to decide which troubleshooter best fits your problem. Figure 23.3 gives you a peek into the Windows 2000 troubleshooter.

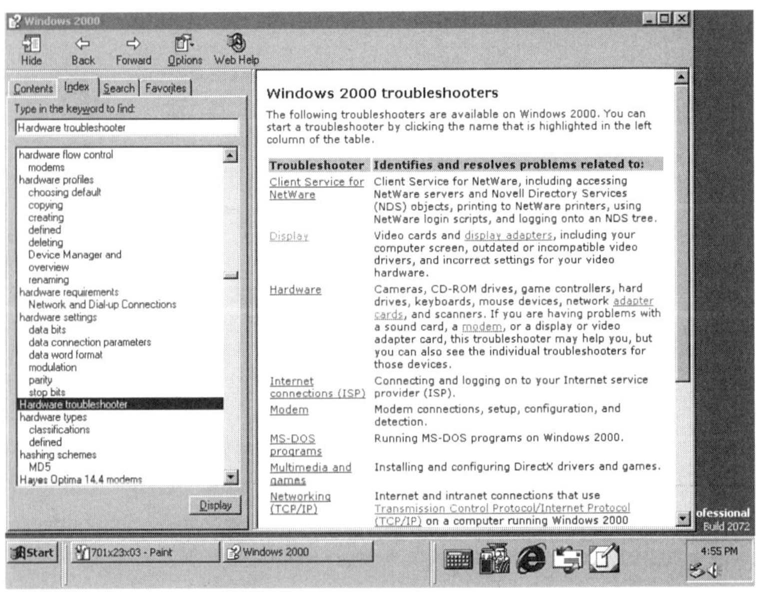

FIGURE 23.4
Windows 2000 Troubleshooter.

Click on one of the blue underlined words to start working through the steps. If you find you've chosen a troubleshooter that isn't what you really need, feel free to click the Display button at the bottom of the screen on your right. This takes you back to the beginning, and you can choose another troubleshooting program.

Summary

In this hour, you should have learned how to introduce your computer to new toys, or in other words, how to install new hardware on your computer. You also should have learned how to uninstall hardware that has outlived its usefulness, overstayed its welcome, or just gone kaput. And finally, you should be able to use the Windows 2000 troubleshooter.

Q&A

Q Would I install a printer with Installing Hardware?

A Although printers are considered a piece of hardware, you have to work through the steps in Hour 17, "Fussing with the Printer."

Q I have three USB devices but only two USB holes on the back of my computer. Help!

A Buy a USB hub. It's a device that plugs in to your computer's USB port and gives you even more USB ports. You can generally plug two or more other USB devices in to the hub, and you can add more hubs, as necessary, to handle the burden of all your computer's USB devices.

Q Can I add an extra hard drive to my computer?

A Sure, most computers can sport two hard drives inside the console and many outside. This is more technical than Plug and Play, however, and I recommend that you have a dealer or consultant install and configure the hard drive for you.

Workshop

The workshop includes quiz questions to help gauge your grasp of the material and exercises to help reinforce your learning. You'll find the answers to the quiz in Appendix A, "Answers."

Quiz

1. If Windows isn't detecting a new piece of hardware you have just physically installed, what is the first thing you should check?

2. What are two reasons Windows might not be able to Plug and Play a piece of hardware?
3. Other than using the Windows 2000 troubleshooter, what is another method of dealing with uncooperative new hardware?
4. *Bonus question*: How old was Napoleon when he conquered Italy?

Exercises

1. Find out what hardware devices are installed on your computer (you must do this by finding the list of USB controllers, not just following the cables that flow from your hard drive).
2. Assuming that you have the necessary security clearance (from the network administrator, your dad, the missus, whomever) and any required software, install a piece of hardware.
3. Now, uninstall whatever it was you just installed. Then, reinstall it. Isn't this just a merry-go-round of educational fun!

Vocabulary

device driver—A program that enables a device, such as a modem or printer, to communicate with Windows 2000.

hardware—The tools and toys you can plug in to your computer to enable it to do more things for you or just do the things that it does, but even better—for example, speakers and a sound card, so you can hear all the bells and whistles on your favorite virtual pinball game (the game itself would be *software*).

Plug and Play—A handy feature of USB that allows the computer to detect a new piece of hardware and, all on its own, reconfigure the other devices to make friends with it—or at least allow them to work together. This saves you a lot of computer nerd-work.

troubleshooting—The process of working through possible solutions to a problem.

USB—The acronym for *Universal Serial Bus*. Aside from facilitating Plug and Play, the USB allows you to install, daisy-chain–style, up to 127 pieces of hardware on your computer, usually without requiring you to shut down or restart the hard drive.

HOUR 24

Time and Sound in Windows 2000

This final hour is dedicated to fun—fun with time, fun with speakers, just plain messin' 'round. Still, this is serious stuff. The clock that my computer displays is the only clock that I refer to in my office. It has to be correct. I listen to music all the time when I work, so my speakers have got to be pretty darn cool. So, although this hour might not help you write a better report or show you how to clean up a disk drive, it should help you work more happily and maybe put a smile on your face.

The highlights in this hour include the following:

- Finding the time
- Setting the PC's speaker volume
- Adding special sounds
- The Address Book

Finding the Time in a System Tray

Off to one end of the taskbar, playing teeter-totter with the Start Button, is what I call the *loud time*. It's a graphic of a megaphone, apparently shouting out the current time of day (see Figure 24.1). Okay, the real name is the System Tray—but that's boring. Loud time is so much more.... Oh, never mind.

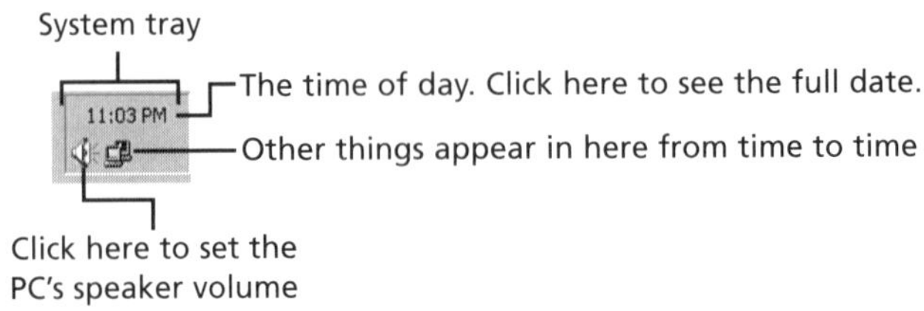

FIGURE 24.1
The time—wow, it's late!

The System Tray shows you several things, depending on how your computer is set up and what it's doing. Table 24.1 lists some of the more popular "guys" you might find there.

TABLE 24.1 The System Tray Table

	The volume button	This enables you to adjust the PC's speaker volume. Double-clicking to open displays the Volume Control dialog box.
	The printer dude	This icon appears whenever you're printing something. Then it immediately goes away. (It stays around longer for network printing.) Opening this icon displays a window for the printer, displaying documents queued or waiting to be printed.
	The modem buddies	They appear when you're connected to an online service or the Internet. Open to display a window detailing information about the connection.
	The networking guy	This one appears when you have a local area network connection. Opening it displays information about the connection. Be careful not to confuse this with the Internet guy; they're similar.
	Other little guys	These might show up in the System-Tray area, depending on what type of software you have installed. For example, some

		utilities and programs display icons in the System Tray to check their progress. If you have an e-mail program, an icon of an envelope might appear when there's new mail.
11:21 PM	AM or PM	The last goodie you'll see is the current time. Double-clicking on this displays the Date/Time Properties dialog box, which enables you to set the clock and date.

> To find more information on any item that shows up in the loud time area, hover the mouse pointer over it. A pop-up bubble appears, telling you more than you need to know about what your computer is doing.

Setting the Time on Your PC

Forget the date? Position your mouse pointer at the time in the taskbar and a bubble pops up displaying the current date in its full format. Doing this, you can find out whether or not it's Saturday, so you can stop working. (My editor is still nagging at me so I have to work on Saturday.)

If you double-click on the time, a dialog box appears (see Figure 24.2), enabling you to set the current date and time for your computer. This comes in handy for those times when your computer has lost track of the time (which it does; computers don't make good clocks).

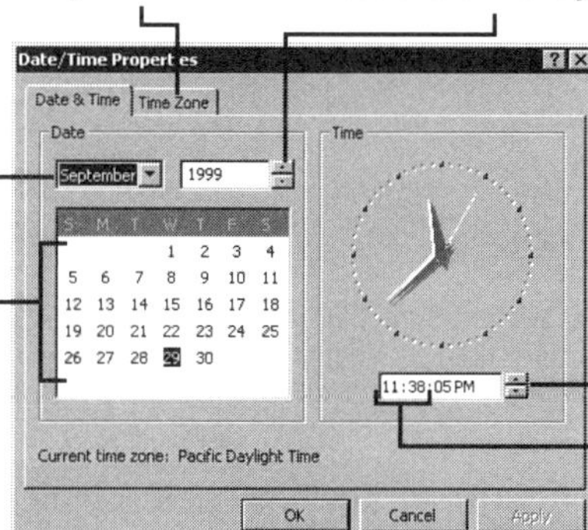

FIGURE 24.2
Setting the time.

Time Zones and Daylight Savings Time

The Time Zone panel in the Date/Time Properties dialog box allows you to select the time zone where your computer lives. Click on the Time Zone tab to bring that panel forward. It shows a global map with the current time zone highlighted (see Figure 24.3). To set a new time zone, click the down arrow and search through the list until you find your time zone.

Click the OK button in the Date/Time Properties dialog box when you're done messing with it.

If you live in one of those parts of the country that celebrates daylight savings time, make sure you click with the mouse in the "Automatically adjust clock for daylight saving changes" box on the Time Zone panel (see Figure 24.3). When the time changes from Standard to Daylight time, Windows pops up a little message letting you know that it's adjusted the computer's clock accordingly. This is one of those amazing things that computers should have done all along, but they are only now coming around to doing.

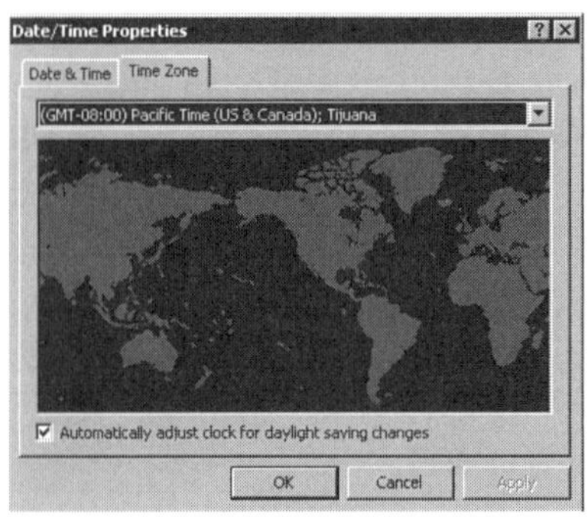

FIGURE 24.3
You're traveling through another dimension—the Time Zone.

Setting the PC's Speaker Volume

If you click with the mouse on the taskbar's Volume button, a volume slider pops up as you can see in Figure 24.4. This is where you can adjust the PC's speaker volume, making the noise your computer squawks louder, softer, or turning it off altogether.

If you click twice on the Volume button, you'll see a multimedia Volume Control panel. Strange stuff, although it does let you set volume levels for every individual thing in your computer that can potentially make noise. Close that window if it bothers you.

FIGURE 24.4
The Volume button adjusts the PC's speaker volume.

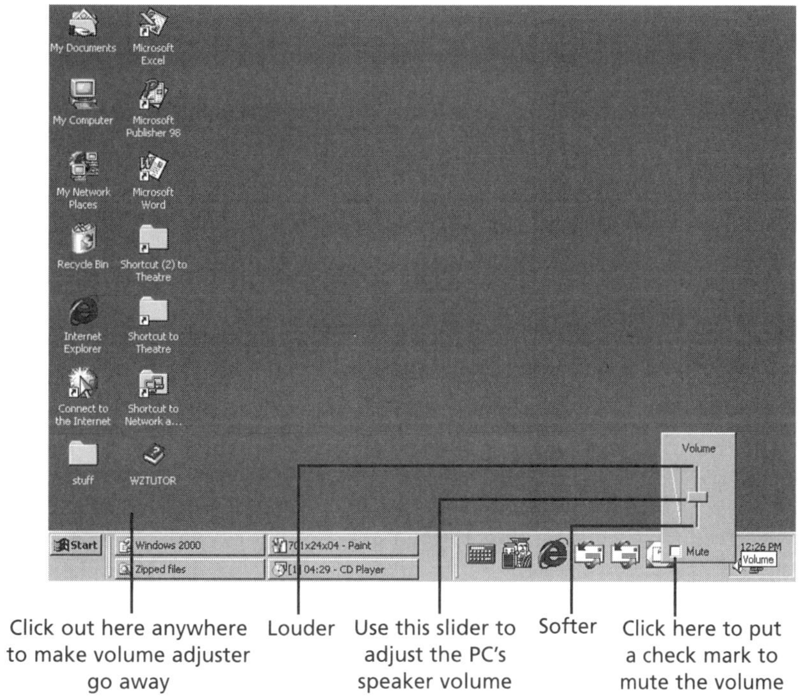

Hiding Items in the System Tray

The System Tray is a handy place to put things and display information. For example, you can glance at the System Tray to see whether your computer is online (on the Internet), or whether you have new e-mail waiting. It can be handy.

On the other hand, some people detest the heap of icons in the System Tray. As you use your computer and install new programs, the number of icons there will grow and grow. But, honestly, not everything *needs* to be there. Most items can be removed quite easily.

Generally speaking, if you right-click on an icon in the System Tray, you might get a pop-up menu, or a dialog box may be displayed. These typically lead to a place where you can reset an option, one that determines whether a System Tray icon appears or not.

For example, if the volume control bugs you, you can remove it.

To Do 24.1: Removing the Volume Control

1. Right-click the volume control icon in the System tray.
2. Choose Adjust Audio Properties from the shortcut menu.

3. Remove the check mark by Show Volume Control on the Taskbar.
4. Click OK.

It's gone!

Other items can be removed this way as well. And some icons cannot be removed, or perhaps their options can only be set by running an associated program (or finding an associated icon in the Control Panel).

If you want the volume control back (or if it doesn't appear in the first place), it's simple to return it to the System Tray.

To Do 24.2: Finding the Volume Control

1. Open My Computer.
2. Open the Control Panel.
3. Double-click on the Sounds and Multimedia icon. 
4. Click on the Sounds panel to bring it to the front.
5. Click in the Show Volume Control on the Taskbar box. This puts a ✓ in the box, which causes Windows to display the Volume button.
6. Click OK.

   The Volume button will appear on the taskbar when the window disappears.
7. Close the Control Panel window and My Computer's window.

These same steps are used to add other items to the System Tray. But it isn't always obvious where to find the options. (One icon in the System Tray on my computer has Remove Icon as one of the options for its right-click shortcut menu.)

For example, to remove or set the clock in the System Tray, follow these steps:

To Do 24.3: Finding the System Tray Clock

1. Click on the Start button.
2. Choose Settings.
3. Choose Taskbar, Start Menu.
4. Click in the box by Show Clock.

   If a ✓ appears in the box, the current time appears on the taskbar. If the box is empty, the clock won't show up. Click with the mouse once in the box to change from the ✓ to nothing or back again.
5. Click OK.

The Taskbar Properties dialog box is retired, and you now have a clock (or not) on the taskbar.

Adding Special Sounds

Your computer has the capability to perform a barrage of noises. Yes, they are loud, annoying, somewhat entertaining noises. And you can schedule these sounds so that anytime you do anything on your computer, such as close a program, exit a window, maximize a window, pop up a window (get the idea), you can have a noise associated with it. Sounding interesting? It is.

To Do 24.4: Adding Noises

To Do

1. Open My Computer.
2. Open the Control Panel.
3. Double-click on the Sounds and Multimedia icon.
4. Make sure the Sounds tab is forward.
5. Click the task you want to add sound to.

   These tasks are located in the sound events section. Figure 24.5 shows that Exit Windows has the sound "ta-da" associated with it. So whenever I exit Windows, I hear "ta-da."

24

FIGURE 24.5
Making sounds for your computer.

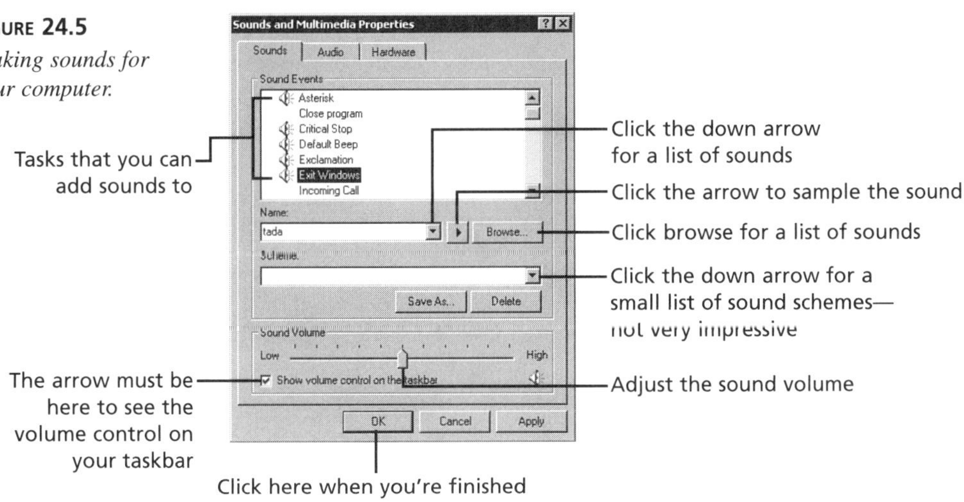

6. Click the down arrow next to Name.

   Here are a list of sounds to choose from.
7. Pick a sound.

8. Click the arrow to hear your sound.

   This arrow looks like the kind you'd see on a CD player.

9. Continue adding sounds.

10 Click OK when you tire of this process.

Sounds on the Internet

Windows 2000 comes with a host of interesting sounds, but never really enough—and hardly enough to appeal to a sound-discerning individual such as yourself!

The easiest way to get a new sound is to search for *Sounds* on the Internet. Use any popular search engine and look for *Sounds* or *Windows sounds* to find Web page after Web page that stores sounds available for you to download. (See Hour 11, "It's a Wild World Wide Web We Weave," for more information on Web browsing.)

When you find a sound file to grab, ensure that you save it to disk; when you click on the link, choose the Save to Disk option. Or, if the sound merely plays, click again, but this time press the Shift key (a Shift-click), which brings up a Save As dialog box.

Choose the C:\WINNT\Media folder for saving the files. If you save the sound files there, they will appear in the Sounds and Multimedia dialog box.

Of course, you can always save sound files in your own personal, C:\MyDocuments \Sounds folder. The Browse button in the Sounds and Multimedia dialog box can be used to fetch sounds from that folder instead of from the Media folder.

> Want to have a little fun? Open Windows Explorer (if you forgot how, review Hour 18, "Maintaining and Cleaning Files"). Find C:\WINNT\Media folder. Click once on the Media folder to open it. The right side of Explorer has a few sounds you can play with. Double click the name of the sound and listen to it play. Try Mozart's Symphony No. 40 and turn those speakers up!

Creating Your Own Sounds

Suppose the Internet bores you. Instead of hearing Big Ben chime when you quit Windows, you would rather be lulled by the cooing of your two-year-old saying, "Night-night." Ahhh, precious little guy!

Your computer lets you create any sound you want and save it to a sound file on disk. All you need is a microphone properly plugged into your PC's sound-input or Mic jack. Any old cheap microphone will do. The PC's Mic jack is on the back of the computer, normally close to where the speakers are connected.

Then you just need a program called Sound Recorder to actually record the sound and save it to disk.

To Do 24.5: Finding the Sound Recorder Program

1. Click the Start Button.
2. Choose Programs.
3. Choose Accessories.
4. Choose Entertainment.
5. Choose Sound Recorder.

Figure 24.6 shows the path to get the Sound Recorder Program.

FIGURE 24.6
The path to your own sounds.

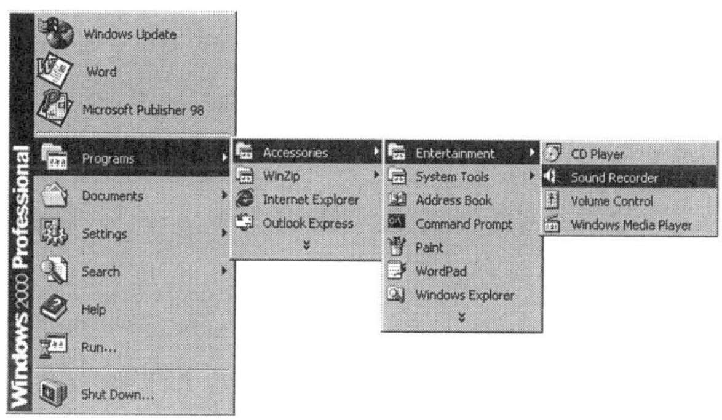

Get the microphone ready to record and then click the red recording button in the Sound Recorder's window. Say whatever it is you want to say, or whatever funny sound it is you can make with your body. Figure 24.7 shows you the sound recorder.

FIGURE 24.7
The Sound Recorder.

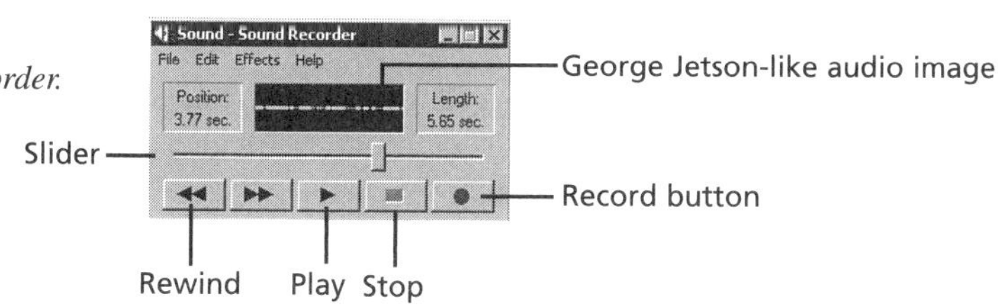

When you're done recording, click the Stop button.

To remove excess noise from the beginning of the recording, position the slider at approximately the point where your sound starts. (Use the Play and Stop buttons and then the slider to backup the sound. The George Jetson-like audio image can help you determine where the sound really starts.) Choose Edit, Delete Before Current Position. Click OK in the warning dialog box, and the sound sample is trimmed.

Likewise, you can remove excess sound from the end of your recording: Click the Stop button when you want the sound to stop. Use the slider to make adjustments, if necessary. Then choose Edit, Delete After Current Position from the menu. Click OK in the warning dialog box.

With your sound nice and tight, you can save it to disk using the File, Save As command. Refer to the previous section for information on where to save the sound file.

> You may need to unmute the microphone to record. Double-click on the volume control in the System Tray. In the Volume Control dialog box, ensure that the Microphone column doesn't have its Mute box checked. (Choose Options, Properties to get at the dialog box that displays the Microphone column. Locate Microphone in the scrolling list and put a check mark next to it to display.)

Importing Sounds

Finally, you can import sounds from other devices, such as your home stereo, TV, or VCR. This is a bit "techy" (but then again, this isn't required information here).

Start by connecting the audio output from some sound-producing device (the left or mono jack) into your computer's line-in jack, (for example, from the VCR's audio output into your computer's line-in jack). You may need an RCA-to-mini-Din adapter, which can be picked up at any Radio Shack.

After the connection is made, use the Sound Recorder program, as described in the previous section, to record the sound from the TV, VCR, or whatever.

> As when muting the microphone, you might find that the line-in jack in your computer is being muted by Windows. Double-click the volume control in the System Tray to display the Volume Control dialog box. Look for the Line-In column and ensure that the Mute box is not checked.

The Address Book

The Windows Address Book is similar to that little black book you keep shoved in the bottom of your briefcase. It holds names, addresses, phone numbers, e-mail, all kinds of information—but the Windows Address Book is kept in your computer, and you can access the information from a variety of places such as Outlook, Internet Explorer, Microsoft Phone System, and NetMeeting.

To Do 24.6: Finding the Address Book

1. Click the Start button.
2. Choose Programs.
3. Choose Accessories.
4. Click on Address Book.

▲ Figure 24.8 shows the path to the Address Book.

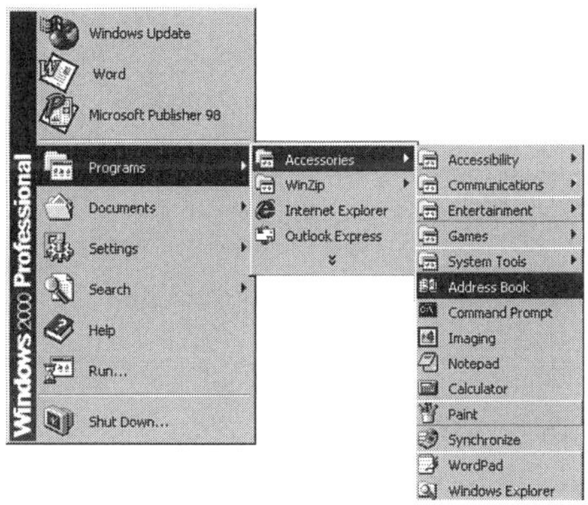

FIGURE 24.8
The path to your addresses.

Figure 24.9 lets you take a little peek at an address book. This is the group of contacts belonging to the poker group.

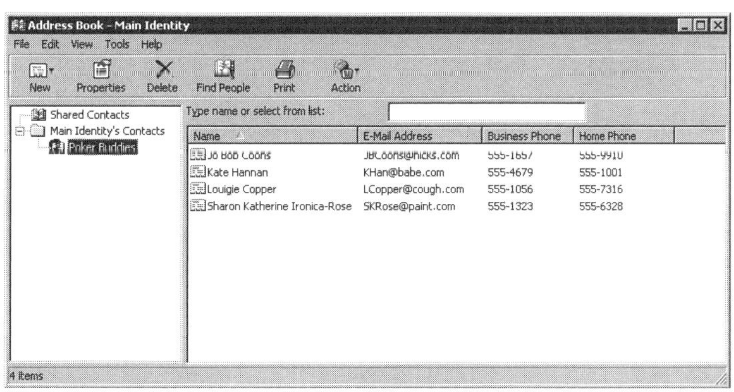

FIGURE 24.9
The address book.

To Do 24.7: Adding People to Your Address Book

1. Click on New.

Figure 24.10 shows a new contact being added.

FIGURE 24.10
Adding a new contact—ho, ho, ho!

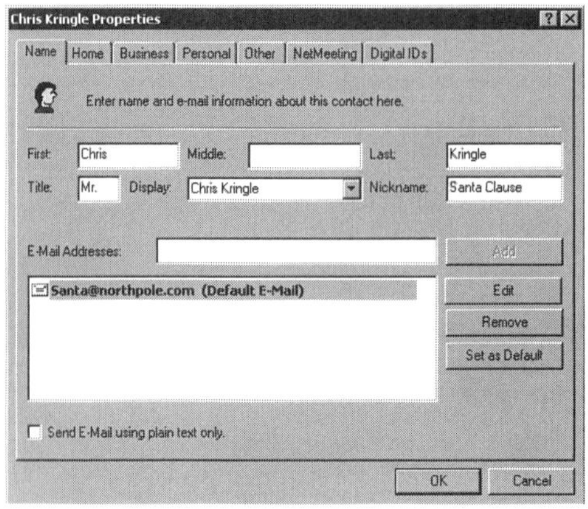

2. Click each of the other tabs to add more information.

   Be complete! You have the room to add tons of phone numbers, addresses, fax numbers, even personal information.

3. Click OK when you're finished.

> If you ever want to add or change information to an entry, click the person's name and then click the Properties box.

Summary

This hour was about time, sound, and places (address book). It could almost be a "Twilight Zone" episode. Be honest, this stuff is fun! Making new sounds and applying them to all your Windows sounds can really customize your computer. Take full advantage of the Address Book, too. If you are someone who keeps contact information, it can come in really handy.

Q&A

Q Why is my clock off a few minutes every week?

A It's part of the computer's inability to tell time. Seriously, the computer does lots of things that "interrupt" the clock. These actions, such as sleep mode, heavy disk activity, or even restarting, might suspend the clock—even if just for a few moments. Those moments add up.

Q I detest music files playing while I view Web pages. What can I do?

A I hate them too. Shocking. And often there is no option to turn off the music (officially known as MIDI music). However, you can mute the MIDI synthesizer in Windows: Double-click the volume control in the System Tray. In the Volume Control dialog box, locate the MIDI column and put a ✓ in the Mute box. Click OK.

Q My modem is still very loud, though I've turned down the volume in the System Tray. Help!

A The modem's volume is controlled using the Control Panel's Modem icon. Open that icon, and choose your modem from the General tab. Click the Properties button. In the Properties dialog box, locate the Speaker volume slider and adjust the sound there. Click OK (twice), and the modem's volume is set.

Workshop

The workshop includes quiz questions to help gauge your grasp of the material and exercises to help reinforce your learning. You'll find the answers to the quiz and exercises in Appendix A, "Answers."

Quiz

1. What is the real term for what was called, "Loud Time"?
2. How do you find today's date?
3. What does the choice Delete Before Current Position do?
4. *Bonus Question*: What did Alexander Graham Bell prefer to say when answering the telephone?

Exercises

1. Scroll the year in the Date/Time Properties to a different year and find out what day your birthday falls on.
2. Turn your volume levels up to the highest level. Now turn them all back down.
3. Record yourself laughing (like an evil, wicked witch type of laugh). Then add that sound to Windows, and assign it as the sound for Close Program.

Vocabulary

System Tray—An area to one side of the taskbar that displays the time and small icons that control various programs or aspects of Windows.

Volume Control—An icon in the System Tray that sets or mutes the PC's speaker volume.

TIMEOUT 5

An Introduction to MP3

The Internet is a nest of latest rages, and the loudest and latest of them all is the MP3 craze.

MP3 is the name of an audio format, one that stores lots of CD-quality music in a file that doesn't eat up half your hard drive space, nor take weeks to download. That makes MP3 music files all the rage for anyone who's into music and has access to the Internet.

What does MP3 stand for? Who cares. The point is that, if you can remember MP3, you can easily get to an MP3 Web page: `http://www.mp3.com`.

That's music central for downloading (saving to disk) music files from the Internet onto your computer. Here are the steps to reach it:

1. Start the Internet Explorer and connect to the Internet.
2. Visit the `www.mp3.com` Web page.

The Web page is the home for most of the MP3 music files that can be had on the Internet. It's like an online music store, although virtually everything there is free: Just find the link to the music you want to hear, click, and download, (see Figure TO5.1.)

FIGURE TO5.1
The mp3.com *Web page.*

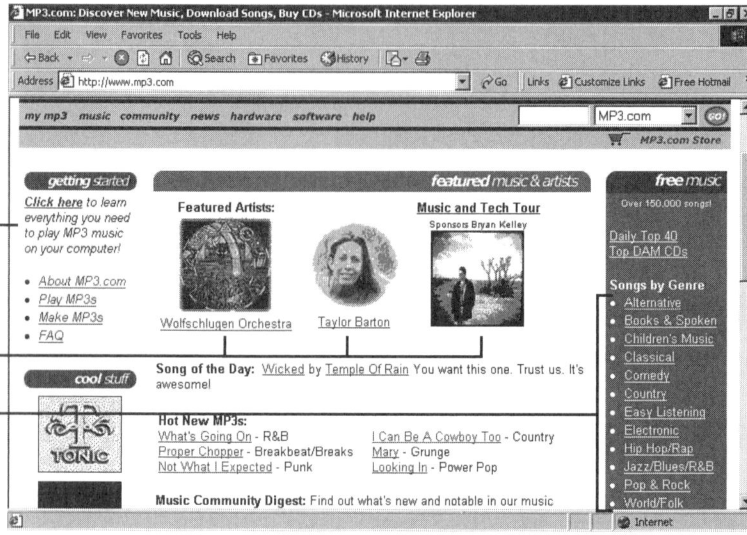

You can browse the MP3 site for music you want, search the site, or click one of the links on the main page, such as the Song of the Day or the Hot New MP3 Titles.

When you find a title you'd like to hear, click on it. That should take you to a page where you can read more information and even download (save) the music file to your computer.

To Do TO.1: Saving Music to a File

▼ To Do

1. Right-click the link.
2. Choose Save Target As from the shortcut menu.

   This ensures that a Save As dialog box will appear in order to save the MP3 file to disk, see Figure TO5.2. (If you just click the link, Windows might only play the music, not giving you a chance to save it to disk.)

FIGURE TO5.2
Right-click the word Play to get the menu.

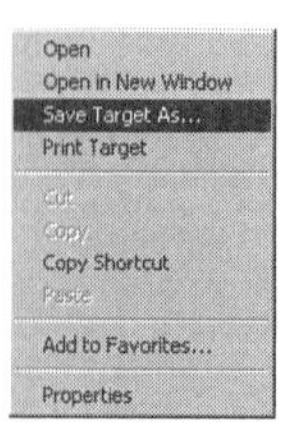

3. Use the Save As dialog box to find a disk drive and folder for the file.

   For example, you can create a new MP3 folder in your c:\My Documents folder. Or get fancy and save your New Age tunes in the c:\My Documents\MP3\New Age folder.

▼

4. Type in a name for the file or use what is automatically inserted.
5. Click the Save button.

   Now sit back and wait as the MP3 music file is sent from the MP3 Web page to your computer, see Figure TO5.3.

   Doh-dee-doh-doh . . .

FIGURE TO5.3
Downloading complete for the MP3 file.

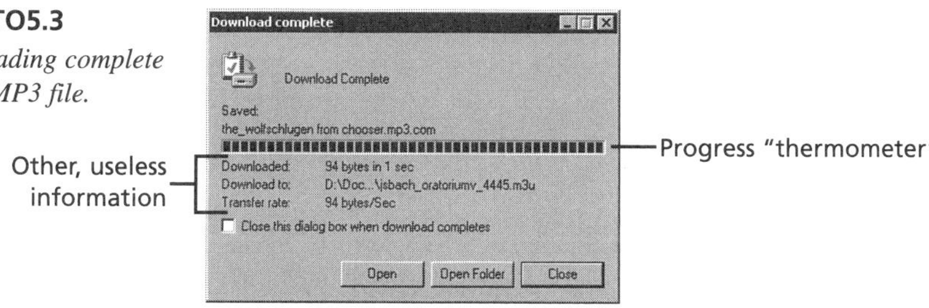

> While you're waiting, you can continue to surf the Web, read e-mail, or even peruse other files and download them. The downloading takes place as long as you're connected to the Internet—although if you download several files at once, the overall speed will be less than if you download one file at a time.

After a while (or after a "spell," if your downloading a Country-Western tune), downloading is done. Close the proper dialog box and get ready to listen to the music.

Playing the song is possible using the Windows Media player that comes with Windows 2000. Merely find the icon for the file you downloaded and double-click.

For example, if you just downloaded some eye-popping, heavy-metal version of Verdi's Requiem, find that icon in the c:\My Documents\MP3\Wake up the Neighbors folder (heh-heh). Double-click the icon and the Media Play starts (see Figure TO5.4).

FIGURE TO5.4
Something bizarre by Bach.

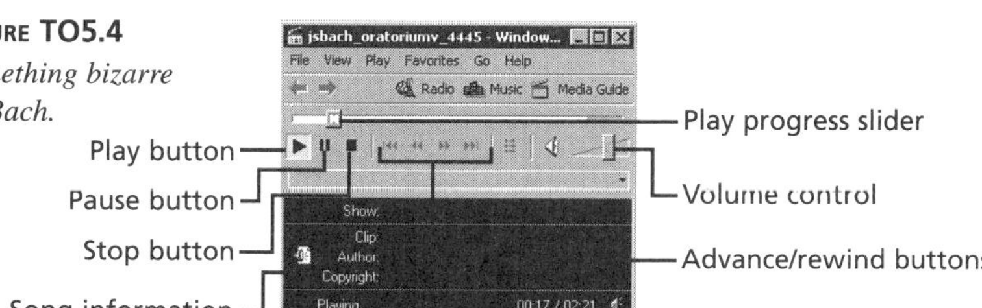

Click the Play button (if necessary), adjust the volume (up), and be prepared to *rock*!

PART VI
Appendixes

Appendix

APPENDIX A

Answers

This appendix contains the answers to the quiz questions at the end of each hour.

Hour 1

Quiz

1. True or False: All Windows 2000 computers come with a network?

   False. Windows 2000 comes with networking software that lets you *use* a network. You must purchase networking hardware to make your PC network-happy. This is not something that all PCs come with; because all networks are subtly different, networking hardware is usually purchased separately from the basic computer.

2. Where is the Internet?

   The Internet is everywhere. It's a collection of computers all over the world that share information and resources. The Internet is as close as the phone plug in your wall.

3. How does Windows 2000 display information about your computer?

   Graphically. Windows 2000 is a graphical operating system, using windows, icons, and other graphical gadgets to help you control both your computer hardware and software.

4. *Bonus Question*: Who was the only president not born in the United States?

   Theodore Roosevelt. (He himself didn't know it.)

Hour 2

Quiz

1. What should you plug all your computer gadgets into?

   A power strip.

2. How many characters can your password be?

   Up to 14 characters long.

3. What is the only option you have for shutting down that does not require you to save your work first?

   Hibernate.

4. *Bonus Question*: What country is Mount Fuji in?

   Japan.

Hour 3

Quiz

1. Which item in the Start menu contains programs?

   Program, Documents, Settings, Search, Help, Run, Shutdown.

2. What type of icons will you find in My Computer?

   It acts as a visual representation of your computer's hard drives, folders, and files, showing you how and where information is stored.

3. How do you close a window in Windows?

   Click the close button (the ×) located in the upper-right corner of the screen.

4. *Bonus Question*: Who was the first Roman turned Christian emperor?

   Constantine.

Hour 4

Quiz

1. What three things are in My Computer?

   There are disk drives, folders, and files.

2. What is the most common way to quit a program?

   Choose File and then Exit.

3. Other than clicking the Start button, what is a way to open the Start menu?

   Press Ctrl+Esc.

4. *Bonus Question*: How long was the Titanic?

   882 1/2 feet long.

Hour 5

Quiz

1. Which key offers the quickest access to Help (otherwise known as the *Help key*)?

   F1.

2. What is the purpose of the underlined words in Help text?

   Windows provides definitions for these words, which may be jargon-ish.

3. How do you exit Help?

   Click the × box (for closing the window).

4. *Bonus Question*: What does Massachusetts mean?

   Great Mountain Place.

Hour 6

Quiz

1. What happens to a program when you move it around, rename it, or even delete it from your Start menu?

   Nothing. The actual program is safely tucked away in the bowels of your hard drive. If you *really* want to delete the program from your computer, see Hour 19, "Installing and Removing Software."

2. What does the Start button start?

   The Start button doesn't really start anything. It just opens the door to the Start menu, which gets you to your programs.

3. What happens to the highlighted *old* name when you begin to type in the Rename dialog box?

   Abracadabra, it disappears!

4. *Bonus Question*: How many people were in the Air Force during World War I?

   50.

Hour 7

Quiz

1. What does each button on the taskbar, with the exception of Start, represent?

   Each button represents a program that is open.

2. When your taskbar becomes too cluttered to be of much use, how do you fix it without closing programs you need?

   You can stretch your taskbar to make room for the programs.

3. How do you ensure that your taskbar is always displayed on top of the windows you have open on your desktop?

   Right-click on the taskbar, choose Properties, and then choose Always on Top from the list of options.

4. *Bonus Question*: In the movie *Star Wars*, what type of pirate is Han Solo?

   A Corrillian pirate.

Hour 8

Quiz

1. What are the three ways to open the Print dialog box?

   Click Print on the menu bar and then choose Print.

   Click the Print icon on the toolbar.

   Type Alt+F, P.

2. What three things must you choose before you can doodle in Paint?

   You have to choose your tool, your tool's options, and then the color you will use to paint.

3. What is the advantage of adding a word processor (Word, for example) when Windows 2000 already comes with WordPad?

Although WordPad is fine for simple documents, it lacks all the nifty features such as spell-checking and page numbering.

4. *Bonus Question*: What is the full name of Rhode Island?

   State of Rhode Island and Providence Plantations.

Hour 9

Quiz

1. In which folder will Windows 2000 automatically save a file if you yourself don't designate one?

   Files will be automatically saved to My Documents—the folder Windows has already created for all your stuff—unless you direct them to another folder that you have so creatively created.

2. What do you do if you want a file saved within two different folders or even on more than one drive?

   After it has been saved in any drive, copy it from Windows Explorer: Right-click on the file; select Copy; find the other place you want this file to live; from Edit, select Paste; and congratulations, you have twins.

3. *Bonus Question*: The red triangle on every bottle of Guinness Stout has what kind of reputation?

   It's the world's oldest trademark.

Hour 10

Quiz

1. How can you avoid having to retype your password each time you want to access the Internet?

   When your Dial-Up Connection dialog box appears, type your password, but check the Save Password option before clicking Connect.

2. Can you use a different password for your e-mail than you use for your dial-up connection?

   Yup. In fact, it is probably preferable if you are concerned about limiting access to your e-mail communications. You can also save your e-mail password, just as you saved your dial-up one.

3. If you think you need the Internet Connection Wizard after your computer has already been configured, can you bring him back to life?

   Yes, by going to the Start menu and then choosing Programs, Accessories, Communication, and finally Internet Connection Wizard.

Hour 11

Quiz

1. What is a quick and easy way to retry a hefty download that has stalled out part way through?

   The Refresh button will often do the trick.

2. What is perhaps the best reason to take an exit ramp off the Information Superhighway?

   You do have a life outside cyberspace; live it.

3. *Bonus Question*: What did the great Buddha die of?

   Intestinal hemorrhaging caused by a large, spicy meal.

Hour 12

Quiz

1. Why should you save an e-mail attachment to disk?

   Because sometimes attachments can carry viruses that will make your computer very, very sick.

2. What kind of files can you clip on to a piece of e-mail as an attachment?

   Pictures, documents, spreadsheets, graphics, music, pretty much any sort of digital document.

3. What are two ways to check for e-mail without restarting Outlook Express?

   There are three ways: Click the Send/Recv button at the top of the screen; click the down arrow *next* to the Send/Recv button and choose an option; or click the Tools button and then Send and Receive.

4. *Bonus Question*: What were the last words of the famous composer Ludwig van Beethoven?

   "Pity, pity—too late!" This was said because he had requested wine to be brought, but it did not arrive in time.

Hour 13

Quiz

1. What is WinZIP?

   A popular program used for archiving.

2. Is it possible to save just an image from a Web page and not the text?

   Yes.

3. What does FTP stand for?

   File Transfer Protocol.

4. *Bonus Question*: One in three Taiwanese funeral processionals has one of these. What is it?

   A stripper.

Hour 14

Quiz

1. What is the first step in setting up a network?

   Installing the network card.

2. What is My Network Places?

   It lists all the computers on the network.

3. How can you tell you have a shared or mapped hard drive?

   Shared drives appear with a little "serving hand" beneath their icon; mapped hard drives appear with network "plumbing" beneath their icons.

4. *Bonus Question*: What is the funny bone?

   The humerus, an unprotected nerve cell.

Hour 15

Quiz

1. Why and when would you need to log on as other than administrator, if you are indeed the network administrator?

   Although you need to be logged on as administrator when you have to change user parameters, it is best to instead be logged on as a user when simply using your computer and its programs. That way, no unscrupulous interfacer can sneak bad stuff into the heart of the network.

2. What is the Multiple User concept?

   This allows several people to use one computer. They can access their own programs and information, while protecting other programs and information from users who lack clearance.

3. Why should you log off of a computer when another user is waiting to use the very same program on which you are currently working?

   Because the computer is recognizing you as the user until you log off. That means anything that happens until you have logged off of that station will be attributed to you. In addition, your access to certain programs might differ from those of the user who is waiting to log on.

4. *Bonus Question*: What is the lowest point on the earth's surface?

   The Mariana Trench, located in the Pacific Ocean around the Mariana Islands.

Hour 16

Quiz

1. Name three items that you are *not* able to remove from your desktop.

   The Recycle Bin, My Computer, and My Network Places.

2. Why shouldn't you put every application you use in a convenient spot right on your desktop?

   Because, the more cluttered your Desktop, the less useful the shortcuts become. Plus, the more stuff on your desktop, the slower your computer gets. Save this kind of access-logic for the front closet and the back of the garage.

3. Under what circumstances might it be more productive to ignore all this Active Desktop stuff?

   Unless you depend on Internet research and time sensitive news-stuff for your work, you might actually find the Active Desktop to be more of a distraction than a help.

4. *Bonus Question*: Dolphins live in the Amazon River. What color are they?

   Pink.

Hour 17

Quiz

1. What is the purpose of designating a printer as your default printer?

   This tells your computer where to print unless otherwise instructed.

2. What is the purpose of the stuff you put in the User Information Sheet?

   That information is used to let the recipient know where and whom the fax is coming from.

3. Which port do most computers use to communicate with printers?

   Most computers use the LPT1 port to communicate with local printers.

4. *Bonus Question*: How big is the actual *Mona Lisa*?

   Two feet by two feet.

Hour 18

Quiz

1. How often should you run the Disk Cleanup program?

   At least once a month.

2. Why are backups necessary?

   To ensure that you have a safety copy of the information on your hard drive.

3. How can you rename more than one file at a time?

   You cannot. Windows lets you rename only one file at a time.

4. *Bonus Question*: How many paintings did Vincent van Gogh himself sell?

   One.

Hour 19

Quiz

1. What icon in the Control Panel is used to add more programs to Windows?

   The Add/Remove Programs icon.

2. How do you remove a program that's not in the list of programs Windows can remove?

   Find out whether your program has a Remove Program feature by browsing through its Help file. Use the Index to look up *Setup* or *Install*. Then, check under that heading to see whether there is an uninstall procedure.

3. What types of programs can you drag to the Recycle Bin?

   Ha! Trick question! You really shouldn't drag any programs to the Recycle Bin. Work through the steps in this hour and remove them properly.

4. *Bonus Question*: The properties of matter are solid, liquid, and gas. What do some scientists consider the fourth to be?

   Plasma.

Hour 20

Quiz

1. What has happened when your files are fragmented?

   Windows has split the files into smaller pieces so that they fit on disk in a more efficient manner. This does not affect the files, but it will slow disk performance over time. The Disk Defragmenter program fixes this problem.

2. Which files does Disk Cleanup remove?

   Temporary Internet files and other files created by Windows 2000 and various applications. You no longer need the files, so Disk Cleanup removes them for you in one handy step.

3. Can Check Disk be made to operate automatically?

   Absolutely. You can preset options and make decisions for Check Disk by clicking the Options button and changing the settings. Then you can use Scheduled Tasks to have Check Disk run every week or so—all done automatically.

4. *Bonus Question*: What is the name of the monster in Mary Shelley's book *Frankenstein*?

   The monster didn't have a name; the creator of the monster was Dr. Frankenstein. Ohh, trick question!

Hour 21

Quiz

1. How do you give yourself a larger work area on your screen?

   Choose a new resolution from the Screen area in the Display Properties box.

2. How do you change the color scheme of your computer?

   Click the Appearance tab from the Display properties box. Choose a color from the Scheme options, or click the down arrow next to Color and choose your own.

3. What was the original purpose of the Screen Saver?

   It was designed to prevent "phosphor burn-in." It was a problem that affected early monochrome and color PC monitors; if you left the monitor on for any length of time, the screen image would eventually "burn" into the phosphor.

4. *Bonus Question*: In Nigeria, all twins have to be given the same names. What are they?

   The first born is always Taiwo, and the second born is always Kehinde.

Hour 22

Quiz

1. Where is the fonts folder located?

   In the Control Panel off of My Computer.

2. How do you preview a font?

   Open the fonts folder. Then double-click on the font name.

3. What is the path to get to the Character Map program?

   Start button, Programs, Accessories, System Tools, Character Map.

4. *Bonus Question*: In 1952, who was offered presidency of Israel?

   Albert Einstein.

Hour 23

Quiz

1. If Windows isn't detecting a new piece of hardware you have just physically installed, what is the first thing you should check?

   Make sure that the device is turned *on*; Windows won't acknowledge its existence until it is powered up.

2. What are two reasons Windows might not be able to Plug and Play a piece of hardware?

   Your computer is not USB-equipped, or the device is too old to be Plug-and-Play compatible.

3. Other than using the Windows 2000 troubleshooter, what is another method of dealing with uncooperative new hardware?

   You can go back to the Add process, click on the troublesome device, and redo all the steps you did to install the device in the first place. Sometimes this will ease the new kid's jitters.

4. *Bonus Question*: How old was Napoleon when he conquered Italy?

   24.

Hour 24

Quiz

1. What is the real term for what was called "Loud Time"?

   System Tray.

2. How do you find today's date?

   Point your mouse at the time in the taskbar and a bubble pops up displaying the current date in its full format.

3. What does the choice Delete Before Current Position do?

   It removes excess noise from the beginning of any recording you do in the Sound Recorder program.

4. *Bonus Question*: What did Alexander Graham Bell prefer to say when answering the telephone?

   Ahoy!

APPENDIX B

Problems and Solutions—Troubleshooting

We tolerate a lot of abuse from our computers. They crash. They die. They refuse to work. They make us cry. Still, we plug along, accepting some ridiculous shortcomings that we wouldn't tolerate in anything else. Or worse, we blame ourselves for something the computer does. Believe me, it's not always our fault.

The following is a list of common problems and suggested solutions. Alas, I cannot list every possible problem and the potential solution here in this brief appendix. The best I can hope for is to train you how to spot and work with errors to best correct them.

Also, please don't forget other sources for help. Your dealer, the computer manufacturer, and the software developer owe you support as well. You paid for it.

General Mayhem

When the computer crashes or something doesn't work right, you'll know. Either Windows will flash an error message your way, or things just won't seem to work right. When these signs appear, you should probably do the following things:

1. Save your stuff.

   Always save your hard work to disk—if you can. Minor system burps and hardware errors make the computer's environment unstable. Saving to disk is your top priority.

2. Quit your programs.

   If possible, try to quit your programs. This is part of a graceful shutdown and will reduce the chances of missing files or lost clusters on the disk.

3. Shut down Windows.

   Quit Windows as you normally would. The instructions are in Hour 2, "Let's Get Ready to Rumble…!"

After Windows shuts down, turn off the computer. Wait a spell (usually a minute or so, just long enough to ensure the hard drives stop spinning). Then turn on the computer again.

In most cases, turning the computer off and then on again (as just described) fixes minor problems. Why? I don't know. I don't even think Microsoft knows. But for some reason the computer gets "tired," and shutting down and turning it back on again fixes several types of minor problems.

Is the Problem Predictable?

Sometimes a computer program is a one-time event. For example, you open a Web page and Internet Explorer gives up the ghost and disconnects you from the Internet. Oh, well. Trying again usually works. Other times, you might notice certain problems always happen always at the same time or under the same circumstances.

If the problem is predictable, such as the system is unable to recover from sleep mode, it's definitely not anything that's your fault. Like the old doctor-doctor joke ("Doctor, Doctor! It hurts when I do this!" "Then don't do that!"), you should probably avoid the activity that crashes your system.

Instead of suffering or living with the problem, consider getting support. If the problem is with a specific application, call the developer's technical support. If the problem occurs when using your printer, you might need to phone your dealer for technical support.

By making note of when or how the problem recurs, you're helping the tech support people help you find a solution.

Problems after Software/Hardware Installation

Many computer problems are common after installing new hardware or a new piece of software. Something in the hardware refuses to cooperate, and your computer seizes. Or maybe the new software interferes with the way an old program works. That happens a lot.

There are two approaches to take. The first is to remove the offending piece of hardware or uninstall the software. Not everything out there is Windows 2000 compatible. Just because it says "Windows" on the box, doesn't mean it's friendly to Windows 2000.

The second approach is to work with the hardware or software and configure it to be more friendly to your system. The manual can be a source of help here; the troubleshooting guide can assist you in nailing down common conflicts and resolving them.

Finally, some programs absolutely refuse to run under Windows 2000. Mostly, these are programs that are not compatible with Windows 2000, so it's a good thing that they don't run. You can try to contact the developer for assistance, however checking on the side of the box for Windows 2000 compatibility is the best clue.

Calling for Help!

When you phone your dealer, manufacturer, or developer for technical support, be aware of a few things. First, the support is offered because they do care about their products. Just the willingness to provide support is a good sign of the company's faith in what they produce.

Second, never use support as an excuse not to read the manual. One of the reasons WordPerfect stopped its legendary (and toll-free) support is that many people were calling to ask how to set up their computers. They hadn't even removed the software from the box! This is abuse of a decent system. Always make sure you've exhausted other resources before you call the company for help.

Third, have information handy. Know the name and version of the program. Have your registration number handy. Know a bit about your computer, too. It runs Windows 2000, but how much memory does it have? Which microprocessor? Knowing this information will expedite the support process. You can also refer back to Hour 20, "Fixing Up Your Disk Drives," and read about System Information, which is the best place to find all the information about your computer.

Fourth, be able to accurately and calmly describe the problem. The more specific you can be, the better the solution they can offer. If you get huffy and just say "The damn thing won't print!," they'll be less likely to help than if you can better describe the situation.

Fifth, accept their solutions. It will take time for them to work with you, following through on their instructions. Be patient. Be nice. Say, "Thank you."

If you get into one of those, "It's not our fault; call someone else" wars, give up and phone your dealer or whomever sold you the computer. At that point, it becomes their problem to provide you with a solution.

Be prepared to wait on hold or even pay money for tech support. Again, this would be intolerable in other industries, but it's the expected norm with computers. Still, the more people follow my previous words of advice, the easier it should be to get quality technical support.

Don't Forget the Troubleshooters in Windows!

Windows tries to help in your woes, as well, and not just be the cause of them!

Don't forget that Windows 2000 comes with a program called the Windows 2000 Troubleshooter. The Troubleshooter lets you work through a series of questions with the end result being that Windows tries to figure out the problem, or at least, narrow it down to the point where you can fix what's wrong. As you might expect, sometimes the Troubleshooter does a good job; sometimes it doesn't.

Hour 23, "Installing and Removing Hardware," gives you a nice introduction to the Windows 2000 Troubleshooter.

APPENDIX C

Basic Windows Concepts

This book, technically, is about how to use Windows 2000. But to be fair, this part of the book has been added to bring those of you out there who may need more background information to bring you up to speed. The basic concepts in this section will help you operate and maneuver around Windows.

If you're familiar with how to use the mouse and work with text, you can skip this appendix. It's not a part of the 24-hour allotted time. This is extra. *Added value*, I believe is the term.

The highlights in this appendix include the following:

- Working with the mouse
- Working with text

Using Mr. Mouse

You're fooling yourself if you think you can use Windows without a mouse. You need a mouse to use Windows. You must have one. Not only that, you need to understand how the mouse works and how to perform some common mouse tricks.

You don't have to have your hand on the mouse all the time you are using your computer. You only need to grab it when something mousy is required, which isn't that often.

The mouse points away from you, with its tail trailing off toward the rear of your desk, back into the bowels of your computer somewhere. So if the other end of the mouse were its head, you'd grab the mouse with its head under the palm of your hand. Remember: The tail points *away* from you, right underneath the tips of your fingers.

The mouse gets going thanks to elbow movement on your behalf; do not roll the mouse with your wrist. Use your elbow to help glide Mr. Mouse around on your table top. The mouse controls a pointer or mouse cursor on the screen that mimics the movements of the mouse on your table top. Move the mouse wildly in a circle, and the pointer on the screen follows suit.

It's best to roll your computer mouse on a soft mouse pad. This allows the mouse's rubber ball, underneath, to get some traction, and it makes for smoother mouse operations.

Understanding the Mouse Lingo

There are five things you can do with the mouse and five terms used to describe them: point, click, double-click, drag, and select or highlight. Each of these terms is elaborated on in the following sections, and a brief description is offered in Table C.1.

TABLE C.1 Mouse Terminology

Mouse Action	*Description*
Point	To move the mouse pointer on the screen so that it's hovering over some object, a button or icon.
Click	To press and release the mouse's main button (the one on the left).
Double-click	To perform two quick clicks in a row, both pointing at the same spot.
Drag	To press and hold the mouse button down and then move the mouse around. In Windows, this technique is used to move objects around on the screen. The drag ends when you release the mouse button.
Select	To click on something, highlighting it.

The Left-Handed Mouse

If you're one of those who are lovingly referred to as southpaws (meaning a left-hander), you can choose to use your mouse on the right side of your computer—like the right handers—or use your mouse on the left side, where it's more intuitive for you. Heck, even some right-handers like a left-handed mouse.

To Do C.1: Making Your Mouse Left-Hand Friendly

1. Double-click My Computer (the icon on your desktop).
2. Double-click the Control Panel.
3. Double-click on the Mouse icon to open it up.

   You'll see the Mouse Properties dialog box, as shown in Figure C.1.

FIGURE C.1

The Mouse Properties not related to Mouse Droppings.

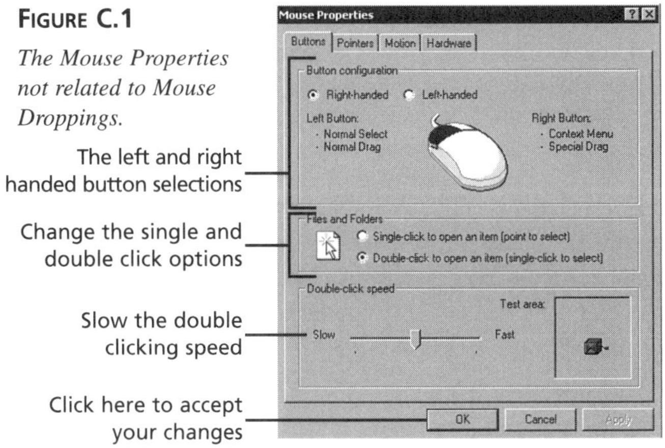

4. Click on the Left-handed option button.

   You'll see the button highlight on the demo mouse change from the left side to the right, which is where you want it. Notice that the descriptions of the left button and right button change when you click either Right-handed or Left-handed.
5. Click OK.

This closes the Mouse Properties dialog box and the Control Panel's window, as well.

You've just switched mouse buttons, so from here on in you'll use the right button to click, double-click, and open things. You'll be using the left mouse button to pop up shortcut menus. Remember that!

Making Changes to Master Mouse

The mouse doesn't have to look, act, or respond in the fashion that it does now. Nope. You can change your mouse pointer, you can change the speed at which you have to double-click, and you can adjust how fast your pointer moves.

To Do C.2: Adjusting with the Mouse

▼ To Do

1. Open the Mouse Properties box as described above.

   Figure C.1 shows you how you can change the speed of your mouse.

2. Click on the Pointers tab.
3. Click the Scheme button.

   Choose one of the schemes and notice all your pointers change. I particularly like the Dinosaur theme. Keep playing until you pick the theme you like.

4. Click Apply.

   Your pointer immediately changes.

5. Click on the Motion tab. ▲

The Speed and Acceleration are both areas you'll have to play with to see how you like the streaks your pointer leaves behind. I must stress to you how absolutely unimportant this area is. Really. Unless the pointer really bugs you, you can completely forget this area. If you do make changes, click OK. You can always go back and make more adjustments if you don't like the outcome of your work.

The Formal Messing with Text

Part of Windows' common approach is that it treats any text or graphic in any application the same way. There is a definite way to edit text, to change its size, style, and so forth. This is a constant, something done the same whether it's in a big program, such as Microsoft Word, or in a tiny text field in a dialog box. The same holds true for graphics on the screen, although there's not as much you can do with them.

Even though Windows is graphical, there is a lot of text. You still need a keyboard, along with your mouse, to make things happen. In fact, I'd say a goodly chunk of your time spent working with Windows will be spent typing in text, either in an application or in a dialog box somewhere. No matter what, you can always rely on the consistent rules in Windows for dealing with text.

Respecting the Flashing Toothpick Cursor

Windows uses two objects when you play with text. The first is the Text Selection pointer, which is what the mouse pointer turns into when you hover it over text. This pointer says you can use the mouse to select text and position the flashing toothpick cursor on the screen.

The flashing toothpick cursor is used to help you edit your text. It marks the position on the screen where new characters appear as you type them. New text appears behind the toothpick cursor, and the toothpick cursor moves to the right as you type.

You can move the toothpick cursor by clicking the mouse at a new spot in the text. This works whether you're working in a word processor or toiling away in some tiny text input box in some obscure dialog box. You can also move the toothpick cursor with your keyboard's arrow keys, as covered in the next section.

Editing Your Text

To create new text, type away. If you make a mistake, you can use the Backspace key to backup and erase your text.

When you're done typing in a line of text, you press the Enter key.

In a dialog box, when you're done filling in an Input box and want to continue to the next field, you press the Tab key.

While you're working with text, you use several special keys on the keyboard to edit as you go. These keys are listed in Table C.2.

TABLE C.2 Windows Editing Keys

Key	*The Function*
Backspace	Backs up the toothpick cursor and deletes the previous character.
Delete	Deletes the next character, the one after the toothpick cursor.
Ctrl+Delete	Deletes all text from the toothpick cursor until the end of the word. (This doesn't work in all applications.)
Home	Moves the toothpick cursor to the start of the line or the first character in an input box.
End	Moves the toothpick cursor to the end of the line or the last character in an input box.
Tab	Moves the toothpick cursor to the next input box in a dialog box.
Enter	Ends a line or paragraph of text. (Use only in a word processor.)
←	Moves the toothpick cursor back one character.
→	Moves the toothpick cursor forward one character.
↑	Moves the toothpick cursor up one line.
↓	Moves the toothpick cursor down one line.
Ctrl+←	Moves the toothpick cursor back one word.
Ctrl+→	Moves the toothpick cursor forward one word.

C

Selecting Your Favorite Text

All text in Windows, whether it's in a word processor or some lowly text in a dialog box, can be edited using the cut, copy, and paste commands, even if there isn't an Edit menu hanging around nearby. What you'll be using instead are the keyboard shortcuts for those commands:

- Ctrl+x (control key plus the x key) for Cut
- Ctrl+c (control key plus the c key) for Copy
- Ctrl+v (control key plus the v key) for Paste
- Ctrl+z (control key plus the z key) for the Undo command.

Before you can cut or copy text, it first needs to be selected. There are several ways to do this in Windows. The best way to select text is to drag over it with the mouse's Text Selection pointer. This is illustrated in Figure C.2. Start the drag at the beginning of your text, then drag to select and highlight. Release the mouse button when you've selected the necessary text.

FIGURE C.2
Text is selected.

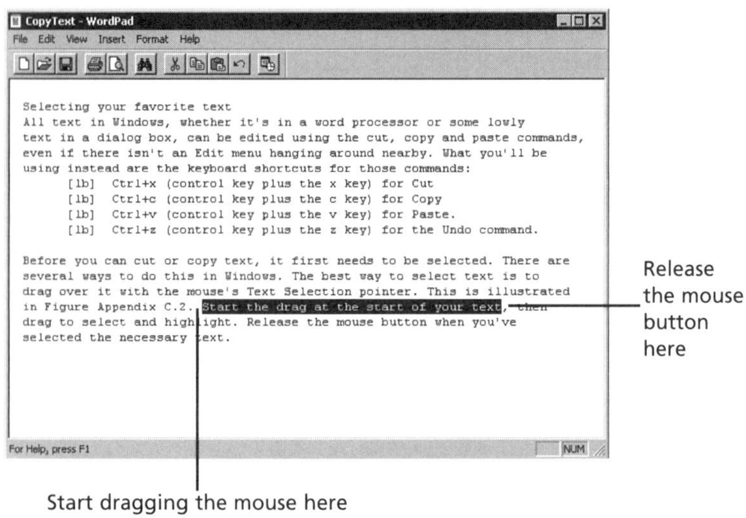

To select all the text in a dialog box, double-click on that box. This highlights all the text.

You can also select text by using the shift key while moving the toothpick cursor. For example, shift+← selects one character to the left of the toothpick cursor. Keep pressing shift+← to select more characters.

After the text is selected, you can use the Cut or Copy commands on it to cut or copy the text; press Ctrl+x to cut, Ctrl+c to copy.

You can also press the Delete key to delete all the selected text.

Press Ctrl+v to paste previously copied text.

Press Ctrl+z, the Undo command, to undo whatever editing changes you've made.

Big Text, Small Text, All Different Sizes

The size of your text can also be changed, from teensy-tiny to relatively huge. The value used is *points*, which is a typesetting term. A *point* is essentially a tiny piece of a letter. Text typically appears on the screen in 8-, 10-, or 12-point sizes. The larger the point value, the bigger the text. If you set the point size to about 72, you get text about 1 inch high.

As with the font, setting a new point size is typically done with a drop-down list box, either on a toolbar or hidden in a menu. You can usually type in a size value in addition to selecting it from a list.

The new point size affects any selected text in your document or, if no text is selected, it affects anything new you type.

INDEX

Symbols

A

B

J

K

L

M

Q

R

T

Other Related Titles

Peter Norton's Complete Guide to Microsoft Windows 2000 Professional
John Mueller, Peter Norton
Sams
ISBN: 0672317788
US $29.99/CAN $59.95

Microsoft Windows 2000 Professional Unleashed
Paul Cassel
Sams
ISBN: 0672317427
US $49.99

Sams Teach Yourself Microsoft Office 2000 in 24 Hours
Greg Perry
Sams
ISBN: 0672314398
US $19.99/CAN $29.95

Sams Teach Yourself Microsoft Outlook 2000 in 24 Hours
Herb Tyson
Sams
ISBN: 0672314495
US $19.99/CAN $29.95

Sams Teach Yourself Microsoft Word in 24 Hours
Heidi Steele
Sams
ISBN: 0672314428
US $19.99/CAN $29.95

Sams Teach Yourself Microsoft Excel in 24 Hours
Trudi Reisner
Sams
ISBN: 0672314452
US $19.99/CAN $29.95

How to Use Microsoft Windows 2000 Professional
Walter J. Glenn
Sams
ISBN: 0672317117
US $24.99/CAN $37.95

Sams Teach Yourself Microsoft Windows 2000 Professional in 10 Minutes
Jane Calabria, Dorothy Burke
Sams
ISBN: 0672317028
US $12.99/CAN $19.95

SAMS

www.samspublishing.com

All prices are subject to change.